Nine Innings
for the King

COMPILED AND ANNOTATED
BY JIM LEEKE

Ballplayers in the Great War:
Newspaper Accounts of Major Leaguers in
World War I Military Service (McFarland, 2013)

Nine Innings for the King

*The Day Wartime London
Stopped for Baseball,
July 4, 1918*

JIM LEEKE

McFarland & Company, Inc., Publishers
Jefferson, North Carolina

Portions of this book appeared in "Royal Match: The Army-Navy Service Game, July 4, 1918," in *NINE: A Journal of Baseball History & Culture*, spring 2012, and in the author's profiles of Ed Lafitte, Mike McNally, Hugh Miller and Ernie Shore for the SABR Baseball Biography Project. Numerous articles cited here appear in their entirety in Jim Leeke's *Ballplayers in the Great War*, also from McFarland (2013).

ISBN 978-0-7864-7870-5 (softcover : acid free paper) ∞
ISBN 978-1-4766-2017-6 (ebook)

LIBRARY OF CONGRESS CATALOGUING DATA ARE AVAILABLE

BRITISH LIBRARY CATALOGUING DATA ARE AVAILABLE

On the cover: Admiral Sims (center) looks on as King George V meets Navy ballplayer Michael McNally, *The Sphere*, London (author's collection)

Printed in the United States of America

McFarland & Company, Inc., Publishers
Box 611, Jefferson, North Carolina 28640
www.mcfarlandpub.com

For Robert Hausafus,
shipmate on the USS *Ranger*.
Hi-yo, Silver!

Sam, ol' chap, shake 'ands! God's
    blessin' on the w'rligig o' time
That 'as brought to London town
    this wonderful red-letter day;
Did you ever know that baseball 'ad
    a touch o' the sublime,
And that Nations' 'earts are welded
    in the 'eat o' manly play?

> —J. W. Bengough,
> "John Bull to Uncle Sam"

Table of Contents

Acknowledgments

Many people helped to produce this book. The author especially thanks Trey Strecker of Ball State University for his early interest and support; Andy Kulina and Lisa Beebe-Strahley for their research in London and Washington, respectively; the late Blair Fuller for sharing memories of his father; Ed Bartholemy for information and photos of his grandfather; Jane C. Clark for proofreading; and Sara Shopkow for editorial guidance.

Many librarians and archivists also offered support and advice. Their institutions include the A. Bartlett Giamatti Research Library, National Baseball Hall of Fame and Museum, Cooperstown, New York; Richland Library, Columbia, South Carolina; Clemson University Libraries; St. Louis Public Library; Boston Public Library; Newport (Rhode Island) Public Library; Chester County (Pennsylvania) Library; Chester County Historical Society; Kinchafoonee Regional Library, Dawson, Georgia; and the President Woodrow Wilson House, Washington, D.C.

Thanks as well to Elizabeth Kirkland for information on Lady Drummond.

Preface

Some books begin by accident. This one began the day a writer noticed a dusty compilation of *The Stars and Stripes* in an antique mall in West Virginia. The U.S. Army had published the newspaper in Paris during the First World War. The tattered volume contained every edition printed at that time, but was almost too fragile to open. Fortunately, a usable copy wasn't hard to find and purchase on the Internet. You can even read *The Stars and Stripes* online if you want to, but browsing actual pages is more satisfying.

The old army weekly had the optimistic voice of the doughboy—*Lafayette, we are here!* The sports section was jazzy and interesting and offered coverage from home along with articles from France and England. Equipped with his compilation, the writer began recycling the baseball stories into a blog he called *Uncle Sam's League*, all about big leaguers in the armed forces during the war. After exhausting the pieces from Paris, he expanded the blog to include stateside papers and, later still, compiled an entire book, *Ballplayers in the Great War: Newspaper Accounts of Major Leaguers in World War I Military Service* (McFarland, 2013).

Several articles stuck in the writer's mind. The *Stars and Stripes'* man in London filed several stories in 1918 about the Anglo-American Baseball League, a Canadian and American military circuit popular in England during the war. The correspondent once mentioned that King George V planned to attend the league's game on the Fourth of July. This was obviously a big deal, U.S. Army versus U.S. Navy at the Stamford Bridge stadium in Chelsea. Curiously, the newsman never mentioned the game again—not in *The Stars and Stripes*, anyway. Nearly a century later, the mystery was irresistible.

1

The writer who owned the compilations had an odd professional resume. Mixed with the journalism and marketing that had long provided him a livelihood were a couple of modest military histories and one season covering major league baseball for a suburban daily. How could he not dig into the Chelsea game?

Each small discovery led to another, all interconnected in unexpected ways. The many Canadian army baseball teams playing in England early in the war led to baseball-starved Yank businessmen in London, who funded the Anglo-American league, whose rosters included former and active major leaguers (among them a future Hall of Famer), which naturally drew press coverage, which helped spark the royal family's interest in a gilded Fourth of July baseball game, which highlighted the importance they attached to U.S.-British relations at a critical moment in the war, which led to breathless headlines on the other side of the Atlantic, all of which culminated in one hell of a good ball game—one seen by tens of thousands of screaming Yanks and astonished Londoners, many of whom hadn't the slightest notion what they were watching but who cheered themselves silly nonetheless. Amazing.

Then somehow it was all forgotten.

Ask a hundred knowledgeable baseball fans today to name the most important baseball game ever played, and not one will cite the Army-Navy game in Chelsea. Yet those nine innings helped solidify the British-American alliance that still endures. What other sporting event has made a contribution half so vital to the national interests of the United States? Energetic Uncle Sam crossed the Atlantic to help exhausted John Bull when it mattered most, when Kaiser Bill might yet have won the bloody Great War in the trenches. The Chelsea game represented what we'd now call a tipping point.

On a baseball diamond squeezed onto a soccer pitch, the Yanks proved to the worried populace of the old country—and to their own folks at home, who hardly needed convincing—that they were fit, willing and dependable allies. The Anglo-American league later dubbed their roaring display of American exuberance and athleticism "the King's game," which was fitting.

It's all so long ago now. Four or five generations have come and gone, through another world war, a cold war and many lesser conflicts. The First World War's centennial gives us an opportunity to revive the King's game in transatlantic memory. It matters today because it mattered then ... and *really* mattered.

Think of the game now as an important chapter in wartime history, or as just a time when grown men played ball overseas on the Fourth of July.

You'll be right either way.

Prologue. The Fourth

The fourth day of July 1918, a Thursday, was unlike any that had ever dawned in England. On this morning, in the fourth year of the Great War, London looked and felt like an American city. The Yanks or Huskies or Sammies or Attaboys—despite many other shortages, the Britishers suffered no lack of nicknames for their allies arriving in limitless thousands on this side of the Atlantic—were all cordially and sincerely invited to celebrate the signing of their Declaration of Independence. In the typically muted British manner, they were nearly *beseeched* to do so, and in the capital of the empire their forefathers had rebelled against 142 years earlier. Their hosts would have been crestfallen had the former colonists behaved more like Londoners, and declined with polite thanks to go off and commemorate privately. "Celebrations are not natural to the British disposition," an American newspaperman observed.[1] But the Yanks were the Yanks, the more the merrier, the louder the better, decorum be damned, and *this* Fourth would be a humdinger.

It was a perfect summer day promising heat, so fine that you might've thought the king had summoned it by decree especially for the Americans. "Every Britisher awoke this morning with a real desire to celebrate."[2]

Fear in London had vanished at dawn like Bram Stoker's vampire count. Danger lived *out there*, across the Channel, in the bloody, godforsaken mud of France and Belgium, in *some corner of a foreign field / That is forever England*.[3] The big ugly German bombers, the *Gothas*, came now only in darkness, dropping bombs like vandals, blowing up innocent families in their beds, antiaircraft guns banging away like thunder. None had

3

U.S. Army troops in England, July 4, 1918 (*Gorrell's History*).

appeared since the middle of May, and they'd paid dearly for *that* raid. And the huge, horrible Zeppelins rarely came over at all anymore, the Boche having lost too many airships, too many airmen, good riddance. Still, London couldn't be too careful about the enemy. Seven fat balloons, "sausages," floated, hovered, on picket duty over the football grounds in Chelsea. A silver dirigible would join them later and pursuit planes were likely standing by at flying fields ringing the city. But now as London shook itself awake, no one in the city felt the least bit threatened.

> Early morning saw American flags on all sides, notably on the Palace of Westminster, in Pall Mall, and in the City. American soldiers and sailors from rest and training camps poured into town and by 10 a.m. a huge crowd had gathered at the Eagle Hut in Aldwych to cheer the raising of the flag. The band of the Irish Guards played national airs while brakeload after brakeload in khaki and blue drove gaily away, cheering and cheered, to visit London, East and West.
>
> The stock market suspended business to cheer for the President; Lloyd's and the Baltic sang "The Star Spangled Banner" and "God Save the King."[4]

The American flag and Union Jack fluttered together everywhere against the high English sky, "getting hopelessly entangled in what looked from below like a serious love affair."[5] The Yanks saw their Stars and Stripes streaming over Victoria Tower and 10 Downing Street and the Guildhall and the Royal Exchange and beside the Royal Navy's white ensign over the Admiralty. "'Old Glory' broke from tens of thousands of London's high places. It was upon the towers of ancient and historic buildings. It hung in countless mean streets from the windows of the humblest homes."[6] And in those streets themselves, on the sidewalks and corners all over town, vendors offered small American flags for sale and found plenty of takers at sixpence apiece. Out at the Stamford Bridge Football Grounds, site of the afternoon's baseball game, the "rather dingy surroundings were shut out by a square mile or two of flags, 'Old Glory' and the Union Jack predominating, but the rest of the Allies not being forgotten."[7]

The British even ran up the American flag over the Houses of Parliament, then dipped the Union Jack three times. It was almost too much for a portly civilian gent from Council Bluffs, Iowa.

> Boys, I felt like an old woman. I wanted to shake everybody by the hand and weep on their shoulders and throw my hat and money and keys in the air, and just roll around on the ground for joy. Then I collared a man and thanked him as an American. He seemed kind of excited, too, and he kept thanking me back. He said, "Well, say, it's still true that no foreign flag has flown supreme over Parliament. Old Glory is no foreign flag anymore in this land." Well, boys, I must have ruined that man's clothes pawing all over him. Did you ever hear anything so great—so wonderful—oh, there ain't no word to describe it![8]

The previous night, July the third, London hotels and theaters had celebrated, restaurants had produced American menus, "and theatreland made the American fighting man feel it was his particular night."[9] Today, on the Fourth, Londoners rang the big bells at St. Paul's, threw open their churches for prayer and Holy Communion, hung an American flag and the Union Jack behind the pulpit at City Temple. Courts and schools and most shops and stores were closed as Britishers readied concerts and teas all over town and handed out free tickets to this, that and the other thing.

The biggest, most important event this morning was something called the Anglo-Saxon Fellowship meeting at Central Hall in Westminster. The big hall overflowed, with thousands more standing outside. One sweet old dear turned away and toddled across to Westminster Abbey, where she prayed for blessings upon America. "Inside, the band of the Coldstream Guards filled half-an-hour of waiting with brave music—most of it music of the American fighting mood—and roars of cheers and choruses sung by the audience en masse, and with the wildest enthusiasm, and stamping, and clapping, and yelling, and whistling, filled the Central Hall with noise and excitement such as rarely inhabit that sedate rendezvous of Wesleyan Methodism."[10]

Political and military leaders delivered speeches during this clambake,

American soldiers and sailors with British civilians, July 4, 1918 (*Gorrell's History*).

which seemed a "magnificent outburst of Anglo-American friendship" to folks back home.[11] The speaker the Yanks remembered most wasn't their own Admiral Sims or General Biddle, or Viscount Bryce or any of the British bigwigs they probably didn't know from Adam, but the Right Honorable Winston S. Churchill. The Britishers themselves, though, weren't quite sure about him. "Col. Churchill, who is half American, can always be depended upon for a stirring speech, but he is not exactly one of our statesmen," the *Daily Chronicle* had sniffed. "It is no reflection on him to suggest that if his efforts were supplemented by such a speaker as Secretary Balfour, former premier Asquith or Viscount Grey, the opportunity would be met much more adequately."[12] But it seemed to the Yanks that the *Chronicle's* scribblers were loony.

　　Maybe not many of the American boys actually knew the pedigree of the proud, headstrong former first lord of the Admiralty, the architect of the disastrous land and sea campaign in the Dardanelles, late lieutenant-colonel (*leftenant*-colonel, they said over here) of the Sixth Royal Scots Fusiliers, an impatient veteran of trench warfare across the Channel, current minister of munitions, and, especially today, doting son of Lady Randolph Churchill, beautiful Jennie, his American-born mother. But the Yanks knew a fine, stem-winder of a stump speech when they heard one.

Churchill was terrific, "defiantly pugnacious,"[13] everybody cheering and clapping, the Britishers shouting, "Hear! Hear!" "*Germany must be beaten until she knows she is beaten,*" Churchill rumbled.[14] And the Fourth of July would never again be only an American celebration, because hereafter England would celebrate both the Magna Carta *and* the Declaration of Independence. "We are glad to know," Churchill added slyly, "that an English colony declared herself Independent under a German King."[15] (George III was also the king of Hanover, you see. Churchill's dig wouldn't appear in tomorrow's newspapers, but a fellow from the Young Men's Christian Association, the Y.M.C.A., would repeat it in his own speech later back home in Philadelphia.)

The "Y" pulled out all the stops in London today, inviting five hundred doughboys for sightseeing, and the speeches, and the ball game, plus dinners and music and dances afterward. These were only a fraction of the Yanks who flooded into the "Big Smoke." Everyone gathered first at the Eagle Hut on the Strand. Here a lonely Sammy or Jackie could find a bed, familiar food, games, movies, French classes, books, newspapers, religious services and even a helpful "hut mother" to darn socks and sew on buttons. Today, especially, the Eagle Hut was packed and buzzing.

The Irish Guards band began the morning with "The Star-Spangled Banner" as the American flag rose out front, followed by a concert inside. "It's the finest fish feathers," an approving soldier said to his pal.[16] The Quiet Room was noisy, Y officials popping in with shouted directions and instructions. "The secretaries in charge told me the boys were consistently hungry, that they had been eating ever since their arrival and were now clamoring for lunch."[17]

A Texas boy got poetic when somebody handed around an album to collect signatures:

> *Kaiser Bill went up the hill,*
> *To take a little peep;*
> *Kaiser Bill came down the hill,*
> *And landed in a heap.*[18]

After they'd all grabbed some chow, the Yanks headed out in every direction. "The sight-seeing parties were taken for drives through the City and the West-end. Their progress was accompanied by much flag-waving and cheering."[19] They couldn't have had a bigger time back home in Dubuque or New Haven.

It wasn't like this just in the British capital, either, not by a long shot.

Bristol, Liverpool, Leeds, Manchester and Southampton all had asked for detachments of Yanks to entertain on the Fourth, and so had lots of others. "In most large towns in England the day was recognized. Historic cathedrals and chapels, St. George's, Windsor, and King's College, Cambridge, among others, saw services. Liverpool was decked in flags and a review of troops was a feature. Manchester opened a Stars and Stripes Club."[20] And the Fourth wasn't just big in England today. "It crossed the Atlantic, overran Great Britain, took possession of France, penetrated Italy, traversed the Mediterranean, where at Corfu the Serbian Government officials attended high mass in honor of the American national holiday. There were celebrations in Egypt, Siam, India, and on into the Pacific, where in Australia demonstrations were made in all the principal cities, and returned home by way of Japan, the Philippines and Hawaii."[21]

And in America—why, at home they were launching ships. Almost a hundred of them, of every size and shape, wooden and steel, tankers and transports and cargo ships, all hitting the water on this single day, the Fourth of July, to "douse the Kaiser."[22] They would launch nearly half a million tons from shipyards on all the coasts, and along the big rivers, and on the Great Lakes, too. The first new ship, the *Lake Aurice*, had already slid down the ways at Superior, Wisconsin, exactly one minute after midnight. *Popular Mechanics* would run a picture of the brilliantly floodlit steamer splashing into black Lake Superior. And to help protect all this fine new shipping, more American tonnage in one day than German U-boats had yet managed to sink altogether, the U.S. Navy was launching fourteen destroyers. "Heartfelt congratulations on this magnificent performance," British prime minister David Lloyd George would cable the president.[23] It was a grand thing.

People greeted the Yanks cheerfully everywhere they went in London today, whether military or civilian, in uniform or mufti. Even the notoriously grouchy taxi drivers crumbled into good humor and generosity. "No charge, thank you just the same," one announced, having maneuvered his Yank passenger through jammed streets to a restaurant in Soho. "I'm hauling Americans free today. Have to do some little thing to help celebrate."[24]

Publisher Lord Northcliffe thought the big ball game in Chelsea was such a fine idea that he'd ensured that his *Daily Mail* had printed articles about it. Much of Fleet Street, in fact, had even tried explaining the rules and niceties of the American national pastime to the innocent Britishers. The city's newspapers offered meticulous illustrations and diagrams, *shortstop* being no more comprehensible to lovers of cricket than *silly mid off* to baseball bugs.

Londoners seemed especially keen on shepherding Yanks to the game, which Britishers kept calling the *baseball match*. An American naval officer standing in a long line for the Tube at Piccadilly Circus had a ticket handed to him by an Englishman who'd just bought it for himself. "He said I would be late to the game if I had to wait much longer, and it wouldn't matter so much if he were a bit late," the lieutenant marveled. "Then he went to the end of the queue again."[25]

One smart American, a doctor touring England and France for the Y, had wisely reserved a taxi to ferry his party to Chelsea. (Cabbies not as generous as the one in Soho were charging one and two pounds for the trip out.) The taxi got an entire block and a half before a bobby stopped it at Piccadilly Circus and asked to see tickets.

"What tickets?"

"Tickets for the ball game."

"But the game is four miles away."

"You can't go on Piccadilly, sir, without tickets."

So Dr. George Earle Raiguel dug out his tickets. His taxi then turned onto Piccadilly, which was banked with people. What did it all mean?

"The Americans going to the ball game, sir!" the bobby said.

A big cheer went up when the Yanks' taxi started down the street. "Standing up to see what royal personages were back of us, and finding no one within sight, we soon saw that we were being cheered because we were Americans! So we cheered back. And this was a continuous performance. Sometimes we stood up and waved our flags and hung out the sides of the taxi. Then we would sit down and think what fools we were, only to stand up again and cheer. ... So, unrestrained, we went the rest of the way to Chelsea."[26]

Tens of thousands of people streamed toward Chelsea from every corner of the city. One group of doughboys and tars, being Americans, naturally stopped at Buckingham Palace to give three cheers for King George. The Yanks were mighty fond of the old boy. They'd each received a printed welcoming note from the king when they'd landed in Great Britain, a memento that some will keep all of their lives. And when every hotel and boarding house and Y.M.C.A. hut in London was full to bursting, a lucky few had even been known to find a night's shelter at "Buck House."

And hadn't George even dropped by the Eagle Hut with the missus just the other day, nobody even knowing they were coming, and visited with the boys awhile, and tucked into a tall stack of buckwheat cakes hot off the griddle? (He probably didn't get to enjoy them all that often at home, poor guy.) Why, the British monarch will even take in the ball game with them today—although not from the cheap seats, if there even *were* any actual seats out where the soldiers and sailors had tickets. So, the king was all right with the kids from Poughkeepsie, Pocatello and Peoria ... three cheers for George V!

Hearing the hubbub, the monarch stepped out with Queen Mary onto their splendid balcony. A couple of hundred boys from the Eagle Hut had already serenaded them just after midnight. Now here were more, cheering them. Their majesties had to be surprised. Certainly, nothing like this had ever happened with their Guards or Highlander regiments or the lads of the Royal Navy. The bemused royal couple gazed upon their exuberant young allies "and smilingly acknowledged the demonstration."[27] Maybe George and Mary also gave the boys a restrained royal wave or two, to get into the spirit.

Not much about the scene would have surprised any of the American women living in England during the war. They understood the doughboys better than anyone else here. They knew, for example, that many of the boys who didn't have tickets to the big game would happily pass the Fourth *playing* baseball instead of watching it. The challenge, of course, was to round up enough equipment.

American sporting goods were scarce now in England. The loss of the torpedoed steamer *Kansan*, consigned to Davy Jones' locker along with a shipment of balls, bats, bases, masks and gloves from the Y, hadn't helped any. Getting ready for the Fourth, the U.S. Army Air Service had snapped up every baseball uniform left in the country. Any Yank ballplayers who didn't already have a set of flannels were out of luck, and would have to run onto the diamond in whatever bits of army khaki they didn't mind getting dirty. Or that's how it had seemed, anyway.

The notion hadn't gone down well with their American sisters, aunts and cousins residing in England. A couple of hundred of them decided to whip out a few more uniforms for the holiday. They rolled up their sleeves and got to work in the workrooms of the American Red Cross in Grosvenor Square. They usually made surgical dressings there, but it wasn't exactly the garment district. One of the ballplayers who'd take the field in Chelsea had loaned them an old uniform to work from. Nobody ever said which one, which was just as well because it could have been any of them. He'd probably stuffed it into his barracks or sea bag before sailing from the States, along with a ball tucked into a mitt and maybe a nicked-up old bat or two.

The volunteers carefully took these flannels apart stitch by stitch and used the pieces to make patterns. They worked for a whole weekend, making uniforms in sizes medium and extra large. Englishwomen pitched in and helped, too, even if these strange baseball suits weren't like anything their Tommies wore to play cricket, rugby or football. By Monday evening they'd turned out three hundred uniforms, enough to outfit thirty teams—

sixty, if they handed them around for doubleheaders—and shipped them out by late-night trains. The boys would wear these homemade togs in the camps and flying fields around London and find them "quite as good as the ones they wore at home."[28] In fact, Yank troops would play ball at more than forty places in England today.

The really big game, though, the King's Game, was in the city, Army HQ versus Navy HQ, at Stamford Bridge. These ballplayers had no worries about *their* uniforms, which were new and handsome enough for play at Braves Field or the Polo Grounds. The soldiers sported blue caps and pale, gray-green jerseys with an "A" on the chest and an American flag on the left sleeve. The sailors wore navy blue with red trim. Everybody looked swell. No general or admiral, colonel or commander, first sergeant or chief petty officer, would be embarrassed when the players took the field today in front of the king and the queen and all the other fancy folks.

A few of the boys had played in big games before. Ed Lafitte had toiled in the big leagues back home and faced Walter Johnson of the Washington Senators while pitching for the Detroit Tigers. And speedy Mike McNally had raced home with the Boston Red Sox's winning run in the second game of the 1916 World Series, in the gloaming at the bottom of the fourteenth inning. His teammate Herb Pennock had pitched with Babe Ruth, who was now tearing up the American League back home. But none of them, in any league anywhere, had ever played with a king peering down from the grandstand.

All of this would come soon enough. Right now, at midday, secluded from all the clamor and bustle outside, the army and navy nines sat down together for a pregame luncheon at the Savoy. This came after their private boxes last night at the Empire, with everything draped in flags and flowers, for a performance of *The Lilac Domino* (an operetta, for crying out loud), where afterward the orchestra had played "The Star-Spangled Banner." For a few of the boys—dashing Ensign Charles Fuller of Harvard; Herbert Pennock, from the posh fox-and-hounds country outside Philadelphia; Captain Lafitte, from New Orleans, Atlanta and Philadelphia; and Ensign Stuart Hayes of Washington, D.C., by way of American consulates in Scotland and England—the theater and the posh dining room were probably enjoyable reminders of peacetime civility.

But for most of the others the Savoy was something out of a fairy tale or Frank Baum's strange kids' story about an emerald city called Oz. Oh, sure, Mike McNally had played in big-league cities, and would play there again when peace rolled around. But in the off seasons, he lived and worked back home in the coal country around Scranton, Pennsylvania. He wasn't the only scrappy, hardscrabble kid dining at the Savoy today, either. With him were Blackmore from Dowagiac, Michigan, Vannatter from the Western League, Tober from Toledo, and Chief Wiskeman from the navy (a career sailor, *Chief* not a nickname but his rank). Most of these men had beaten the baseball bushes from Norfolk to Des Moines, Martinsburg to Salt Lake City. For them, lunch at the Savoy could have been trumped only by supper at the White House, and nobody was expecting an engraved invitation anytime soon from President Wilson.

What unfathomable quirk of military life, what strange, million-to-one chain of events, had set them down amid the crystal and silver and linen at the Savoy? Nearly everyone else wearing khaki or blues today would wolf down whatever was ladled out in a chow hall or on a mess deck or, much better, something tasty over at the Eagle Hut. Or maybe instead they would spend the holiday with a kindly British family, sharing their bland, heavy food and warm beer. Why exactly the ballplayers were *here*, at the Savoy, none of them could have said.

When the dreamlike luncheon ended, and it was time to head for the ball yard, transportation stood waiting outside. No squadron of black taxicabs for them, nor one of the city's distinctive red double-decker buses, nor even a lorry or camion sent from one of the military camps. No, these boys, on *this* day, left the Savoy in four-in-hand tally-ho coaches, like characters out of a Sherlock Holmes story. Mike McNally and the others must have shaken their heads in wonder.

Lady Luck just had to be a baseball fan, to haul off and smooch a guy that way.

1

The Canadians

The Britishers had a cartoonist, W. Heath Robinson, who had a penchant for drawing odd, impractical machines. During the war, he drew such outlandish contraptions as "A New Mortar for Sending Luncheon Baskets Up to Aeroplanes"—although, in Robinson's imaginings, these were all German devices.[1] "The master minds of Krupp have turned out nothing like the inventions of Mr. Robinson's pencil," a reviewer wrote about the cartoonist's perfectly titled little book, *Hunlikely*.[2] (Robinson would draw more enemy machines in the *next* world war, but it would be very difficult indeed to find much that was humorous about the Nazis.)

Over in New York City, too, every now and then, a cartoonist drew odd, elaborate and even more impractical machines. His stuff clearly was the work of a genius or a wickedly funny lunatic. Take the invention he called "Simple Way to Shine Your Shoes Without Going Near a Bootblack Stand."[3] Sure, it was just a simple little device, which involved only a pistol, a dog, a flea, a windmill, a blob of wax, a sugar cube, a pulley and a goat's whiskers. And those weren't even half the items that constituted Step A through Step S, each vital to completing the weird, extended sequence that finally produced a shoeshine for a man standing on a box.

This cartoonist didn't yet draw many of these machines. He was still too busy drawing other panels for syndication to newspapers across America. Eventually, though, he would draw more and more of his machines. In time, they would make him beloved and ridiculously famous, his name mentioned with a smile by scientists, engineers and dreamers well into the next century.

Rube Goldberg would have adored the weird, convoluted history of the great Fourth of July baseball game.

The phenomenon had started with one thing, which led to something else, then to this, and next to that, followed by a whole unrelated thing, until finally George V of England was learning to throw a baseball for the ceremonial first pitch at Chelsea. Except that, unlike in any Rube Goldberg machine, the marvelous mechanism that became known as "the King's Game" had no single, inspired creator. Nor did it have a clear starting point, the Step A in an unlikely string of connections.

You could have argued that it began with boys from Yellow Knife and Quebec who crossed the Atlantic with the Canadian army. Or you could have declared that it actually started with a pair of hustling American sports promoters who created a circuit they called the Anglo-American Baseball League. Or with a washed-up baseball star and diamond comedian. Or a U.S. Army quartermaster nobody had ever heard of before. Or an American admiral, or a pair of imaginative officers in a British propaganda office, or even the king himself. All of them or none of them might have constituted Step A.

Or, with equal justification, you might have argued that Fate had ordained the game, or that History was its true father. You might even have believed that the game had somehow assembled *itself*, across three nations and an ocean. That it had somehow, all by itself, slotted together all of its interconnected cogs and springs and wires and levers. Surely, no one person or team, however inspired or determined, could have devised anything so perfect, so essential to British morale and resolve in this year of desperate armed struggle. And yet, somehow, there it was. Go figure.

But if you absolutely *had* to identify Step A in some endlessly argumentative hot-stove league, the Canadians were a good place to start. And to get to the Canadians, you had to go back even further, to the assassination of an unknown (to Americans) Austrian archduke in the summer of 1914. The chain of events that had then somehow brought about the Great War was a sort of Rube Goldberg antimachine—incredibly complex, completely unnecessary (many will still argue today), and utterly, horribly tragic. "The lamps are going out all over Europe; we shall not see them lit again in our life-time," British foreign minister Sir Edward Grey had mourned as he sensed disaster coming.[4] He was not far wrong. Soon the guns of August, to use the title of Barbara Tuchman's fine history of the whole mess nearly half a century later, were firing in France and Belgium. Millions of Britishers cheered their Tommies off to the front, while others hunched their shoulders, steeled their nerves, and struggled onward beneath the same dark cloud as Sir Edward.

Men in every country shaded in pink on world maps reported to their territorial military units or stood in line at local recruiting offices. "BRITONS," shouted posters in Great Britain, above an image of Lord Kitchener, without even his name, just Kitchener pointing straight out, stern, composed, mustachioed, "WANTS YOU." And below that, "JOIN YOUR COUNTRY'S ARMY! GOD SAVE THE KING." Dominion troops weren't Britons, strictly speaking, but George V was their king and they answered the call of the mother country. Soon hundreds of thousands were aboard troop ships steaming toward England.

The Canadian boys quickly reached the eastern side of the Atlantic, but the front lines had already grown static, the armies dug deeply into endless lines of trenches. By late October 1914, thousands of Canadian troops not already on the Continent were scattered across four isolated camps on England's Salisbury Plain. Naturally, along with their army kit, they'd brought over quite a few bats, gloves and baseballs. These tough, rangy kids from Ontario, Saskatchewan and Alberta were just as baseball-crazed as the boys still living in peace below the 49th parallel.

By spring 1915, England was accustomed to having Canadians milling everywhere, even if they did sound like Americans and weren't particularly keen on the monarchy. "Today's weather is springlike," read a dispatch from Shorncliffe. "A party of arrivals from Canada gave their British comrades initiation into the mysteries of baseball today."[5] Soon enough, Britishers embraced this Canadian invasion. "The seaside resort and Continental packet station of Folkestone is becoming more Canadianized even than Salisbury. It has recognized the wisdom of accepting a dollar bill for four shillings; a café proprietor has opened 'The Canadian Café'; Canadian bands are engaged to play on the Leas promenade on Sunday afternoons, and postcards are being struck off in honor of the Dominion boys. Moreover, the townspeople are being given frequent opportunities to see the game of baseball."[6]

Folks in the city of Bath would actually *miss* the game when nearby Canadian troops relocate their camp later. "It was through them that many Bath people received their initiation into the mysteries of baseball, and they would have been glad if circumstances had permitted the Canadians to add to the education of citizens as regards the peculiarities of the great game of the North American continent."[7]

Ban Johnson, president of baseball's American League, in May 1915 pitched in to equip the Canadian boys fighting on the other side of the English Channel. Stories had reached Americans that their northern neighbors had taken to playing ball in back of the trenches in France, with enthusiastic if baffled British Tommies and French poilus rooting them on. "An appeal has been made to me to provide a big assortment of baseball paraphernalia, consisting of balls, bats, chest protectors and gloves for use of the Canadian soldiers in France," Johnson wired to the mayor of Toronto. "I am prepared to arrange for this donation. The American league club owners and players will cheerfully make the contribution. Kindly instruct me to whom I will send this shipment if it is wanted."[8]

The Canadian minister of militia accepted this gear for the country. Johnson also promised to send five gross (seven hundred twenty) of balls, fifty bats, six masks and chest protectors, and six new sets of uniforms. This wouldn't exactly equip the whole Canadian army in France, but it seemed a reasonable and generous gesture to many Americans.

"Johnnie Canuck is not radically different from a Yankee," a smug Buckeye wrote after a trip north from Youngstown. "He plays the great American game of baseball with the same fervor that is displayed on any diamond in Ohio. He talks the latest Yankees slang and has the most recent ragtime hits on his lips. Even his enemies have admitted that the Canadian soldier is some fighter and that is not strange when it is remembered that he is from the continent of North America."[9]

By summer 1915, a ball club of neutral American civilians had popped up to play the Canadian soldiers. They all got together in June during a military sports festival at Stamford Bridge. There the Duchess of Connaught's Canadian Hospital played "a team of Americans organised by Mr. Jack Norworth, the popular comedian," a squad also known as "Mr. John Gibson Lee's London American team."[10-11] The northerners took the game, 10–6.

The same two teams went at it again a week later. "A team of London Americans on Saturday beat the staff of the Duchess of Connaught's Canadian Hospital by nine runs to seven in a baseball match at Taplow, where an excellent diamond had been laid out on the fairway of Mr. Waldorf Astor's private golf course at Cliveden."[12] This time the Yanks came away winners, 9–7. A month later these teams met again at Taplow, with the Canadians back on top, 15–6.

The powerful Astor family was famous on both sides of the Atlantic, of course. *The landlords of New York*, people called them. Waldorf Astor was a member of the British parliament, and in the early months of the war had handed over his Taplow estate to the Canadian Red Cross for use as a hospital. He and Nancy Astor, his wife, along with J. G. Lee, would soon become important figures in baseball circles in England—and not just because Waldorf had built that ball field on his estate along the Thames, an hour's train ride outside London.

In fall 1915, Canadian baseball encroached even on the holiest of British sporting holy sites, Lord's Cricket Ground, the fabled home of the Marylebone Cricket Club in London. "Lord's is the epitome of all that is English on the field of sport as applied to games where muscle, skill and defence each play their part. The history of Lord's is unique, and its green playing fields have been the foundation of the education of some of the greatest cricketers in the world."[13]

The Yankee team battling the Canadians was again J. G. Lee's London Americans. (Comedian-songwriter Jack Norworth seems to have dropped out of the picture. He is remembered today as the fellow who wrote "Take Me Out to the Ball Game.") Lee a few years earlier had played on the Tottenham Hotspurs club in the short-lived London Baseball League, one of several failed attempts to transplant America's national pastime to the mother country. A

"**Wounded Canadians at Mrs. Astor's hospital, playing ball,**" with nurses looking on. Circa 1915, probably taken at Taplow (Library of Congress).

Britisher and a civilian, he nonetheless would be a huge force in Canadian military baseball during the war. At the moment, his game at the holy cricket ground was a very big deal.

> For the first time in a quarter of a century a baseball match was played at Lord's yesterday, when Canadian soldiers from Shorncliffe beat American residents in London by fourteen runs to four. The game was more interesting and closer than the score indicates until quite near the finish, when the superior condition and constant practice of the soldiers gave them a great advantage. H.R.H. Princess Louise was amongst those present, and in the fourth innings the teams were presented to her Royal Highness, who still maintains a deep interest in anything concerning Canada.[14]

Feisty, artistic and independent-minded, sixty-seven years old, Princess Louise was the fourth daughter of old Queen Victoria and also King George's aunt. She had lived on the other side of the Atlantic in the last quarter of the last century, when her husband, John, marquess of Lorne (the Britishers had such lovely titles), was the governor general of modern Canada (1878–

1883). Louise hadn't really cared for Ottawa, truth be told, and probably wasn't much fonder of baseball, if she had ever even seen it before. But she was a princess and it was wartime, so she dutifully went to the ball game on September 11 and cheered for those fine Canadian boys, who were also rooted on from the stands by their pals, including wounded soldiers.

"The interest which the game excited was shown when the teams adjourned for tea. Then the Canadian spectators holloaed [*sic*] disapproval, asked the teams to bring out their beds and lie down, and were as uncomplimentary as they could be in order to show their own tireless enthusiasm."[15] Yep, the Canadians sure were like their American neighbors. And they trimmed the London squad, either 14−4 or 15−4, depending on which paper you believed.

The fighting ground on into 1916, a slow-moving disaster for every nation under arms. The Battle of the Somme alone cost hundreds of thousands of soldiers on both sides. In England, at least, another season of baseball offered respite and relief for the boys from North America. With the Britishers' own sports in a shambles, many of their great stars dead or disabled, decades of stiff-upper-lipped resistance to the game slowly crumbled. The Canadians began forming leagues, especially at military hospitals in their camps at Orpington, Buxton and Bovington, "where baseball takes over in the evenings."[16]

"Baseball has at last obtained a firm foothold in England and is being played to such an extent in and around London by Canadians whom the war has brought over that a league has been formed among teams drawn from the army pay office and other colonial units, the staffs of the various Canadian military hospitals and munition workers," the *New York Times* noted. "The Canadians having intimated that they would welcome the entry of an American team into the league, one is now being formed by J. G. Lee of Central Buildings, Westminster. In addition to the London district, four teams have been organized at Taplow, while at Epsom, Hampton, Bramshot and many other centres farther afield, the game is being played."[17]

Lee had tried building a league once before, in the last summer before the war, after midshipmen from the U.S. Naval Academy had visited England. The middies had come over on the battleships USS *Missouri* and USS *Illinois* during their summer cruise. They'd made a well-publicized visit to London and played ball against a British team in the stadium at Shepherd's Bush. Lee was the Britishers' pitcher and the organizing secretary of something called the British Baseball Association.

"This year we are contenting ourselves with exhibition games; but about the end of the year we shall be holding a meeting in London to organize a league," Lee said. "Next year [1915] we hope to have a big league competition, in which clubs in London, Liverpool and other large cities will participate."[18]

Lee wasn't alone in daydreaming about this league. A group of well-known Americans living in England, including barrister R. Newton Crane, gave the scheme financial and moral support. "Thanks to the generosity of some American gentleman who are desirous of seeing the game played here," Crane told newspapers, "we have obtained an ample fund to guarantee us against loss."[19] None of these sporting gentlemen had consulted the Kaiser, however, and their venture was spectacularly mistimed. Tommies were fighting spike-helmeted Germans on the Continent before the Yank middies had returned home on their battleships.

England's version of Ban Johnson kept plugging away and finally managed to get a league up and running in 1916. The Military Baseball League wasn't exactly the circuit he had envisioned two years earlier. It was largely a Canadian affair, with a modest schedule of twenty-eight games. "There is not a great supply of necessary balls, gloves, masks, and bats, but the Canadian Government understands for what reasons a Government exists, and is sending more over as military supplies."[20]

Lee's league also included the London Americans, a squad of Yanks living and working in the metropolis. Editors around the globe have always known that all news is local, so Lee's little circuit made news as far away as Manhattan thanks to a shining name from high society.

"Baseball has gripped England and is now being played in many parts of the country before big crowds, due principally to the presence of large numbers of Canadian soldiers," the *New York Times* reported. "Mrs. Waldorf Astor has given a cup for competition and the Canadian Red Cross Society has offered one for the runners up."[21]

Nancy Astor of Virginia is familiar to art lovers today because of a famous portrait painted by John Singer Sargent in 1909. Her husband, Waldorf, born in New York, was a British army officer, and he and Nancy both took a good deal of interest in supporting various war charities. William Waldorf Astor, Waldorf's father, despite also being American-born, was the newly minted first Viscount Astor (money and prestige clearly having their uses).

Lee's new league had eight clubs—Canadian Army Pay Record Office ("Paycord"); 623nd Company, Mechanical Transport, Army Service Corps; the Duchess of Connaught Canadian Red Cross Hospital at Taplow (this nine was called the "Astorias"); one team apiece from the Canadian military convalescent hospitals at Bushey Park, Epsom, Plumstead and Bearwood; and the London Americans.

The Canadian teams proudly wore maple leaves or regimental crests on their flannels. At least one nine wore colorful heliotrope shirts (*bluish-red*, to Americans). The London Americans' spangles bore an emblem of British and American flags separated by a large *L* for London. The league's nines played decent ball, and passed along their gate receipts to war charities.

"We have as good a team as there is in the league, but of course, that does not say a lot for us," wrote London American George Van Dyne, an ex–Georgetown University ballplayer attached to the U.S. consulate general. "Mrs Astor and a number of other ladies and lords, princesses, &c., are deeply interested, and have offered numerous silver cups for the winners of certain games and of the pennant. The champion team will have quite a display if interest does not flag before the middle of September, the end of the season."[22]

Attention didn't flag. If anything, enthusiasm was higher by September. Britishers with titles in front of their names and initials behind them noticed the seven Canadian teams and the one scrappy American squad. "The London American baseball team proved to be in fine fettle yesterday, when, at Chalkwell Park, Westcliffe-on-Sea, they beat a Canadian nine and so secured absolute possession of the 'Jones' Cup, having won two of the series of three games played for the benefit of local military hospitals. The winners had thirteen hits to the losers' six, and made no errors. At the conclusion of the match both sides were congratulated on their excellent display by the Mayor of Southend, who was amongst the 4,000 spectators."[23]

There was even a 1916 postseason of sorts, as several nonleague games made the sports pages across Canada, Great Britain and the United States. The first was between Canadians and the Yanks on September 23 at The Queen's Club (capital *The*, if you please) in West Kensington. Britishers called the game there a "charity baseball match."[24] A paper in America called it "the first important ball game since the Giants and Chicago Americans played their exhibition game in February 1914, on the ground of the Chelsea Football Club, at Stanford Bridge."[25]

Sir Sam Hughes, Canada's minister of defense and the fellow who had accepted Ban Johnson's baseball gear for the Canadian troops, threw out the first ball. A fine looking fellow in uniform, the very model of a modern major-general, Sir Sam had armed his troops with a lousy Canadian-made rifle rather than the reliable Lee-Enfield, and was soon to be sacked for incompetence and general cussedness. Also in the crowd was an impressive array of empire bigwigs, including the duke and duchess of Devonshire (the *ninth* duke, about to become the new governor-general of Canada), Earl Grey (the *fourth* earl; the tea being named for the *second*) and A. J.

Balfour (a failed British prime minister early in the century, but considered something of an elder statesman today).

Lady Julia Parker Drummond of Montreal also attended. She had come to England to work with the Red Cross, and the proceeds of the game would go to a fund that she'd set up to help widows and orphans of Canadian soldiers. One of those soldiers was her son, Lieutenant Guy Melfort Drummond, who had been killed in action in April 1915 at the second battle of Ypres—or "Wipers," as Tommies called that tragic place. The newspapers were kind and didn't mention her loss when they might've gotten weepy over it. No one recorded Lady Drummond's reaction to the game, or what she might have thought while watching it. Probably, like Princess Louise, she was just doing what she considered her duty.

Several thousand spectators, aristocrats and commoners alike, watched the game in "superlatively fine weather," which was no small blessing in an English summer.[26] The teams played under the eye of an amateur umpire, Wilson Cross, an American executive for Vacuum Oil in London. He displayed no evident bias for the Yankee side, which was his mistake. "Despite what the American colony, present in force, thought ample provocation, Mr. Cross escaped from the grounds uninjured."[27] American rooters got understandably sore after watching the boys from up north smack the ball hard all around the yard. "Nine Canadian soldiers with schrapnel [*sic*] distributed through their anatomy made monkeys of nine able-bodied American baseball players at Queen's club, West Kensington, yesterday afternoon in the fastest exhibition of the game ever seen in England. The score was 9 to 1 in favor of Canada. ... It was Sergeant 'Billy' Doyle, of Medicine Hat and the Canadian mounted rifles who mainly put the kibosh on the Americans' hopes. From his place on the slab Doyle pitched a game which proved his right to travel in league company. He had the enemy guessing from start to finish."[28]

Sergeant Doyle was actually from Halifax, but baseball coverage in England was a little lax. It was no disgrace for the Yanks to lose to him, since Doyle had won seventeen straight games for Epsom that season. Still, a London scribe's innocent observation that the "Canadian thrower bowled very well indeed" was too much for a United Press correspondent. "O 'ell, yes: he bowled jolly well," he huffed. "The Canadian strikers batted well, too, and the chap with the odd-looking mask played a ripping game as wicket keeper." The UP man did concede that the Yanks hadn't played classy baseball. "There was a man at first with a glove and uniform but he didn't seem to belong to the club. ... There were more American errors than the final shows. The scorer got tired in the fourth inning and began counting them by twos."[29]

A week later at Woodcote Park, the London Americans "turned the tables on the baseball team from the Canadian Convalescent Home, Epsom, by winning an exciting game, which was played in the presence of some thousands of spectators, by three runs to two."[30] The following Saturday, back again at Queen's and playing before three thousand people (it was too much, really, to call them *fans*), the Canadians turned the tables right back, besting the Yanks, 8–4. "The Lord Mayor of London threw the first ball, and the play was level at the end of the sixth innings—three all. In the eighth innings of the Canadians an umpire's decision upset one of the American team, and there was trouble, people flocking on to the playing pitch. However, officers came to the rescue, and, after a time, play was resumed."[31]

This might have been the first rhubarb ever on British soil, and a unique international incident. (Newspapers didn't say whether the arbiter was again Wilson Cross.) The beef hardly mattered, though, and the pair of games at Queen's raised two hundred fifty pounds for Lady Drummond's widows and orphans.

America's entrance into the war in April 1917 changed everything— but not right away. Promising to kick the stuffing out of Kaiser Bill was one thing, while putting a few million men into the field was something else entirely. The U.S. Navy was in fighting fettle and swung into action right away. The U.S. Army, on the other hand, had barely managed to keep America's southern borders safe from Pancho Villa in 1916. Gearing up for the trenches of France was going to take time.

The 1917 baseball season in England again was mostly a Canadian affair. Lee's circuit was now called the Military Hospital Baseball League and had just six teams. Again, the league included Pay Records and the London Americans, plus nines from the hospitals at Epsom, Orpington, Taplow and Uxbridge. Posters would advertise one of the league games as a "BASEBALL CONTEST ... Soldiers & Sailors Half Price. Wounded Free."[32] Unfortunately, there were plenty of wounded men in England to use those free passes. Convalescing Tommies wore a distinctive blue uniform, which they didn't like much and that stood out among the normal khaki. The London American ballplayers noticed these men in the crowds that watched their games at Canadian military hospitals.

"The side lines will be as noisy as the bleachers of home—the cheers will be for our opponents (Canadian-London baseball teams) and the jeers will be for us; yet we're happier that way for the fans are wounded 'Tommies,'" American pitcher Leon Vannais wrote home to Hartford, Connecticut. "Mother, you can't conceive of how wonderful they are! Bright blue suits, bright red ties, clean white bandages, many slings, numerous crutches; if it were not for the faces, one would weep to look at them—

but one has no desire to feel sad except in a sub-conscious way. The cheerfulness of the men is contagious. They sit there—their eyes sparkling with mirth and interest—their shouts full of the old familiar rooting expressions made wonderfully fresh and greatly supplemented by their witty mixing in of the new slang of war. No wonder we don't mind who they cheered for, it's enough that we're able to give them an afternoon of real sport."[33]

The 1917 season featured another game at Lord's on July 2, the Pay Records nine beating the London Americans, 7–3. "Practically all the winning side have been in France, and most of them have been wounded."[34] The Yanks also played twice more at Queen's, the lord mayor of London throwing out the first ball for the second game, and raised two hundred fifty more pounds for Lady Drummond's fund. "The bantering and the exhortation—all part of the game—from the various 'corners' of the crowd were quite properly fulfilled. Such 'music' seemed strange to English ears. It was at least amusing, and made it possible to imagine what a real baseball show is like on the 'other side.'"[35]

It was a second game at Lord's this season, on July 28, that really grabbed attention on the western side of the Atlantic.

Five or eight or ten thousand people (British newspapers rarely agreed on anything involving baseball) saw the Taplow Astorias beat Lee's London Americans, 12–3. Colonel William Lassiter, the American military attaché, threw out the first ball. Vice-Admiral William S. Sims, commanding the U.S. Navy in Europe, watched from the stands. So did Princess Louise and Lady Drummond, along with Nancy Astor, Martin Hawke (seventh Baron Hawke, a cricketing great), George Harris (fourth Baron Harris, another cricketing giant), a Mr. Vanderbilt (there were several in England; the newspapers didn't specify which) and A. J. Balfour. Mrs. Astor also auctioned off "a giant edition of the Stars and Stripes" donated by department-store magnate Harry Gordon Selfridge.[36]

"There were lots of girls in pretty white frocks wandering with officers and soldiers in regulation khaki, and I was amused at noting the once aristocratic sanctity of the pavilion, now turned into a sort of barracks for the use of a cadet corps which has its quarters at Lord's," a British Lady (capital L) wrote for an American audience.[37]

The rooting started even before the game, which was natural enough to Canadians and Yanks, but very strange to British ears. "Players making preliminary throws or taking preliminary catches were told all their faults through a megaphone in language and tones which made the advice the more pungent. Many Londoners heard baseball for the first time, for there seems to be as much to hear as to see in the game. ... This will not be the last baseball game in London this season, and the interest taken in the match on Saturday shows that baseball is growing in popularity in this country."[38]

The Astorias soundly whipped the Americans, Leon Vannais taking the loss. Except for a seven-run fourth, Vannais hurled a decent game, especially for a pitcher who worked during the week as a Price, Waterhouse accountant. The game was considered a rousing success in America, despite the loss. "Baseball took a decided spurt on Saturday the twenty-eighth of July," *Baseball Magazine* trumpeted.[39]

Lee was jubilant. "Baseball is going strong this year and with the advent of the American boys things will be much better," he wrote a few days later. "So far I have arranged about 150 games around London. ... Of course you know it is an up-hill job, but I am positive in a few years Baseball will be well in hand. Well the game at lord's [*sic*] was one of the best sights in London for some time and it just made the English people stand up and wonder. But I obtained lots of publicity and the game got a big jump through this, so much so that I have been asked to organize teams in the British navy. So you see what is coming."[40]

Before fall arrived the baseball contagion had touched even the royal family, although Lee had little to do with it. On Saturday, September 1, a team of the Canadian Forestry Corps beat the Epsom club 1–0 in a game at Windsor. Princess Mary took in the game and apparently talked about it later at the castle. The king and queen went with her to the Foresters' next game the following Saturday. A brief account on the outing in the British press read like a scene from an Oscar Wilde play.

> The King and Queen, who were accompanied by Prince Albert and Princess Mary, motored from Windsor Castle on Saturday afternoon to the Canadian Forestry Corps Camp in Windsor Great Park, and witnessed a game of baseball between the Canadians and a team from Orpington Hospital. Princess Helena Victoria, Princess Marie Louise, the Marquis de Soveral, and Lady Perley (wife of the High Commissioner for Canada) were also present. Their Majesties were received by Brigadier-General McDougall and Lieutenant-Colonel Penhorwood.
>
> At the conclusion of the match, which was won by the Canadians by two runs to one, the Royal party were entertained at tea by the officers of the Corps. Before leaving the King informed General McDougall and Colonel Penhorwood how much he had enjoyed the afternoon, and alluded to the enthusiasm of the Canadians and the excitement they exhibited during the game.[41]

England got another little taste of the American national pastime later that month when in "a well-planned attack near Brighton a small party of

Americans completely demoralized a Canadian force, supported by heavy rooting artillery. Casualties, 13 to 1." The story that reached the States didn't say whether the Yanks were soldiers, but their uniforms didn't match the London Americans.' "They played in blue uniforms with gray socks, each wearing an American flag. The Canadians had gray uniforms with the initials of the Ontario Military Hospital."[42]

The writer's artillery reference was unfortunate, since the hooting spectators included wounded Canadian soldiers and several hundred Canadian officers on leave for the day. "Many of them were legless, many in basket beds. Quite a few were swathed from head to foot like mummies, and mingling with the perfume of gorgeous gardens surrounding the athletic park was a heavy essence of iodine, arnica and iodoform. The rooting gayety of these convalescents, however, was little affected by bandages, blindness, the awful discomfort of plaster casts or missing legs or arms."[43]

British and Canadian casualties were everywhere in Great Britain. In late October, Lee took his London-Americans and a Canadian squad across to Ireland, where they played two games to benefit wounded troops in the Emerald Isle. (Ireland was still undivided and under British rule, the Easter Rising there having failed in 1916.) In Dublin, twelve thousand people watched the Canadians beat the Yanks, 10–6, poor Vannais again taking the loss—although he didn't seem to mind, later recalling the trip fondly. The funds the teams raised benefited the Dublin Castle Red Cross Hospital. John Graham Hope de la Poer Beresford (fifth Baron Decies), who was married to an American, "presided at a dinner given to the teams, and presented the members of both teams with miniature silver cups of Irish design."[44]

The Dublin contest proved such a smash that Belfast asked for a game, too. Lee obliged and took his team north. Another large crowd watched the teams play to a tie, the newspapers not recording the final score. The receipts this time went to the hospital of the Ulster Volunteer Force. In both cities, Lee also auctioned off bats and balls to boost the take for the war charities. *Baseball Magazine* now proclaimed him "the father of baseball in England."[45] Maybe Lee thought such good ink would carry his league even higher the following year. But he would discover before the 1918 season that another crew of hustling Yanks had plans of their own.

"Next summer 'ball' will carry everything before it," some smart cookie wrote home to America that winter, "as the presence of the American boys will give a decided fill to the strong foundation laid by the Canadians during the last three years."[46]

2

Arlie Latham

The Rube Goldberg machine that was the King's Game wasn't linear. Step A didn't always lead to Step B, or Step B to Step C. Sometimes, depending on who diagrammed its many whirling components, Step B might sit ticking away off to one side, while (*whilst*, to the Britishers) Step A rolled or whacked or glided its way toward Step F or G. If that's how the machine worked, then Step B was one Walter Arlington Latham.

Latham's history was long and colorful, so it was noteworthy but not surprising when he bobbed up in wartime London in 1917. The energetic fifty-seven-year-old was discovered suiting up with the London Americans— and not as a coach, mind you, but as a player. He might, in fact, even have been fifty-*eight*; the hand-written records of his times don't agree. Latham was born on March 15 in West Lebanon, New Hampshire, in either 1859 or 1860 (the latter being the more likely, according to his biographer and other students of the game), a year or two before the start of the American Civil War in 1861. His convoluted path to England was something of a Goldberg machine itself.

Universally known as "Arlie," Latham was a magnificent Yankee amalgam—a ballplayer, shoemaker, bar owner, vaudevillian, jokester, brawler, delicatessen owner, big-league coach, and natural-born hustler and salesman. He'd been the bane of major-league owners, managers and opponents for decades, while remaining a fan favorite the whole while. Arlie had broken into the big leagues with the Buffalo Bisons in 1880 and, incredibly, lasted long enough to take the field with John McGraw's New York Giants twenty-nine years later.

"Arlie and baseball grew up together, beginning in the early days when ... players wore no gloves, catching the heavy, fast-flying symbol of American vitality with their bare hands," his biographer would write a century later. "He and the game survived rule changes, and the birth and death of leagues that few remember. He watched the game go from his style of smart, calculated play to the era of the big bats."[1]

Henry Latham, Arlie's father, was a shoemaker. In the fall of 1864, three and a half years after the start of the Civil War, Henry enlisted as a bugler in Company H of the First New Hampshire Heavy Artillery. His regiment served mostly in the defenses of Washington, and Henry survived the war to return home a corporal. He later moved his family south to Lynn, Massa-

Arlie Latham, coaching with the New York Giants, 1909 (Library of Congress).

chusetts, which offered more opportunity for a shoemaker.

Arlie apprenticed as a shoemaker, too, although it's hard to imagine that the trade suited him or that he liked it very much. He became a good athlete in the 1870s, taking up baseball first as a catcher, than as an infielder. He got good enough to play for several local clubs across Massachusetts. He married for the first time in 1879 without much enthusiasm, taking a quick break in the middle of a game to tie the knot before hurrying back to the field. His son Clifford was born six months later.

If no role model as a family man, Arlie was a fine ballplayer and his run in the big leagues was remarkable. After his lackluster rookie year in Buffalo in 1880, he broke in with the St. Louis Browns in 1883. He remained with Prussian-born owner Chris Von der Ahe's club until 1890, playing with and for Charles Comiskey, who was first Arlie's teammate, then his manager. The Latham-Comiskey relationship was often contentious, but nothing compared to the legendary Latham-Von der Ahe combination. The

Browns' third baseman was constantly broke, often in trouble and continually running some scam or bluff, whether on the field or off. Each time, Von der Ahe would fine and forgive his bad boy and the whole cycle would start over. "Arlie," the owner once despaired, "I have fined you over a million dollars and never collected a cent."[2]

Arlie's fondness for good clothes and high living earned him the nickname Dude. Even playing in four consecutive championship series with the Browns (1885–1888) couldn't keep him in adequate funds. He returned in the off seasons to a Massachusetts shoe factory, where he used his only other skill outside of baseball. In later years he ran saloons and pool halls, played on roller-hockey teams (a popular sport before the turn of the century), and for a time starred on the vaudeville circuits.

"A gentleman remarked recently, after seeing Arlie Latham in 'Fashions,' which Knowles & Morris bring out at the Grand Opera-House next week: 'He must have been practising a song and dance about third base all Summer.' 'Fashions' is a combination of laughable situations strung together, as the author claims, for no other purpose than to amuse the public."[3] *Fashions* included a song especially written for Arlie, "The Freshest Man on Earth," after the nickname bestowed on him by Cap Anson. Cap hadn't meant it especially as a compliment, but it was the sort of nickname that stars need and sportswriters love.

The baseball diamond was an even bigger stage for Arlie. People loved his capering and joking. He couldn't help playing to fans in St. Louis, or to fans in other teams' parks, too. Once during a game in Brooklyn a loud bang and clatter rose from a quarry next door. "Don't be alarmed, folks," Arlie hollered to the crowds. "That merely was [Brooklyn owner] Charlie Ebbets falling down the stairs with the day's receipts."[4]

Probably the best-known stunt attributed to Arlie was lighting candles to protest an umpire's decision to keep playing a crucial 1889 game, also in Brooklyn, despite rapidly falling darkness—or already *fallen*, in the Browns' view. Sportswriters loved the tale and repeated it for decades, despite the fact that it was actually Von der Ahe who "decided to place a row of lit candles in front of the Browns bench."[5] Arlie later wrote that his own role had been to run back into the clubhouse, find nine old candle stubs, and pass them out among his teammates. "We lit the candles and sat on the bench looking over the flames at the black field like mourners at a funeral."[6]

This infamous game, "one of the wildest of the 19th century," had already featured a unique example of baserunning by Arlie, who shaved about twenty feet off the right angle when rounding third.[7] The tactic somehow went unnoticed by the ump, who perhaps missed it in the failing light, but was instantly picked up by the crowd. Later, illuminated only by candles and the lights of a passing elevated train, the contest ended with manager Comiskey pulling his team off the field, the Browns slugging their way out of the park, a St. Louis forfeit (later reversed) and a full-blown riot by the Brooklyn fans. Life with Arlie and the Browns was rarely boring, but generally not quite as exciting as this.

For years, Arlie was a fan favorite as a hitter, clown and base stealer. He swiped so many bags during his early years in the show that he created his own sliding glove, a "highly unusual contraption" that wouldn't become commonplace for another century. "I bought a stout buckskin glove—the sort a railroad engineer might use, with a gantlet over the wrist," he remembered decades later, "and had a shoemaker sew an extra piece of stiff leather on it to save wear and tear on my forearm."[8] The glove helped preserve his hide and fingers, but sometimes sparked fisticuffs when a second baseman noticed Latham charging down on him wearing an armored glove.

Using his fielder's glove was something else entirely, although Arlie still managed to please the fans. During a game in 1887, he dodged a scorching line drive, more out of self-preservation than anything else. "But it was the effect caused by his brazen sidestepping that seems to have made a light bulb go off in Latham's busy, attention-seeking brain. He couldn't have failed to notice that that single move had, quite simply, slayed the crowd."[9] Arlie often wouldn't bother to dive for hot line drives after that. His signature *olé* move as the ball shot past into the outfield entered the baseball lexicon as an *Arlie Latham*.

After leaving St. Louis, Arlie spent the 1890 season with Chicago in the short-lived Players' League, then moved on to Cincinnati as time began to run out. He hurt his arm, and balls shot past because he couldn't handle them. He played in the Queen City with the Reds through 1895, then returned to St. Louis in 1896—but with the Cardinals this time. After a final brief stop with Washington in 1899, he disappeared from big-league diamonds. He bounced from team to team in the low minors, still seeking the limelight, never finding a home.

The old third-sacker even tried his hand as an umpire, working the bush-league circuits. He retained his showman's flair, once fetching a tape to measure the length of the first baseman's and runner's feet before calling a close play at the bag. But he wasn't good at umpiring and didn't like working in leagues where the clubs might be managed by aging ballplayers he'd known in the show. One day in Little Rock, Harry "Farmer" Vaughn, a former Cincinnati catcher, skippered the opposing Birmingham team. When Arlie rang up a batter with a called third strike, Vaughn charged hotly out to argue.

"Hello, Harry," Arlie said pleasantly. "How is your liver?"[10]

Like many famous clowns, Arlie had a dark side. It would have been charity to call him an indifferent husband, and he was physically abusive to his first two wives. His third marriage somehow lasted nearly sixty years—despite, or maybe because of, lengthy separations. Arlie also associated with gamblers, which wasn't especially unusual in his era, but still raised eyebrows and suspicions. One of his later acquaintances, Arnold Rothstein, a silent partner in a billiards hall owned by New York Giants manager John McGraw, helped fix the 1919 World Series, the "Black Sox" scandal that got "Shoeless" Joe Jackson and seven Chicago teammates permanently booted from baseball.

Just as bad to modern eyes, Arlie in 1887 signed a petition by Browns players who refused to play an exhibition game with the Cuban Giants, an African American club. "We're all good Democrats and can't think of meeting the black birds," he told outraged Von der Ahe in a team meeting.[11] Years later, Arlie would work a few African American ball games as an umpire.

In February 1909, after the former star had been out of the majors for a decade, hot-stove leagues heated up with reports that manager McGraw might sign Arlie for the Giants. The idea seemed preposterous, but there was one critical twist. "Latham as a player is impossible," sportswriter Bozeman Bulger explained in the New York World. "His arm is so bad that he could not even throw a fit; but on the coaching lines he can easily hit .800. That is the only purpose for which McGraw will sign him."[12]

"It sounded like a joke when McGraw announced that he had signed Arlie as comedian-coach, but the 'Joints' look upon the humorist as anything but a joke," agreed a sportswriter in Spokane. True enough, there was Arlie, signed and in the Giants' camp at Marlin Springs, Texas. "Latham will do coacher's duty, going through his performance for the edification of opposing players, and it is possible that many a close game will be changed unless Latham has lost his ability to make pitchers laugh at the wrong time."[13]

The Brooklyn Eagle figured that McGraw had made a typically shrewd move in signing Arlie, who "could do more in a high class way to unnerve a pitcher than anybody who ever wore a shoe."[14] Tom Loftus, Arlie's former teammate and manager, recalled: "He never raved and yelled at the pitcher, but the minute one of his side cracked out a nice hit Arlie was right on the job with that old oily talk of his. 'Well, well, well, Mr. Pitcher'—always the mister—'that was a little hard luck for you. Oh, and look who's up now! But never mind: the trouble will all be over in a minute. We'll make it as easy for you as we can.' That line of talk is what gets a pitcher every time. Because he can't say anything back. Call him lobster and a pitcher is back at you in a flash, giving as much as you can send; but get under his skin with the polite conversation and the pitcher hasn't got a chance. That was easy for Latham."[15]

Arlie performed just as expected with the Giants in 1909—coaching from the bench and beside the bags, delighting fans and keeping the club loose. Four times during the season, McGraw even used the old man between the lines when his bench was empty. Arlie went oh-for-two at the plate, scored once and fielded two balls at second base—this by a coach who was then forty-nine (or maybe fifty) years old.

"The outstanding feature of the first game was the introduction of Arlie Latham to run bases for O'Hara in the ninth inning," a New York daily reported of an August doubleheader in Philadelphia. "He and Shafer worked a double steal successfully and the crowd went wild."[16] A century and more later, Arlie is still the oldest big-league ballplayer ever to steal a base. He might have paused to remember that particular game a time or two later in England, when Lieutenant Billy O'Hara was fighting with a Canadian regiment in France and shy Arthur "Tillie" Shafer was on the American west coast learning to fly float planes for the U.S. Navy.

The Giants were only a one-year deal, then Arlie was again out of baseball. By 1915, he had gone into business, without much success. "'Arlie' Latham Batting .106 in the Delicatessen League," a headline declared, above a photo of Arlie outside his display window, wearing a white jacket and long apron and standing next to his dog. "Great game, baseball. I love it, always will. Was in the game thirty-five years, you know. But 'Ma' and I realized that it was almost time we put something by for the old rainy day and we opened this shop, and were doing very well, thank you, and going to do better. ... I will be in the .300 class as soon as the season is under way and things get warmer."[17]

Arlie couldn't have peddled that much baloney behind his own counter. He left the deli business less than two years later and sailed for England in January 1917, three months before America entered the war. He went alone, no doubt wisely in wartime, without his third wife or their four children. Exactly what he expected to do "over there"—or even what he *hoped* to do—remains unclear. He listed his occupation as salesman, and stated on his passport application (perhaps not exactly understanding the question) that the object of his visit was "Foot Arch Supports Manufacturers."[18] In a registration form he filed with the U.S. consulate general, he said he was in London on "commercial business, on behalf of Walter A. Dunbar of Lynnwood, Massachusetts."[19] Arlie's biographer has concluded that he might have been working for the Spalding & Bros. sporting goods company, but adds, "Knowing Latham's infamous inability to hold a regular job, he might have arrived in England only to quit the company that had brought him over."[20]

However he earned his living, Arlie was soon testing his ancient baseball skills against the Canadian military nines, playing for J. G. Lee's London Americans. His teammates were Yank accountants, businessmen and consular officers, all half his age or younger—and the old Brownie was having the time of his life. As improbable as it must have seemed to many, Arlie played right field in the July 28 baseball match at Lord's. Even British newspapermen marveled.

"A white-haired player, 'Daddy' Latham, an ex-first-baseman of the Cincinnati Reds and a Big League player in the 'nineties, hit one of the prettiest strokes of the day. He played a game that many of the younger men might envy," London's *Times* said.[21] That fine and fastidious newspaper didn't record whether any khaki-clad spectator might have bellowed that time-honored British accolade, "Well done that man!"

Newton Crane, the expatriate lawyer who had helped bolster J. G. Lee's dreams of starting a league back in 1914, might have been the first person to recognize the old Brownie cavorting amid his countrymen in a league game earlier in the season. Crane had often seen Latham play ball at the height of his skill and fame in St. Louis. "I would have given a great deal to have you with me last Saturday afternoon at a game between our London American club and another in the league," he wrote home to an old friend in the Mound City.

I saw a man go to bat who arrested my attention by something familiar in his movements. He was long past youth and the adherents of the visiting club began to jeer him, calling out that "grandpa is afraid of the pitcher, see him strike out, etc." The batsman feigned terror and wobbled his knees and went through several antics, which turned the crowd from jeering to good-natured laughter.

When he made a hit and ran on his toes to first base, I could hardly believe my eyes, for I recognized in the player none other than our old friend, Arlie Latham, whose antics and tricks and amusing patter at third base were the delight of the "rooters" for the St. Louis Browns in the old days when you and I were such regular attendants at the ball park.

Latham is now playing right field for the London Americans, which is a purely amateur nine, and yet it puts up a very good article of ball.

I heard that Latham is over here as a teacher, but of what I have not the slightest idea. His hair is nearly as white as mine, but he is still full of ginger and bears no trace of age in his movement. Although we might possibly get a more effective player, we could have no one on the team who would be such a steady influence and attract so much attention.[22]

Sports editors and columnists in the States slapped their thighs in delight and reached for their pencils when they learned of this fine wartime story ... which, of course, many promptly got all wrong. "Arlie Latham, veteran ex–National leaguer and for some seasons one of the game's most popular comedian coaches, is now a member of a Canadian regiment in London," read the caption of a widely syndicated photo—this, despite the fact that an American flag and not a maple leaf was clearly visible on his uniform. "At a recent game between Canadians and Americans, Arlie was there to make the Sammies happy with the comic capers that have made him a hit with every American fan."[23] That bit, at least, was accurate.

The discovery of the irrepressible Arlie playing ball, in England of all places, delighted everyone. But the person who mattered most was Newton Crane. A week before the war's end, a wire service would even mistakenly report that Crane had summoned Arlie to England "as the one man to put the new game in motion on the other side."[24] The Latham-Crane connection would indirectly lead, however, via a dozen strange swerves and detours, to King George V attending the great army-navy baseball match a year later in Chelsea.

3

The Anglo-American
Baseball League

If Arlie Latham was a bright, whizzing whirligig in the Rube Goldberg machine of the King's Game, Robert Newton Crane was more like a clear glass marble rolling down a curved channel between the charismatic old diamond star and the founding members of the Anglo-American Baseball League. Crane was an important but not especially dazzling component of the machine.

For decades the man was always referred to in print as R. Newton or Newton Crane, never as Bob or Newt—but that was British formality for you. Crane was a lawyer and former managing editor of the *St. Louis Globe-Democrat* who had first come to England as the United States consul at Manchester in 1874. He was appointed the U.S. dispatch agent in London in 1904, a largely honorary post involving the forwarding of official mail and documents. By a sort of gentleman's agreement, the actual work was handled by a Britisher with the fine Dickensian name of Mr. Petherick.

During all his years living and working in London, Crane never lost his love of America's national pastime. He helped found the National Baseball League of Great Britain in 1889 to promote "a vigorous campaign to make baseball one of the prominent field sports" in the country.[1] Despite financial aid from American sporting goods magnate A. G. Spalding, the league lasted just a single forty-four-game season, although "Preston, Derby, Birmingham and Stoke-on-Trent acquired a small number of enthusiastic fans who took an interest in the welfare of their respective clubs."[2]

No doubt remembering the old St. Louis Browns, Crane kept sowing seeds on rocky foreign soil. "He would be the true north for British baseball for the next two decades, as the sport struggled through fits and starts to gain a toehold."[3] Had he been a ballplayer himself, Crane would have been one of those pesky, scrappy sorts who slap bingles all around the yard. He never gave up trying to keep the British leagues going, and in 1894 helped form the London Base Ball Association. The new circuit somehow got noticed on the far side of the Atlantic. "Newton Crane, a name no American ever heard before, should be remembered and treasured now. He has just been elected president of the first baseball league in England."[4]

In spring 1911, after twenty-plus years of seeing British ball clubs and associations come and go, rise and fall, Crane was the honorary president of the Baseball Association. "Before a good sized crowd he tossed the ball into the Crystal palace grounds and the annual schedule began. Six teams have been formed and play every Saturday in and about London. Baseball is kept alive in England by a few American enthusiasts and by the American colony, which contributes generously towards any deficit that arises."[5]

Three years later, in February 1914, the New York Giants and Chicago White Sox visited London on their world tour. The big leaguers played at Stamford Bridge, with the king among the twenty-five thousand people in the stands. "His Majesty was received by the American ambassador, who sat with him and explained the points of the game, the King asking many questions. His Majesty remained until the end of the match, which resulted in a win for Chicago by five runs to four."[6] George V was a good sport about everything, but baseball still didn't catch on.

The World War began just six months later. As the first Canadian boys came over with their bats and balls, things began to change. In May 1915, the 19th Service Battalion of the King's Liverpool Regiment even formed a ball team to play the local championship nine. (The 19th was one of four local outfits known as the Pals battalions because so many friends volunteered together. What happened to them in the slaughter along the Somme and at places like Passchendaele was hard to think about later.)

By 1917, Newton Crane had been living permanently in England for more than three decades. He was now a barrister of the Middle Temple, no small potatoes. As his home country got deeper and deeper into the war, Crane seemed to think a lot about baseball—and he wasn't alone.

"With great numbers of 'Yanks' on British soil, it follows that a good deal of attention will now be devoted to the pastime mentioned," a British editorial read, "and it is equally certain that it will be watched with a polite assumption of interest, but the worthy souls who suggest that exciting conditions will kindle an enthusiasm previous exhibitions of baseball failed to arouse, are, we believe, doomed to disappointment."[7]

Well, maybe. Too much these days—everything really, if you could bear thinking about it—was completely uncertain, including which side would win the damnable war. So who knew what might happen with baseball?

Crane was nearly seventy years old when he spotted Arlie Latham playing for the London Americans. Did he take it as a sign of baseball's future? He certainly got excited, and his letter to an old friend about Arlie playing at Lord's ran in many American newspapers. Maybe baseball's time in Great Britain really had come at last, during the biggest and most horrendous war the world had ever seen. Anything might happen now. Yes, the war was horrible, but baseball continued and even flourished in strange ways.

R. Newton Crane was right in the middle of it all.

People back home first heard about the Anglo-American Baseball League in February 1918. That is, they read about the *idea* for an overseas circuit—which naturally, over time, would become something quite different. Sportswriter Fred Lieb introduced the league to readers in his column in the *New York Sun*.

> An overseas professional baseball organization to be composed of six clubs, and to be known as the Anglo-American league has been launched, according to W. A. Parsons, who was in this city yesterday on a hunt for players. Howard E. Booker of San Francisco, who has been active in English sporting circles and on the turf for the last eight years, has received permission from the British war office to start the league in England.[8]

Parsons and Booker thought that London, Paris and Brighton were all sure bets for their new league. Recreation centers for American troops in France would host the other three clubs, Aix-les Bains and Vichy being the most likely candidates. The AABL (an acronym that nobody actually used at the time) would play only a five-month season, April 1 to September 1, as the rainy season in London worked against playing any later.

A Stateside paper would call the AABL "the crest of a baseball mania which has followed American soldiers and sailors wherever they are based in Europe."[9] Arlie Latham agreed. "Every American warship which has touched these shores since America joined in, every American troopship which has come across—and the hundreds more that will come—contain two, three, four, half a dozen baseball players who are among the front rank in the United States, and dozens of others of less ability to whom the game is the only one that matters when they have a little time to spare,"

Arlie said in London. "We are going to cater for them, and we figure that, by the end of this summer, when we have played games in the principal centers of population in the United Kingdom, Saturday after Saturday, baseball in England and Scotland, Wales and Ireland will have come to stay."[10]

British and French officials strongly endorsed the new league, or so Booker told Fred Lieb. The sportswriter was silent, though, on just what well-placed Yank officials thought of the scheme. "The games naturally are expected to draw well at the American camps," he wrote, "especially at the recreation centers, where professional baseball is expected to make Uncle Sam's fighters feel at home."[11] There was plenty of interest in London, too, according to Booker, who dropped Arlie's name into the interview as an associate in the venture.

Working from an office at 96 Washington Street in Newark, New Jersey, Parsons had already signed up thirty American ballplayers for the league. He and Booker planned to fill out the rosters with Yanks and Canadians who were either too young or too elderly to be snapped up by the draft. The pair figured that the AABL might somehow equal a Class B league, and that it would continue after the war in the leading cities of England and France. Lieb must have needed a column that day, because he not only ran with the story, but added a sappy postscript: "A world's championship series of real worldwide interest ceases to be an idle dream of the thirty-three degree fan. By ten years it may be a reality."[12]

You bet.

Still, unlikely and even miraculous things happened in wartime. And, despite being professional sports promoters—never the most trustworthy species—the odd couple of Booker and Parsons could claim some credibility.

At thirty-one, Howard Elliott Booker was the younger and more dynamic partner. Newspapers called him a horseman active in British turf circles, an ex-champion roller-skater and a boxing promoter. Before the war, Booker had promoted a 1913 bout in Paris between Jack Johnson and Jim Johnson, as well as roller-skating exhibitions in England, France, Belgium and Germany. In August 1916, two years into the war, he had made a trip over to England, "accompanying my wife on visit to her people." He sailed to England again in July 1917, to "close my business and ship race horses as all racing has closed down in England."[13] His passport photos showed a slim, dark-haired man, handsome in his way, with an expression that had grown more serious as the war continued. A Boston writer described him this way:

> Booker came from San Francisco, where his father was prominent as
> treasurer of the San Francisco Company Water Works. He is a little fellow

with a great personality and a reputation for being square that has made him a very successful promoter. His standing in London is high. That Booker is behind any project compels faith in it. He it was who inaugurated the movie shows first in the English and Canadian camps and later in those of the Americans.[14]

William A. Parsons was the elder partner. Born in Massachusetts but now living in Brooklyn, he had just turned fifty. In a passport application before the war, Parsons had listed his occupation as salesman, which was inadequate but accurate as one label among many. In a postwar application he would change it to "amusements" and "Theatrical Business," which came nearer the mark.[15] His photo revealed a graying, distinguished-looking fellow who could have passed for a banker or even a horseman like Booker. No doubt this solid appearance was an asset for the former president of an organization called the American Skating Rink Corporation.

The same Beantown columnist who composed the portrait of Booker described Parsons as a "veteran baseball and roller polo player and manager and international sport promoter. Before the war Parsons conducted a chain of skating rinks in Germany. ... Parsons is one of the lessees of the Boston Arena, and upon his judgment largely will depend whether Boston will be represented in the roller polo league now being formed. He excels in experience in the game any man connected with it."[16]

Parsons also had baseball bona fides. Lieb said he was "an old minor league promoter, and formerly owned the Portland and Lawrence New England league clubs. At Lawrence he developed the old Dodger star, Gene De Montreville."[17]

Arlie Latham would have appreciated Parsons' experience in both sports, particularly roller polo, also called roller hockey, which was played with a ball rather than a puck. Arlie had played it for fourteen winters in the baseball off-seasons in Lynn, Salem and Boston. Many years later, he told a writer about playing roller polo at the old Grand Central Palace in New York City.

"I remember what a racket the pipe organ used to make there," Arlie said. "Along with our roller polo we'd give, as an extra feature, demonstrations of baseball: how to pitch a curve, how to slide, and how to guard a base."[18] Arlie pulled out his unique base-stealing glove for these sliding exhibitions, to guard against splinters from the hard wooden floor. Yes, he would have been glad to swap tall tales in London with Parsons about his baseball and roller hockey days.

Whether by circumstance, design or a happy combination, Arlie, Booker and Parsons came together in England during the world war. In mid–February 1918, this odd triumvirate began promoting their Anglo-

American league to the English-speaking world. In little more than a month, Newton Crane was in the picture as well. These four Yankee civilians, representing three generations, hailing from the Middle West and both American coasts, combined their drive, talent, ambition and experience to promote their national pastime in a land that had never before warmed to it.

What could possibly go wrong?

By the time Arlie's name popped up in a British newspaper again in mid–March, the very nature of the AABL had changed. The plan to bring ballplayers over from the States was already out the window. "He hopes to draw his players from the American and Canadian troops and from the Consulate staffs. Negotiations are in progress for taking over the Chelsea football ground, and it is intended to make a start in May. Latham very wisely wants the boys to take to the game, and he proposes to give facilities for Boy Scouts to play."[19]

George T. Bye, an American correspondent in London, soon added several more details. Bye wrote for the *Stars and Stripes*, the great army newspaper published in Paris for the American Expeditionary Forces (AEF) and for several other papers and syndicates back home. Bye would later become a famous literary agent, representing Eleanor Roosevelt, Charles Lindbergh and a few not-yet-famous writers now serving with the army paper in France.

"An Anglo-American baseball league is being organized on the framework of one that was in existence last season but had no A.E.F. participants," Bye reported. "There will be eight teams, four American and four British. And it's not going to be as soft for the Yanks as you imagine. There are two crack teams among Canadian hospital hands in these parts, and in the gradual Americanization of bonny England quite a number of sporty cricketers have forsaken the wickets for our national pastime."[20]

The AABL, in other words, now looked awfully like J. G. Lee's old military hospital league, except that Lee wasn't mentioned anywhere in Bye's story. The correspondent told his army readers that Uncle Sam's teams would include U.S. Navy Headquarters, U.S. Army Headquarters (which the army called Base Section No. 3), the American embassy and consulate combined, and American civilians (who sounded a lot like the London Americans). It was possible the civilians would be squeezed out for a joint army-navy squad, though, and any British participation was still up in the air.

"One team has already been made up of A.E.F. men," Bye added. "Its organizer modestly hopes that the boys will make a good showing. His modesty is cruel. My heart goes out to those innocent boys in blue who wear the inverted peg-top panties. They don't know what they're up against—a utility infielder late of the Brooklyn Nationals, a star battery from the University of California, and a shifty-footed shortstop from Leland Stanford U. And the modest organizer says he does hope to pull a little surprise in the shape of an Iowa corn-shucker who seems to know something about first base. Cru-el, cru-el for the Navy."[21]

Bye was half right about the Yank squads. The army and navy HQs would play in the league, but the embassy-consulate and the civilian nines would not and neither would any British teams. The league eventually would land a ton of talent, especially among the Yanks. The rosters would include the names of former pros from the American, Pacific Coast, New York State, Southern, Western and Illinois-Indiana-Iowa (3-I) leagues, among others, plus some good amateurs from semipro and collegiate teams.

The AABL couldn't have pulled all this together without one major figure who had nothing to do with baseball before the war. Vice-Admiral William Sowden Sims, USN, commanded the American naval forces in Europe. You can look him up today in histories of the U.S. Navy. A biographer has pegged him this way: "An aggressive personality of the Nelsonian tradition, he should have become a swashbuckling sea-fighter, but he never gained the opportunity to do so."[22]

Before the war with Spain twenty years earlier, Sims had studied the French, British and Russian navies as the American naval attaché in Paris. He fit the part, looking more like a brainy spymaster than a naval officer. At the start of *this* war, he had swung his ships very quickly into action, especially the quick, U-boat-sinking destroyers.

The admiral had a nice touch with the Britishers, too—maybe, in part, because he'd been born to American parents living in Canada. After the Span-ish war, Sims had pushed the U.S. Navy to adapt British gun-

Rear-Admiral William Sowden Sims, U.S. Navy (Library of Congress).

nery practices because American shooting was frankly lousy. (Fortunately for the *yanquis*, Spanish shooting was absolutely terrible.) President William Howard Taft had reprimanded Sims in 1910 for an unauthorized speech he'd given about Anglo-American solidarity. The admiral was now a favorite of Stateside editorialists and poets, and not just for the lovely cadence of his name.

> *"And when can you be ready," flashed the Briton to the Yank,*
> *when we slipped across the dampness of the little swimmin' tank,*
> *And then flashed back an answer in a way to glad your glims;*
> *"We're ready now! we're ready now!" says William Sowden Sims.*[23]

Admiral Sims would be an unofficial but very important influence on the AABL once the season got under way. His army counterpart in England would have just as much juice in the fledgling league as Sims did. Major-General John Biddle was a former commandant of the long gray line at West Point, now commanding American troops in Great Britain. The United Press explained to readers back home how these two military men helped shape the AABL.

> For a time this spring England was threatened with an invasion of two teams of professional ball players gathered from bush league clubs throughout America. Admiral Sims put his foot down on this plan, and Booker then decided upon the plan to popularize baseball through the simon-pure athletics of army and navy players.
>
> General Biddle crimped the arrangements for a brief moment when ... backers wanted to divide the proceeds among British and American war charities.
>
> "Give it all to British charities," said General Biddle. "We Americans have come over here to do and give— not to receive."
>
> The promoters "got" him.[24]

Major-General John Biddle, U.S. Army (Library of Congress).

Like Sims and Biddle, Arlie Latham also saw his profile rise on both sides of the Atlantic. A London sporting paper positively gushed over the old Brownie: "Now there is in England one Arlie Latham, an American sportsman of the best type, who knows all there is to know about the national game of his countrymen, who can play it and talk it and write it, who has been long enough in this country to study the psychology of an English crowd and who believes that the time is ripe for educating the public to the advantages and delights of the summer game in which he has earned a well-merited name on the other side of the Atlantic. ... To hear him talk of baseball is an education."[25] How Arlie must have enjoyed that *best type* line! He hadn't often read as much in the Stateside papers.

The final pieces of the AABL fell into place in April. "The American Baseball Club and the Anglo-American Baseball league have now joined forces, so that besides their lease of the Stamford Bridge ground the league will have an opportunity of arranging matches on the Arsenal ground at Highbury, which had been taken over for the summer by the London Americans."[26] Stamford Bridge and Highbury, both normally used for British soccer (*football*, to the Britishers), would be the league's two showcase venues during the summer.

The league was finally set by the first week of May. The AABL was an eight-team, all-military circuit, the Yanks and Canadians having four squads apiece. The London Americans were civilian and so weren't invited, although one well-known player would still suit up for a Yank team. The Britishers didn't participate in the league at all, although this didn't seem to disappoint anybody.

As with everything else involving baseball, the English newspapers rarely agreed on what to call the eight teams, some referring to the command or hospital, others to the location. It probably reminded Yanks of the American Civil War, with the Union army naming battles for the closest body of water, while the rebels looked around for the nearest town. The league itself listed the teams this way:

American	Canadian
U.S. Army	Epsom Hospital
U.S. Navy	Sunningdale Hospital
Hounslow Barracks	Pay Office
Northolt Aviation Camp	Records Office

The Yank teams were all new in 1918, since there hadn't been enough American troops stationed in Great Britain in the summer of 1917. Sunningdale was a convalescent hospital, as was Epsom, which had played in J. G. Lee's military league. Pay Office and Records had participated, too, as the Paycord team.

Unlike many of the American and Canadian military nines scattered across Great Britain, the AABL wore real baseball uniforms. They were a fairly colorful lot, too, and couldn't be confused or mixed up on the diamond. The U.S. Army wore light green; U.S. Navy, dark blue; Hounslow, white; Northolt, gray; Epsom, gray with a blue stripe; Sunningdale, bluish gray with a maple leaf on the pockets; Pay Office, white with a black stripe; and Records Office, dark green with red and white socks.

Northolt and Hounslow both fielded teams from the Yanks stationed at the aerodromes, where squadrons generally lived in tents. Neither nine was strong, although Hounslow did have Private First Class Walter Brockley of the 264th Aero Squadron, who'd pitched in the Ohio State League. Brockley would even beat the U.S. Navy nine once in the early going. Realistically, though, both Air Service teams looked at the AABL as a step above their usual inter-squadron games—they didn't have the players to do otherwise. U.S. Army and U.S. Navy, on the other hand, were headquarters teams, as were the Canadian Pay Office and Records clubs. These four squads tended to look at things differently. In the HQs, people worked in fine offices and didn't sleep or eat under canvas.

Anybody who naively expected headquarters teams of pale, bespectacled tangle-foots more comfortable with pens and eyeshades than bats, gloves and balls was in for a surprise, especially from the American side. The U.S. Army headquarters staff included one hundred fifty Air Service officers and men. HQ wasn't above borrowing good ballplayers from aviation units based at the fields and camps outside London, too. Lieutenant Mims' team nabbed men from at least three squadrons, which sometimes lost their own ball games with their best players off playing in town. The U.S. Navy squad included a commissioned aviator whose regular mission was to fly patrols over the English Channel—no job for a wallflower. The honored word *ringers* would be applied more than once to the Yank headquarters teams. And on the Canadian side, Epsom and Sergeant Billy Doyle had already proved that hospitals could play a very fast brand of ball, too.

Having Canadian nines in the AABL didn't mean that Dominion leagues were finished in England, either. A new Canadian Military Athletic Association was formed early in 1918. CMAA teams were numerous and the competition fierce all over the scepter'd isle. "Some three hundred matches were played in May by men of the 2nd Canadian Division alone, while a further 250 were played at Shorncliffe the following month."[27] The Dominion boys hardly had to depend on others to see good ball.

Geographically, the AABL was somewhat scattered. The headquarters teams were all in London. The Yank HQs were within walking distance of each other, the American Embassy and Buckingham Palace. The Canadian

Record Office was in Green Arbour House near the Old Bailey. (*Record* was the correct name for the HQ, but for some reason it was generally *Records* when talking about the ball team. And wasn't *Green Arbour House* a lovely name for a place where death notices came from?) Pay Office was near the river, south of the Houses of Parliament. The HQ buildings were so posh that some later became foreign embassies.

The four remaining teams were all outside the city. The Epsom hospital was located at stately Woodcote Park in Surrey, southwest of London. The Sunningdale hospital was in Berkshire, west of the city near Windsor Great Park. (Sunningdale was also the headquarters of the Canadian Forestry Corps. The king had seen the foresters play ball the previous fall, and this year the nine would play a number of games with Yank aero squadrons.) Hounslow and Northolt were British flying fields on the heaths west of London. The Yanks learned how to maintain Avros and S.E. 5s at Northolt in Ruislip, Middlesex. At Hounslow, a few miles to the south, it was Camels, Sopwith Pups, Avros, S.E. 5s and Dolphin aeroplanes, and Mono, Hispano Suiza, Clerget and Gnome motors.

You'd have thought that Northolt and Hounslow might lend a little dash and romance to the league, but that wasn't so. The Royal Flying Corps on April 1 had become the Royal Air Force—a legendary name that still thrills history and aviation buffs a hundred years on. The Yank air branch changed its name a month later, too, from the Aviation Section of the Signal Corps to the Army Air Service. Staffed by the likes of Eddie Rickenbacker and Billy Mitchell, the Air Service kept its thoroughly unheroic name on through the Armistice, like some tattered remnant of Professor Thaddeus Lowe's Balloon Corps from the American Civil War. It would finally become the Army Air Corps in 1926.

Yank infantrymen passed quickly through England on their way to France, but the aviation boys were different. While individual squadrons came and went, the Air Service was in England to stay. The first aviation detachment had stepped off the Cunard liner *Aurania* at Liverpool in September 1917. By the following May, fifteen thousand men were scattered across seventy aerodromes and stations. Some Yank birdmen were getting ready to fly in France, or were training as mechanics (sometimes called *mechanicians*) and other specialists. Others served in U.S. repair squadrons working on several types of aeroplanes.

Northolt is still an operational RAF base today, while the Hounslow field has been closed for decades and lies under the flight path of Heathrow Airport. Despite their headquarters scrounging talent from other squadrons, the two Air Service teams managed to field some decent players. They didn't have nearly as many as "over there" in France, though, where the doughboy leagues dwarfed the AABL. London's *Times* would print a good theory about this late in the season.

> The first-class baseball player, of whose wages and exploits and privileges such astonishing stories are told, is not so well represented in England as in France. Here he can be counted on the fingers; over there he needs figures to compute his numbers. The reason is that, generally speaking, the Americans who remain in England long enough to settle down at baseball are craftsmen of some kind, mechanics or men with technical training. The baseball giant, on the other hand, has been educated to baseball and very little else, and consequently, when he becomes a soldier, is the ordinary fighting man, and goes with as little delay as possible to the quarter where he is most needed. The American aviation camps in England supply a large proportion of the baseballers we see.[28]

One thing the AABL completely lacked was good team nicknames. Except for the inevitable *doughboys*, *swabbies* and the like, no team had a catchy handle, not even something with local meaning like *Astorias*. There were no Sunningdale Slammers in the AABL. No Northolt Hammers. Army fans briefly tried pinning *depth bomb throwers* on the navy, which responded with *grenade throwers*. But these were weak examples even of military wit, and neither caught on.

A new set of front-office execs and other suits was now attached to the league. Although they still headed the AABL, Booker, Parsons and Latham had a lot of partners. (Papers back in the States mistakenly had Arlie down as the coach and manager of the Army HQ team and even ran a couple of team photos showing him in uniform, one of which was clearly doctored.) Top among the AABL partners was Arlie's old admirer, Newton Crane, who undoubtedly was the common connection among all the others. Crane was perfect to head the revamped AABL. No American had better credentials with the Britishers. He had three sons in the British army and his daughter was a driver for the French Aviation Commission.

Newspapers on both sides of the Atlantic pegged another American bigwig as the real power behind the league. "Originally the Anglo-American league was the work of Wilson Cross, formerly of Cincinnati, but for the last sixteen years with the Vacuum Oil company in London," an American correspondent wrote later. "Twenty years from now he will be the Henry M. Chadwick of British baseball."

> He got together thirty Americans in London and induced them to form a limited company to be called the Anglo-American Baseball league, and to be underwritten for $30,000. He did this simply and solely as a baseball fan. He secured no help from the states, except that one of his stockholders is W. A. Parsons, of New York City, who owns about all of Coney

island, and whose former London manager, H. E. Booker, has become managing director of the league. It will show how rapidly the league has grown to cite the fact that an office force of six persons is now required to help Booker at the offices of the league.[29]

Born in Cincinnati, Cross listed his hometown as Pittsburgh. As well-known in London as Newton Crane, "Pick" Cross was still dapper at forty-seven and the vice president of the American Chamber of Commerce. An American magazine would call him the "chief baseball introducer in England."[30] Cross was also the umpire who had escaped death or dismemberment at The Queen's Club in 1916 after showing insufficient bias toward the London Americans. The abuse from the stands might have come naturally. A full, prominent lower lip gave Cross the pouty look of a rich kid who's just had his ball swiped by a ne'er-do-well. He was extremely well connected in England, and it was Cross, rather than Crane, who generally got his picture taken with the high and mighty. (Crane wrote that when he finally got himself snapped with Admiral Sims and General Biddle, "I couldn't believe that I was the old man in the photograph."[31])

The AABL front office now looked like this:

President—Newton Crane
Vice presidents—Wilson Cross, Bill Parsons
Treasurer—Robert Grant, Jr. (Boston banker)
Secretary—H. H. Lukens (DuPont executive)
General manager—Howard Booker
Head umpire—Arlie Latham

The league's investors were impressive fellows. The one really famous man among them was Harry Gordon Selfridge, the London department-store magnate. Then came a brace of oil executives; a covey of bankers from New York and Boston; a flock of fellows from Spalding's; various rubber, typewriter and engineering execs; and someone from the O-Cedar Mop company, who was no doubt as respected and accomplished as all the others.

The AABL was ready to play. The league plastered colorful posters on lampposts and walls all over London during the season to announce the games. Ticket prices were as low as eight pence (sixteen cents)—a fact to make fans clap their hands to their heads and shout *What?* all over the United States.

U.S. Army's home field was Stamford Bridge. U.S. Navy and Pay Office shared the Arsenal ground in Highbury, which the London Americans had called home the previous summer. Records Office apparently played home games on the ball field that Waldorf Astor had built at the convalescent hospital on his estate at Taplow. The Canadian hospital and American Air Service teams had their own small diamonds. Teams occasionally went on the road for league games in other British cities, including Brighton and Birmingham. Certainly, there would be enough baseball for everybody ... but whether Britishers were actually able to understand and enjoy it was debatable.

"We are to have another opportunity to solve the mysteries of baseball this summer," said a newspaper in Hull. The phrase *mysteries of baseball* popped up in sports pages all across England, but the AABL stood ready to help solve them. The question "is to be tackled with characteristic American thoroughness. Each visitor as he passes through the turnstiles is to be given a simple explanation of the game, and experts are to go amongst the crowd with megaphones to tell what is happening."[32]

The king's loyal subjects must have wondered whether the American baseball cowboys had let things go to their heads a bit. "We are going to torpedo cricket," an AABL promoter crowed.[33] But Britishers preferred to determine that sort of thing for themselves.

4

Opening Day

The 1918 baseball season got off to a quick start in England, but the AABL didn't have a lot to do with it. Two army nines from a North Midlands camp (unnamed in the newspapers because of wartime censorship) drew a good crowd on April 20 for a game sponsored by the Y.M.C.A. at the Trent Bridge Ground in Nottingham. The mayor and a British brigadier were there, along with quite a few Yanks. A second army game on May 21 drew three thousand curious spectators, including the duke and duchess of Portland. To the duke went the honor of tossing out the first ball.

"Now that we have seen the great American game of baseball we appreciate its excellence," the duke said later. "We shall come again and again to hear more about it, and we hope that baseball will be one of the means of cementing more firmly the friendship of our two peoples."[1]

The quality of play in Nottingham didn't impress everybody, though. "I think it is rather a childish game," a reader who signed himself "L. W." wrote to the local paper. "It reminds me somewhat of my school days when we used to play rounders or handball. As for baseball being exciting, I do not see where it is in the least. I saw it played in America some four years ago and with more energy than in Nottingham."[2]

The AABL moguls apparently agreed, and one of the thirty investors blazed away in print after an army game in June. Like fellow Pittsburgher Wilson Cross, J. M. "Joe" Armel of Wallasey was an executive with Vacuum Oil. Armel hadn't liked the brand of baseball that he'd seen played at the Tower Ground in Liverpool—never mind that he mistakenly called his own circuit the *British*-American Baseball League.

Armel wrote to a Liverpool newspaper that, unlike the unnamed army nines, AABL players "have got the vim in them. They are well groomed in uniform, and we dislike very much to see such exhibitions put on as on Saturday, where the men were ungroomed, were playing listless baseball, and were not even on second class amateur quality, and we who are backing the thing and giving all the returns to charity feel that it is an injustice to the game, and will in very short time be bringing two teams here to play in Liverpool."[3]

As promised, the ABBL played a league game in the port city a few weeks after Armel's diatribe. And in Nottingham, the rare instance of British grousing was firmly but politely put right by L. W.'s fellow Britishers.

"I think it very childish indeed to pass remarks on another nation's pastimes," one reader replied on the same sports page. "Have not the very people who play this game come over to play a bigger and stronger game in France? When you criticise a people's pleasures you are treading on very uncertain ground. Let the boys play a game that pleases them best."[4]

The AABL started its season on May 4 with an exhibition game in

British children greeting American doughboys passing through England (National Archives).

the Welsh coastal city of Swansea. Fifteen thousand people showed up to see U.S. Army face a Canadian hospital team. This was the Army HQ team from London, not some unknown squad from the Midlands. For reasons not explained in print, the army squad had only seven players. One of these was civilian Stuart S. Hayes, a former London Americans player attached to the U.S. consul general. The army manager assembled the full nine players only by borrowing two from a natural rival, the U.S. Navy team in London.

The identity of the Canadians is somewhat obscure. Writing for the *Stars and Stripes*, George T. Bye called them "the Taplow Canadians, champions of England for two seasons."[5] A Nottingham paper mentioned Taplow, too. In the spring of 1918, *Taplow* generally referred to the No. 15 General (Duchess of Connaught Canadian Red Cross) Hospital at Taplow, on the Astor estate west of London. But the two-time champs of England were the nine from the Convalescent Hospital at Epsom. Dozens of Canadian general hospitals, convalescent hospitals and casualty depots were scattered across England, and American and even British correspondents often mixed them up. Whoever they were, the Canadian boys cleaned the clocks of the combined Yank soldier-sailor squad, 10–3. The gate receipts went to the South Wales Prisoners of War Fund.

"The result demonstrates the value of an effective barrage of preparation," Bye wrote for his doughboy audience. "The Eskimo neighbors bombed their way to seven runs in the first push, then were held until the seventh, when they got another, making the final two in the ninth. The Yanks bayoneted their three in the fourth, fifth and seventh innings."[6]

The AABL's two Canadian headquarters teams, Records and Pay Office, played an exhibition at Stamford Bridge the following Saturday, May 11. It ended with an identical score, 10–3, Records coming out on top. The Canadians' game, though, was completely overshadowed by a bunch of Yanks ... not ballplayers this time, but infantry battalions marching through London. The sight was exactly what the Londoners needed.

"London people cheered yesterday as they have not cheered for many a month, from the moment when the first battalion detrained at Waterloo, to the accompaniment of cheers from business London which was on its way to the office, to the last minute of farewell when the crowd called out: 'Come back soon' to the departing soldiers, the day was one of heartening friendliness," said *Lloyd's Weekly News*. "But from the first moment to the last it was the women who gave a special welcome to the marching men. 'God bless you,' they cried all along the route. Mothers lifted their children, that they might have a sight of the soldiers from across the sea who are going to fight side by side with daddy."[7]

The doughboys were the 325th Infantry Regiment from Camp Gordon, Georgia. The officers were mainly southerners, but most of the boys hailed from New York and the northeast. The bulk of their division, the Eighty-second (the "All-American" division), landed at Liverpool, and after short stops in English rest camps embarked at Southampton, England, for Le Havre. That's the way it was for most of the infantry—they passed quietly through England on the way to France. But the Britishers needed and wanted to *see* their Yank allies, so the 325th Infantry was routed through London instead. There was hardly a dry eye anyplace.

The Britishers pulled out all the stops. The Yanks marched along to a Sousa march from their own regimental band and to fifes and drums from the Scots Guards, Irish Guards and Grenadier Guards. They swung out from Wellington Barracks, along Birdcage Walk, up Horse Guards Parade and through the Arch to Whitehall. They passed the War Office and Trafalgar Square, tramped along Piccadilly and turned at Hyde Park Corner toward the American embassy at Grosvenor Gardens, where their ambassador waited to greet them. All along this splendid route, Britishers cheered. The boys marched along with an envelope in their pockets, each marked with the royal arms. Inside was a note of welcome on Windsor Castle paper with a printed facsimile of the king's handwriting. It was a very fine thing.

And so the boys marched on, past their embassy in their long ranks, to the Victoria Memorial and Buckingham Palace. The king personally came out to see them, wearing the uniform of a field marshal of the British army. With him were Queen Mary, Queen Alexandra, Princess Beatrice, the duke of Connaught and all sorts of lords and ladies and other important people. Woodrow Wilson himself couldn't have received a better greeting. "The cheering was renewed again with great fervour, and continued until the last man in the column had passed before the King. Colonel Whitman, commanding the regiment, was beckoned to break away from the column, and take his position beside the King, while his men marched past, General Biddle giving place to him. ... As the commanding officer of each battalion reached the saluting point he too broke away and was presented to the King, who shook hands with each of them."[8]

After the royal review, the boys marched down the Mall, around St. James Park and back to the barracks. They came, they saw, they conquered. Oh, it was swell. The Londoners couldn't have been nicer or more excited. But one of the best things that happened all day had come when the first battalion got off their train on the other side of the Thames. "As the first battalion swung out from Waterloo Station on its way to Westminster Bridge and Wellington Barracks, the temporary headquarters of the visitors, someone in the crowd called to a friend that they were a 'real husky lot.' The word pleased the fancy of the crowd, and soon everyone with a voice to use was calling for cheers for the Huskies—and the Huskies they remained for the rest of their London visit."[9]

The 325th soon rejoined their division, later to fight in France at St. Mihiel, the Meuse-Argonne and Lorraine. It really was too bad the AABL's U.S. Army team never took up the nickname the regiment had earned and left behind in London. *Huskies* beat *grenade throwers* all to hell and back.

After the big parade and the exhibition ball games, the league finally got ready for the official season to start the next weekend. The opening game on May 18 promised to be a beaut', U.S. Army versus U.S. Navy at the Arsenal grounds, Highbury, on Saturday afternoon.

"It was to have been between the Ay-ee-effers and a Canadian team," Bye reported in the *Stars and Stripes*, "but the enterprising manager of the league, wishing to swell receipts for the British Red Cross Society, decided there would be more sensation in a season-opener between the Army and the Navy of the U.S.A., and made the change, which is announced in flamboyant posters all over London."

Bye also demanded to know which team the U.S. Marines would be cheering—a hard choice for the leathernecks. "Some of them are detailed at the base section here, and A.E.F. rest camps in England; some are at Navy Headquarters and at Navy bases. They haven't made up their minds yet, but there is a r-r-reckoning going on, believ-v-v-ve muh. They're comparing notes as to the numbers of times they have been insulted on board ship by some snip of a stub-toed sea swab, and the number of times that monkey-eared doughboys have been rude to them when they were on police duty in France."[10]

Stateside papers took note of the game, especially in New York. "Admiral Sims will demonstrate literally that he 'has something on the ball,' by pitching the first one over. Major-Gen. Biddle, commanding all the American troops in England, will catch it—if he has not forgotten how. Whereupon, they will retire to the grand stand and drink pink pop, while the regular ball players will show the great crowd of Englishers how baseball is played and what kind of fellows play it."[11]

Opening-day ceremonies are usually good for a laugh, and the two middle-aged brass hats made this one special. Biddle, an old West Point ballplayer, stood waiting in his fine general's uniform and boots, armed with a catcher's mitt but no mask. Sims apparently had never played ball in his life. The admiral knocked his own hat off—and caught it again—during his windup. He crow-hopped his delivery, bouncing the ball at least a foot in front of the plate. Biddle made a half-hearted attempt at the ball as it bounced away. Britishers might have thought this was all proper and correct, the way grown men played baseball in the United States.

Silent newsreels don't tell whether the American boys in the stands razzed their commanders, but Sims didn't look the least bit rattled. In fact, in a syndicated news photo widely published across the U.S., the bare-headed admiral looked positively athletic, a natural right-handed hurler.

Sims autographed two balls, which he handed to Lieutenant Mims and Ensign Charles Fuller, the two team captains. As expected, he then retired to the stands, where he enjoyed excellent company. There was a British admiral, of course, and a bunch of other officers, plus the duchess of Sutherland, Lady Clonmell, Lady Helmsley, Lady Celia Coates, Lady Ward, and lots of other bigwigs. But the one who got the most ink—and whose picture naturally was in the papers—was Princess Patricia of Connaught. Rank hath its privileges, and one of Sims' was to watch the ball game with Patricia.

Her aunt, Princess Louise, had dutifully attended a ball game in 1915, but Patricia probably truly enjoyed baseball more than any other royal except the king. She knew the game, too, because her father was the duke of Connaught and Strathearn. Like the marquess of Lorne before him, the duke had been the governor general of Canada, where they knew a thing or two about baseball. All of North America—Yanks and Canadians alike—had buzzed when he'd taken his family across to Ottawa in 1911.

Patricia was "the prettiest member of the royal family," fond of music and outdoor sports, and in 1911 still stubbornly unmarried at twenty-five, having turned away "continental princelings whom her parents picked out for her."[12] The former colonists, of course, couldn't get enough of stories like that. "Princess 'Pat,' as she is called by her intimates, is known to have refused two Kings, one King Alfonso of Spain, the other King Manuel of Portugal."[13] And on top of it all, the whole Connaught family happened to like Americans. "For two years they have spent the Christmas holidays at Cliveden with Mr. and Mrs. Waldorf Astor."[14] It was no big mystery or surprise, then, when the Canadian hospital at Taplow was later named for Patricia.

The princess was always on show in Canada. She *was* a princess, after all, and beautiful to boot. "She's fair game, Joe," Eddie Albert would say to Gregory Peck forty years later in *Roman Holiday*. "It's always open season on princesses."[15] And just like Audrey Hepburn in that movie, Patricia was a good egg. She threw herself into the roundups and rodeos, her popularity flaring and dazzling like the northern lights. When the war began in Europe, the doting dominion named a crack regiment for her—Princess Patricia's Canadian Light Infantry, "the Patricias." The family went back

Princess Patricia of Connaught, a favorite of Canadian and American troops (Library of Congress).

home in October 1916, and people loved Princess Pat even more for her devotion to their soldiers in England. In 1917, Canada put her portrait on the dollar bill.

Patricia was a peach of a princess. She looked out for the boys from Saskatoon and Montreal, and worked with Mrs. John Jacob Astor to help convalescents at the Canadian hospital at Orpington (and not in the one named for her at Taplow, which you probably could call modesty). So, if Canadian soldiers in England happened to love a game that her own countrymen found odd, why, Princess Pat loved the game right along with them. And if their allies the Yanks loved it just as much as the Canadians, all the better.

On opening day, she settled down beside Admiral Sims to watch the game at Highbury. The Arsenal football grounds were almost new and named for the Royal Arsenal in Woolwich, where workers had started the club in 1886. Supporters called the team the Gunners, but nobody was gunning for anything now because British football had been shut down since 1915. It was a nice change to see Yank baseballers running across the grass.

"I suppose it will be like the game I saw in the Middle Ages, when I witnessed Arlie Latham and the other championship Browns and spent the afternoon explaining to my girl why the pitcher could not hit the ball," said an American who'd been in the country for years.[16] (Although not identified by name, this had to be Newton Crane.) Arlie was now on the field in Highbury calling the game as the AABL's chief umpire. The soldier and sailor nines certainly didn't disappoint anyone, adding a couple of extra innings into the bargain. "The American rooters were so excited in the ninth inning, with the score a tie, that three airplanes sailed over the field almost unnoticed. The grandstand was colorful with the women's dresses, the American and British khaki and the various shades of the blue worn by the American and British sailors. It was ideal baseball weather and many fans were without their coats. When the Americans 'stretched' in the seventh inning the police started an investigation."[17]

American newspapers loved the notion of Britishers being flummoxed by the seventh-inning stretch and made a big deal of it. Why, the poor folks over there didn't know the simplest thing about baseball!

"Yesterday it seemed as if these 4,000 people made more noise than we hear from 100,000 people on Cup Final day at the Crystal Palace," said a British paper. "But the crowd was part of the game. Every sailor in his picturesque white hat and every soldier in khaki regarded it as his right to shout his instructions to the men on the field. The players themselves kept up a running comment, and there was also the loud voice of the umpire proclaiming the 'balls' and the 'strikes.'"[18]

This was the *grenade throwers* versus *depth bomb shooters* game, with navy the home team. Cheered on by hundreds of Canadian soldiers in the stands, the army team suddenly looked stronger than it had a few days earlier. "It is rumored that the army team is packed with 'ringers.' Anyhow five total strangers arrived yesterday afternoon from a certain aviation center. They are all ball players, who suddenly became attached to the army headquarters which is playing today."[19] Navy would remember and adopt this tactic with a vengeance a few weeks later.

The opposing pitchers in the opener were army Private Robert Rawlings of Washington, D. C., and navy Chief Yeoman Swanson. Neither could actually *take the hill*, since British fields didn't have mounds. Pitchers threw from flat ground, usually with a wooden plank for a rubber. "Shag" Rawlings was from the 657th Aero Supply Squadron at Woodley Camp near Southampton. He'd been a dandy hurler and outfielder in the amateur leagues back home, before enjoying a cup of coffee in 1916 with the Martinsburg, West Virginia, club in the Blue Ridge League. His little brother, George "Reggie" Rawlings, a star in the Blue Ridge circuit, was now with the Quartermaster Corps in France.

Chief Swanson—we don't know his first name—was no slouch, either, having hurled for a crack navy team in Newport in 1917. A handful of semi-pros and minor leaguers also took the field today. This league opener, Bye wrote, "was no town lot game by any manner of means."[20]

"Many Londoners in the jammed stands, accustomed to see cricketers play in immaculate flannels, could not understand the rough and ready outfits of the Americans," wrote another newsman, "but when the latter began sliding into bases like so many snow ploughs, they realized there was need of padding."[21]

The Yanks put on an exciting, seesaw game for the Britishers. U.S. Army scored three times in the third inning, once in the fourth and again in the seventh. U.S. Navy scored one run in the fifth, then twice more in both the seventh and eighth, tying it up.

"British or United States, it was an American crowd in the grandstand, and to judge by the furious kidding of the umpire, Arlie Latham of the Giants, the games must be getting mighty slow back home. All the kidders from Kidderville were there with the family megaphones," an American correspondent reported by mail—probably Bye again, although the story didn't carry a byline. "But what finally got a rise out of Arlie was that, after giving a ball on a doubtful pitch and finishing a short talk with the pitcher, a sergeant sitting on the Army bench strolled over to the plate and brushed the dust off with pointed deliberation. The ump started for the bench and arrived at the same time as the sergeant; what pleasant remarks they exchanged could not be heard for the delighted yells and counter-yells of the fans."[22]

The game was a revelation to British novelist Thomas Burke. He got almost giddy, trying to describe it later in an article widely published on both sides of the gray Atlantic.

"The whole scene was barbaric pandemonium. A Chinese theatre is nowhere near it and that's saying something. I never dreamed that that hard, shell covered business nation could break into such frenzied abandon," Burke wrote. "You should have heard Admiral Sims as college yell leader when the Navy made a home run hit with his 'Attaboy! Oh, attaway to play ball! Zaaaaa!' And when they got an 'error,' he sure handed the Navy theirs."[23]

The novelist loved the Yank soldiers' and sailors' rooting—what the Britishers called *barracking*—and jotted it all down.

Aw, well, well, well!

Ah, you pikers, where was you raised?

Hey, is this a corner lot or is it a ball game?

Say, buddy, you can play ball—maybe.

'At's right, Navy—on yer toes the Navy, all the time.

Hey, pitcher, quit the plate and send yer li'l brudder.

Aw, buddy, dear, gimme some barb' wire, I wanna knit a sweater fer the piker.

Oh, watch this, watch this! He's a bad actor—kill the bad actor!

More ivory, more ivory!

Get a step ladder to it.

Oh, you quitter. Oh, oh, oh! Bonehead—bonehead—BONEHEAD! Ahhh!

Go-ing up! Go-ing up! Go-ing up! (This, when a pitcher was throwing.)

"Yes, I've caught it," Burke wrote. "From now I'm a 'fan.' I'm going to see every baseball match played anywhere near London. I shall never be able to watch with excitement a cricket or football match after this; it'd be like a tortoise race. I shall take all my friends with me to the next match to join me in rooting and killing the umpire."[24]

It wasn't cricket—that was for sure.

The game itself was really good. Navy catcher Ensign Fuller scampered home with a late run, which was followed by a pinch-hit homer for army in the ninth. The game went into extra innings, tied at six. Army finally plated another run in the eleventh when the navy shortstop missed a throw, and won the AABL's opening game, 7–6.

"Some game," young naval aviator Fuller said afterward. He had caught as a Harvard freshman in 1916 and now flew antisubmarine patrols over the English Channel. "We'll get hunk with those doughboys next week. Honestly it seemed natural to play baseball in London, as some of the crowd was great, cheering us like mad. The English women cheered like the Americans. We had the best rooters, for the navy seems to be more popular in England. The field was fine and better looked after than our fields at home."[25]

The Britishers did seem to enjoy the day, and maybe not simply for the baseball. The Yanks looked fresh and athletic, which was just what Londoners needed and wanted to see in their allies just then. "This beats cricket into a cocked hat," one sporty type said. "The spirit of youth and energy of baseball typifies America as a nation, and especially her methods in war."[26]

The other AABL teams played on opening day, too, but none got any publicity. Northholt, Epsom and Sunningdale chalked up victories, while Hounslow, Pay Office and Records all lost. Diplomats in winged collars couldn't have hoped for better. The Yanks and Canadian split the four games, each winning and losing two.

The league rolled through its second week of play, then paused for a special, nonleague game on Memorial Day. "It is the day on which the graves of Northern and Southern soldiers killed in the Civil War are strewn with flowers by the school children of the nation," a London paper explained.[27] Four manned kite balloons floated overhead as U.S. Navy again met U.S. Army, this time at the latter's home field at Stamford Bridge. The proceeds went to the British National Milk Hostels. Princess Patricia came out again—the newspapers announced days ahead of time that she was coming—and the boys let her know they appreciated it.

> Princess Patricia of Connaught (whom the Jackies especially greeted on her arrival and departure with exclamations of "Oh, you Pat") gave the event a pretty send-off by appearing on the field just before the game was started and shaking hands with Captain Mims, of the United States Army team, and Captain Fuller, the crack catcher of the Navy.
> She was escorted to her seat by that gallant sea dog and fan for fair, Admiral Sims, U.S.N., and General Biddle, who gingers up for his job of commanding Uncle Sam's troops in these isles by being a boy again at a weekly ball game. The sailors declared that her Royal Highness was among their successful rooters, but the soldiers confessed to have lost heart when the popular princess left the ground during the seventh inning at the end of two hours of such speedy work on the diamond as is seldom beaten.[28]

The game featured duchesses and viscounts and lords and ladies in the stands and hardly needed another posh name attached to it, but the navy third baseman supplied one anyway. He was Arthur Bonaparte, "a descendent of Jerome Bonaparte, brother of the great Napoleon, [who] was admired for his dandy crimson striped uniform."[29] Young Bonaparte knocked in the sailors' first run in a 7–3 win—which, unfortunately for navy, didn't count in the AABL standings. Although a success in attracting publicity, the game didn't draw much of a crowd.

> It cannot yet be said, of course, that the ordinary British sportsman has taken baseball to his heart. The stands at Stamford Bridge were crowded with British officers and their wives, sisters, and friends, generally, but the public "surrounds" of the great inclosure, so often, in the days when football was played, black with people, were a waste. The weeds growing, everywhere, so that from the stands it looked as if the "surrounds" had been turned into allotments, were an eloquent testimony to the fact that there was a war on. Only a sprinkling of people occupied this part of the inclosure and many of them were American soldiers. Nevertheless the officials of the Anglo-American League are full of enthusiasm, and the Stamford Bridge game showed an increasing interest on the part of the British public.[30]

In most leagues, rosters routinely change during the course of the season, as players move up or down or out of their organizations. In the Anglo-American league, managers also had to deal with what the brass hats liked to call *exigencies of the service*, a fancy phrase meaning that a sailor's skills might suddenly be needed at sea, or that an Air Service mechanic could be more useful working in France than giving classes outside London. Orders would be cut and off they would go, often with time only for a quick handshake with a pal or two. Life in the armed forces wasn't easy.

But as quickly as the AABL squads lost men, they gained replacements. As the league got ready to roll into summer, another baseball organization was suited up and playing back in America. It soon contributed a couple of ballplayers who would be counted among the AABL's biggest stars. This wasn't another military league, but a single, superbly talented navy team that could have clobbered any club in the Anglo-American league or the whole league rolled together. Any baseball bug in Massachusetts—or in most of New York, for that matter—could've told you exactly which club that was.

Jack Barry's Charlestown Navy Yard nine.

5

Wild Waves

Yanks in the armed forces played ball all over the map during the war. Why, warships sailors had marked out a diamond somewhere in the British Isles—probably Queenstown, although the dateline said London because of censorship—practically as soon as they got there in 1917. But that was in Ireland and well out of the spotlight. The club destined to have the greatest effect on the AABL was Jack Barry's nine in Boston.

The team's player-manager, Jack had once starred in Connie Mack's $100,000 infield in Philadelphia. "Barry is the weakest hitter of the quartet, but his hits are always timely and his sensational fielding is something that cannot be computed in cold, soulless figures."[1] More important than his days with the Athletics was Jack's tenure as the player-manager of the Red Sox. He'd been leading the Boston club when America jumped into the war in 1917.

Jack hadn't seen much of a drop in talent from the Sox to his navy squad, though. In fact, they were pretty much the same players—which requires some explanation. Nothing connected with the Rube Goldberg machine called the King's Game happened in a straight line.

Several ballplayers from the Braves and the Red Sox, the two major-league teams that called Boston home, had hopped into the war early. But *early* by the standard of the major leagues wasn't saying much.

Braves catcher Hank Gowdy was the first active big leaguer to join the colors, enlisting in the Ohio National Guard in June 1917. He rode the train up from Cincinnati, where the team was playing, to Columbus, his hometown, where he raised his hand and took the oath. Gowdy reported for duty later that summer. He soon sported a sergeant's chevrons, and a year later was "over there" with the Forty-second Infantry, the famous "Rainbow" Division—*rainbow* because it included units from twenty-six states. Gowdy saw combat in France and came home from the war as baseball's most popular warrior, and deservedly so.

Many other Boston players preferred having steel decks rather than muddy trenches under their feet, and acted soon enough to have a choice in the matter. Jack Barry was their leader and example.

Jack enlisted as a yeoman in the United States Naval Reserve Force (USNRF) in July 1917. Red Sox club secretary John Lane enrolled with him. It was a spur-

Jack Barry, with the Philadelphia Athletics (Library of Congress).

of-the-moment decision for both, never really explained. Maybe they just felt particularly patriotic that day. "Until yesterday, Manager Barry said he had no idea of taking this step," the *Boston Globe* reported.[2] Lane had planned on joining the army and attending an officers' training camp in upstate New York. Maybe it just came down to the fact that although the military draft hadn't yet taken a single big-league player, everybody saw it coming.

"I consider it my duty to do all I can for my country," Jack said, as much an explanation as he ever gave. "I'm no slacker. If I can be of any use, I'll gladly quit baseball."[3] More than one sportswriter compared him to Commodore Jack Barry, one of the founders of the American navy. The navy didn't need modern Jack right away, so he managed the Red Sox for the rest of the season and finished second behind the white-hot White Sox.

Several of Jack's players followed their skipper and enlisted in the Naval Reserve either during the season or soon afterward. Jack reported for duty at the Charlestown Navy Yard in November 1917, along with infielders Mike McNally and Del Gainer, outfielder Chick Shorten and pitcher Ernie Shore. Walter "Rabbit" Maranville, the Braves' dandy little shortstop, signed up, too, although he'd lost his wife early that year and could have got an exemption from the draft to raise his little girl. Red Sox outfielder Duffy Lewis took the oath as well, but served at Mare Island near San Francisco.

Other major- and minor-league players signed up in Boston over the winter, along with a handful of good collegiate players. Pitchers Herb Pennock and King Bader and outfielder Jimmy Walsh of the Red Sox and rookie catcher Art Rico of the Braves all donned the blue jumper while the snow was still flying. So did infielder Lawton Witt of the Athletics, despite the fact that he'd been the first big leaguer drafted for the army. He'd somehow wrangled his way into the Naval Reserve instead. It hadn't hurt any that Witt (born Ladislaw Waldemar Wittkowsky, called "Whitey" for his pale blond hair) had been a schoolboy phenom' at the Goddard Seminary in Winchendon, Massachusetts, and was well known in Boston. Other guys wouldn't get away with Whitey's enlistment maneuver just several months later, as star twirler Grover Cleveland Alexander of the Chicago Cubs learned the hard way. Alex was a knucklehead in dealing with his draft board, and before long the club was forwarding his mail to the army field artillery somewhere in France.

By spring 1918, Jack had the makings for a first-rate navy ball club. Navy athletic officers probably always planned for him to manage the team representing the First Naval District, based in Boston. And why not? Jack could have penciled in the name of a big leaguer at every position, including his own at second base. Lane was the team's secretary and Roy McGillicuddy, Connie Mack's son, was the treasurer. "I'd hate to have that bunch against me in a league race," a big-league manager said.[4]

Several of the Navy Yard ballplayers and Jack himself were rated yeomen first class. The rank was equal to an army staff sergeant and five steps above a seamen recruit. This wasn't particularly unusual in wartime, when armies and navies were expanding like crazy and somebody had to be in charge of things. Still, it made people wonder about favoritism for ballplayers. Jack soon got promoted to chief petty officer. Chiefs wore a different uniform from the seamen and petty officers below them, and were the men who *really* ran the navy, no matter what their officers might think. Duffy Lewis, on the Pacific Coast, would make CPO, too, and lead a pretty good ball club of his own. Lane rose higher still, to warrant officer.

Jack had a unique group of boys at the Navy Yard and they drew the kind of attention nobody wanted. *Yeoman* was (and still is today) a clerical rating. In earlier times, a yeoman was called a *ship's writer*. The yeoman's rating badge is two crossed quill pens, oddly similar to the crossed bats on baseball programs and memorabilia. It's not surprising that the whole notion of a yeoman-ballplayer seemed absurd to lots of people. Nobody exactly pictured a second sacker or right fielder taking dictation or jotting down figures in a big, cloth-bound ledger.

The *Sporting News*, for one, didn't like it a bit and quickly took to sniping at Jack's boys, mostly ignoring the fact that nearly all his yeomen had volunteered before any official or board had come calling. "These players are enlisted for the period of the war, according to reports that seem to be authentic and while the yeomen-players may never smell gunpowder or feel the agonies of seasickness, they will be kept doing something or other in the service," the newspaper sniffed.[5]

The truth was that many of Jack's men were, if anything, overly qualified as yeomen. Jack and Ernie Shore were college-educated, the skipper at Holy Cross in Massachusetts and his pitcher at little Guilford College in North Carolina. Witt, Rico and Pennock had all gone to good prep schools in New England and Pennsylvania. The squad also had boys who'd joined the navy directly from Harvard, Tufts and Holy Cross. Altogether, Jack might've had the best group of yeomen in the navy. This argument didn't wash with the *Sporting News*, though, or with other flag-waving publications.

The Navy Yard team looked like a powerhouse, especially compared with other military clubs. But Jack's boys played in Boston, where sentiments and loyalties were often divided. Many Red Sox fans seemed to expect their 1917 player-manager to wrangle a long leave from the navy and lead the team again in 1918. Jack was advising the club over the winter, which probably kept the rumors flying. Still, club owner Harry Frazee practically hopped up and down denying that retaining Jack was ever considered. Oh, heaven forbid!

"There is nothing in worse taste, nothing more foolish," Frazee fumed just before Christmas, "than to talk these days of obtaining exemption or furloughs for professional baseball players. A number of Red Sox players have entered the service, but I want to tell you right now that the country can have as many more, and can have me, too, if it wants me and I can be of any service. As for furloughs for my ball players who have entered the navy, I never dreamed of such a thing. Make that as strong as you can. How extremely nonsensical it is at this time to even talk about such things."[6]

It was all malarkey for the newspapers.

A month later, Frazee talked with an assistant secretary of the navy, a well-connected fellow from New York. The owner wanted Franklin D. Roosevelt to arrange extended furloughs for Jack and Duffy Lewis. Not that the magnate ever actually *asked*, mind you. *No, no, Nanette.* It just came up naturally in conversation. Roosevelt asked for and got a letter explaining the situation.

"I have on my roll twelve players who have joined the colors," Frazee wrote. "Most of the boys are in the Navy, and all cheerfully responded to the call when the season closed last fall. I do not have to say to you that if I am without the services of all these players during the season of 1918 my club will not only be out of the running professionally but that my business investment will be practically wrecked."[7]

The Boston owner, never a baseball genius, was completely wrong, of course. His Boston club would win the 1918 pennant and the World Series against clubs just as weak from the war as the Red Sox. Either the baseball gods love justice or have odd senses of humor, or maybe both, because this would be the Sox's last championship until the next century. Not to mention that the team they'd beat in an early and fairly shameful Series— when players threatened to strike because they were unhappy with their cut of the gate—would be the Chicago Cubs.

Between Frazee's finagling and the newspapers' stink about special leaves for the ballplayers, nobody in the navy was happy. Captain William R. Rush, commandant of the Navy Yard, refused to release Jack Barry or anybody else unless ordered to do so, and Roosevelt didn't press it. The brass down in Washington wondered if they shouldn't just ship everybody overseas and be rid of the problem. "They could do a lot of good on foreign service," a commander in the Navy Department said on a long-distance call to Boston. "They were talking about it here the other day. Sims is getting a baseball field at Queenstown [Ireland]. Those players could do a lot of good at Queenstown and Bath and places like that."

"Of course, we want them—as far as they can in connection with their duties—to get a good baseball team for our own," an officer replied from the yard. "I think Captain Rush would be very much disappointed if you take any of them away."[8]

Pay Clerk Lane, the former Red Sox secretary, later reported that the ballplayers themselves "unanimously asserted that none of the members wanted to play 'league ball,' and they would not accept a furlough unless they were ordered. Barry was the only Red Sox player who was not at the meeting."[9] Duffy Lewis checked in by mail to say that he thought furloughs were a lousy idea, too.

There's no way of knowing now why Jack wasn't in the meeting. Maybe he wanted the boys to speak freely without him. Maybe Lane didn't invite him, which doesn't seem likely. There's no way, really, to determine what anybody in the navy or organized baseball might have told or promised or asked of Jack, or even what he might've wanted. He kept quiet, and that was that. But his boys' hard line in their meeting probably helped turn the tide for the Navy Yard. The yard's athletic director later drove a spike into any lingering hopes that Frazee or Red Sox fans might have cherished.

"It has been definitely decided that Jack Barry will remain in the service of the Naval reserve for some months to come," the officer announced in January. "That should set at rest any rumor to the effect that he is to be back with the Red Sox this summer. The other professional ball players in the service are in the same position as Barry: they are in the service to stay as long as their services may be required by the navy."[10]

Captain Rush, bless him, was clear about what he wanted. He wrote to his chief of staff, "It is suggested that you go ahead and fix up a fine baseball team, one that can tackle anything in the country, which you can call the First Naval District Baseball Club, or something like it."[11] Which is exactly what the Navy Yard did.

Frazee stalled a while longer, then hired Ed Barrow as his new Red Sox manager. He probably hoped the whole time for a sudden, improbable armistice that would give him back his ball club.

Jack's ballplayers called themselves the Wild Waves. That was according to *Stars and Stripes*, anyway, reporting from the far side of the pond. Nobody else seems to have called them that, and the *Stars and Stripes* never mentioned it again. But it was a great nickname, and the AABL clubs in England could have used one or two names even half as good. *Wild Waves* was apt, too, because the boys swept over their competition like North Atlantic rollers in midwinter.

"It would not be hard to find several major league managers who would be willing to take the Navy Yard ball team just as it stands and put it into the big circuit without asking any questions," columnist "Sportsman" wrote in Boston.[12]

Before the season got under way, Secretary Lane had in mind a grand, three-month tour to play big-league, semipro and collegiate squads, with proceeds going to the Navy Welfare Fund. Interest ran high but the tour fizzled. The first problem was meteorological—a spring snowstorm wiped out the Wild Waves' first three scheduled games in April. The second, and much bigger, problem was naval. The navy wouldn't sanction the fourth scheduled game, with a local team from Maynard, and wouldn't say why. Jack's club prepared to open the season on April 23 against the fifth planned opponent, Boston College at Alumni Field. The navy abruptly canceled that game, too, just four hours before the first pitch. "It is impossible for Jack Barry to put his team on the field, but if a chance to play Boston College presents itself, arrangements will be made later, it was stated."[13]

Again, the navy didn't say *why* Jack couldn't field his team. It was all very strange. A few papers reported that Rear Admiral Spencer S. Wood, who commanded the First Naval District, had disbanded the club, but nobody was really sure. "Looks as if some of the members of that proposed Navy Yard team will be splicing the main brace before they get into much action on the ball field," Sportsman wrote.[14] The issue hinged on Wood, a former battleship captain who wasn't thrilled to have reserves or ballplayers under his command. This wasn't a rare sentiment for a senior military officer in wartime, but ballplayer-reserves—at least, any playing ball at the Navy Yard—didn't appeal to Wood at all. And *that*, as anyone from the enlisted ranks could have told you, was a no-win proposition.

After a week, the navy finally said that, yes, the team *would* continue, but under strict limitations. No admission could be charged, no collection of any sort taken, and all games had to be played in or near Boston. These rules emerged one at a time, Wood's strict interpretation of navy regulations. Army ball teams didn't have similar restrictions, and navy nines playing in other parts of the country and the world didn't have either— although the navy later agreed with the admiral. Wood clearly lacked Admiral Sims' love of baseball, or maybe just didn't share it in the same way. He certainly wouldn't use pro ballplayers in any meaningful way to boost navy morale or fill the coffers of any welfare fund benefitting his sailors.

Baseball fans and sportswriters didn't warm to Wood, although the *Sporting News* applauded him. Boston's mayor even wired an appeal directly to Secretary of the Navy Josephus Daniels to let Jack's boys make their planned tour. The secretary supported his admiral. "The need of men for ships fitting out is urgent," Daniels replied, "and the navy department does not consider it practicable to permit the considerable number of men on a baseball team to make an extensive tour."[15]

The Navy Yard squad finally began its season on May 4 against Harvard, which had let the sailors use the Crimson batting cage over the winter. Jack repaid this generosity with a 12–0 shellacking at Soldiers Field. The only minor-leaguer he put into the game was Marty Killilea, a third baseman from Double-A Buffalo. Jack even had to send Witt, a shortstop at Philadelphia, to play right field because Rabbit Maranville was at short.

Jack's boys faced an army team from Camp Devens at Braves Field the next day. The army skipper was another Red Sox player, infielder Hal Janvrin, who had somehow bucked the Boston tide of naval enlistments and joined the Signal Corps. The Navy Yard nine put on another show, Ernie Shore beating the doughboys 5–1 in a tidy hour and 45 minutes. Janvrin's boys didn't feel badly about losing to "Long" Shore. A season earlier, he had relieved pitcher Babe Ruth after the first batter in a game with Washington. The Bambino had blown up after walking the guy and punched the umpire, with predictable results. Shore saw the runner get caught stealing, then retired the next twenty-six batters in what for a long time was considered a perfect game. With players like that, the Wild Waves squad impressed even the newspaper boys in Manhattan.

"There were more major leaguers on those teams than there are in the majority of major league teams this season," one wrote. "The Navy Yard team is a wonder, and would class well with any major league club in the country."[16]

As they would do for several military teams that summer, the Braves donated the use of their park for the Navy Yard–Camp Devens game, and even furnished the ushers and other employees. Both umpires donated their services, too. But not one of the forty thousand fans who showed up for the clash donated anything at all, because Admiral Wood wouldn't allow it. No fan paid a nickel to get in, or contributed a cent to the Red Cross, the Navy Welfare Fund or any other worthy cause. It was a debacle, and the *New York Sun* wasn't alone in fuming over Wood's—and the navy's— edict against passing the hat for a good cause.

"The Admiral's statement comes as a great surprise, for if there is any such rule it is not being enforced in this section," the *Sun* said. "We do not see why there should be a rule of that kind. The Boston fans came to the park not only ready but anxious to contribute to the athletic funds of the men in the service. They did not come in the expectation of seeing a ball game for nothing, and they rather resented the fact that no collection was taken up."[17]

Admiral Wood also annoyed people on a different front. The navy had begun enlisting women to serve as yeomen, so the fleet could release shore-bound sailors for sea duty. It was a smart and worthwhile move, and American women responded just the way everybody expected they would—with enthusiasm, and in big numbers. The newspapers took to calling them *yeowomen*, for no good reason except that it made a catchy headline. A hundred years later there are still yeomen in the navy and they're all still called yeomen, no matter their gender. Some of the female yeomen in 1918 were assigned to the Navy Yard, where their commanding admiral didn't quite know what to make of them. "A delegation of the yeowomen had a conference with the Rear Admiral and complained that frequently their salutes are not recognized nor returned. Rear Admiral Wood at first thought the girls could very well omit the salute, but the girls insisted they are members of the Naval forces fully entitled to their hand salutes being returned. The Rear Admiral now agrees with them."[18]

These determined women not only reminded Admiral Wood about basic naval etiquette, but also helped him get rid of his ballplayers—not that this was ever their intention. The navy dropped the axe on the team on May 8, abruptly transferring McNally, Pennock, Maranville, Witt, Gainer and former Brooklyn Dodger Leo Callahan. All six got the news at morning practice.

A transfer was okay with Maranville. The Rabbit had been clamoring for sea duty for months, and had already talked his way out of work ashore for duty on a navy tug. Now he went happily off to report on board the battleship USS *Pennsylvania*. Shipping out was just fine with Herb Pennock, too, and he and Mike McNally now headed for the fleet together. All six sailors left the Navy Yard the following afternoon with new orders— "sealed orders," according to the *Globe*, as if these yeomen had top-secret assignments to track German U-boats. "Whitey Witt felt badly about going away, but the others seemed cheerful and all were the recipients of scores and scores of handshakes. Just before the Brave-Robin game started yesterday afternoon Maranville met many of his old friends as they were going into the park and his hand was nearly worn away from the shaking it received."[19]

Sealed or not, the yeomen's orders tore the heart out of the Wild Waves' team. Being a dutiful chief petty officer, Jack Barry said nothing and kept going with the players he had left—and he had plenty. It might have made him feel better later to know that Admiral Wood was never any happier with his female yeomen than he'd been with his ballplayers.

The Wild Waves kept winning. They trounced the 302nd Infantry in Worchester. They beat the Brooklyn Navy Yard before fifteen thousand fans in New Haven. On Memorial Day, when Princess Pat sat watching the AABL game in London, the Waves played their only road game, at Norfolk (identified in the *Globe* only as "Base 2"). They faced an Atlantic Fleet team that ironically—or maybe by design—now included Witt, Gainer and Maranville. Jack's boys won a thriller, 3–2, in fourteen innings before ten thousand fans. "Jack Barry said that it was as good a game of real baseball as he had ever taken part in," said the Navy Yard's newspaper—whose editor, incidentally, was a yeoman first class named Elizabeth Burt.[20]

The Memorial Day game was the highlight of the team's season. The Wild Waves next shut out the Newport Naval Reserves at Braves Field before fifteen thousand fans, then beat Janvrin's squad again at Fitchburg in ten innings. A few days afterward, the navy again pulled the plug. "A rule of the navy allows men six months' duty on-shore. Except Marty Killelea [*sic*] all the players have had that much time on land."[21] The navy let Jack play one more game, on June 18 against an alumni squad from his alma mater, Holy Cross, in Worcester. His boys won this last game, too.

In their short season, Jack's boys played just eight games and won all of them by a combined score of 57–9. The stats are fuzzy, but the club played for at least eighty-five thousand fans and probably closer to a hundred thousand. Altogether, Jack put thirteen major leaguers on the field.

News of the club's demise didn't hit the national wires until August. The reason for exploding the club, of course, was *exigencies of the service*. This wasn't entirely true, but not an outright lie, either. However you looked at it, the great Navy Yard club was gone, a casualty of friendly fire. *"BANG!"* said a widely syndicated headline, above an illustration of a detonating baseball.[22]

Secretary Daniels reversed the navy's policy against charging any admission to navy baseball games a few days later. Admiral Wood obeyed the directive, but didn't like it. "It is said that most Naval officers hereabouts regret the decision, which is contrary to the custom of the Navy."[23] By then, it hardly made any difference.

The navy scattered several of the Wild Waves among teams in a big new navy league formed in Boston. "It is believed that ample athletic gear should be supplied in order that as large a number of men as possible may participate in athletics rather than to supply special outfits to the first team men in order that these specially selected men may win contests," said a new navy regulation.[24]

To his credit, Wood supported such sports programs for his sailors— as long as they didn't include flashy squads of professionals. Instead of watching former Braves and Red Sox face off against the army at Braves Field, the swabbies now saw such stellar contests as Bumkin Island versus the Navy Radio School. Jack no longer managed any team, but gave up his chief petty officer's rank and reported to Harvard, where he attended an officer training school with Ernie Shore. The war would end before they finished, but Shore stayed in the navy long enough to earn his commission.

Mike McNally and Herb Pennock, meanwhile, were now on the far side of the Atlantic. Over there, the two former Red Sox soon discovered that William Sowden Sims had a much keener appreciation of baseball than Spencer S. Wood.

6

Gothas and Milk

England was exhausted in the spring of 1918—a guy only had to look around to know that—but the Britishers still did everything they could to make the Yanks feel at home. The boys appreciated it, too. Nobody was dropping bombs on their folks in America like they were over here.

"I went into London the other night and I think it is some city too," an Air Service boy from Oklahoma wrote in February. "There are hardly any lights at all in England at night and especially in the larger cities on account of the air raids. We have had two nights this week."[1]

The Germans launched another raid on London before dawn on March 8, when seven or eight Gotha bombers broke through to London. The Gothas were monsters, twin-pusher biplanes big enough to stand up in. "The machine is known as a bombing battleplane and has a wing spread of 78 ft., which, for comparison, is more than three times as great as that of the famous Nieuport speed scout used by the French and British. Aside from its size, which enables it to carry a pilot, two gunners and more than 800 lb. of bombs, its outstanding features are found in the arrangement of the fuselage."[2] In 1927, Americans would see a Gotha up close in the silent war film *Wings*. (*"A giant Gotha, mightiest of German bombing planes, takes on its deadly load for a dash across the lines...."*)[3]

The first time the Gothas had appeared over London, in the spring and summer of 1917, they'd come in broad daylight. Later they began raiding on moonlit nights. Now they were coming even when there was no moon. Eleven people died in the March 8 raid, forty-six were hurt and several people were missing. The reason that German aviators reached

Wreckage of a Gotha bomber in England (Library of Congress).

London that night was surprising. "The raid is designated as the 'Aurora Borealis' raid, as a glow in the northern sky gave a light resembling summer, which was ample to enable the aviators to steer over the North Sea."[4]

"I was awakened by the guns in the outer defense at 4:30 in the morning, and then the inner defense guns began to bark," a Yank naval officer wrote home to Ohio.

> These guns make a quick, sharp bark just after the initial explosion, the effect being like this: Boom-bar-r-k! The moon made a slim crescent in the sky, and it was a beautiful night, although cold. Presently the faint drone of the raiding planes could be distinguished and there came the reverberating rumbles of bombs being dropped. The difference between the sound of the guns and that of the bombs is very noticeable. The latter reverberate, and, if sufficiently near, have a tendency to rattle the windows. Finally the noise of the motors died away and the guns ceased firing. Fifteen minutes later the guns on the coast could be heard, throwing up their barrage at the returning Hun planes, and at about 6 the buglers were sounding "all clear" through the streets.
>
> These raids have gained nothing for Germany. They have strengthened Tommy's determination to beat them at any cost. The Briton "plays the

game" almost too square. It has taken years for him to even consider air-raid reprisals.[5]

The king and queen went to the bombed areas the next day, talked with the people, congratulated them on their bravery or quick thinking, and even climbed through the wreckage a bit. It wasn't the first time they'd done something like this, and it made the papers. Few Yanks were caught in the raid because the Gothas had hit northwestern London rather than the aero-dromes or army camps, but the boys all knew about it and their folks read about it back home. The naval officer's letter ran in the *New York Times* and just about every other newspaper ran at least a wire story. It made lively reading.

Six days later, three Zeppelins came over England.

In earlier seasons, "Zepps" had often reached London and dropped death into her crowded neighborhoods. But that was before British pilots, anti-aircraft gunners and searchlight crews had developed the tactics and incendiary ammunition to bring the huge airships down in flames—before they'd seen their blackened, twisted frameworks lying crumbled in streets and farm fields. This time, the raiders reached only the northeastern coastal towns. "Only one ventured to approach a defended locality, namely, Hull, where four bombs were dropped. A house was demolished. One woman died of shock. The two remaining airships wandered for some hours over remote country districts at great altitude, unloading their bombs in open country before proceeding out to sea again."[6]

Zepps never again seriously threatened London, but the Gothas came back on the night of May 19–20, a day and a half after the AABL opener at Highbury. Maybe it was payback for a British air raid against Cologne on Saturday a few hours after the game. The Germans claimed the Gothas' bombs fell with good effect between the Admiralty and the West India docks. Thirty-seven people died. The Britishers said they shot down four of the behemoths, one actually within London. "It had a crew of three. The two officers' Iron Crossed bodies were picked up far from the wreckage."[7] A fifth Gotha, they said, had fallen flaming into the sea. Maybe all this was true or maybe none of it was. You never really knew in wartime.

Army pitcher Shag Rawlings' outfit, the 657th Aero Supply Squadron, had let many of the boys go into town that night. The raid is mentioned in the unit's typewritten history.

> At 11;30 [*sic*] this night, the first Air Raid this Squadron ever was in, and the first one on London for over 3 months, it started with a heavy bombard-ment by the Anti-Aircraft guns, made a tremendous noise, and of all the flashes and colors that blended the sky, the 4th at home is a drop in the

bucket, it sure was a real battle. ... It sure was wonderful to see the raid and come out alive, for it seemed every minute as tho. our very camp would be wiped off the earth.

A couple of superstitious boys who'd always believed they would die if ever caught in an air raid actually came through it just fine, while several others "nearly ran themselves to death, to get to cover."[8] Six others got restricted to camp later for writing letters about the big raid and their trips to London.

The raid was one hell of an experience even all the way out at Northolt, whose AABL team had beaten the Hounslow nine on Saturday. "At eleven o'clock orders arrived to place light flares on the Airdrome and it was not long before the Coast Defense guns started to rumble," says another squadron history. "The Hun raiders were coming. Soon London seemed to awake, rockets of warning were fired and the rumble drew nearer. Anti-craft [*sic*] guns were fired in the nearby town and the earth fairly jumped. The raid lasted about an hour and a half and the bursting shells and rockets made a wonderful display. The firing died down. The Hun had gone but only to catch his breath and in about ten minutes returned and the raid did not finish until about 2:30 the following morning."[9]

Diary of a Man About Town, a popular column in a London newspaper, later quoted a Reuter report saying that the Germans had been flying *super* Gothas. There was no such thing, as it turned out, but the blighters had come at night, so how was anybody on the ground to know? "There is nothing in the least discouraging in the circumstance that the Huns are trying machines that carry about two tons of bombs," the diarist assured everyone. "These aeroplanes are so big and clumsy that they make far easier targets than the ordinary Gothas."[10]

The bigger they were, the harder they fell—it made a weird kind of sense. The raiders hadn't hit much of anything and one had been shot down, so maybe *Man About Town* was right. Still, even on nights when the Gothas didn't come over, the British capital could feel like a lonely and dangerous place.

"In London, as in all great cities I am sorry to say, sinister forces are afoot in the darkness between midnight and dawn," Lady Lister Kaye, an American, wrote for Stateside newspapers. "They lie in wait to trap Tommy on his furlough, while the pay is still jingling in his pocket. They watch for Sammy, who is now arriving in London by thousands to do his bit in the great world war. London is no worse than New York or Chicago or Paris, but no city plunged into utter darkness by military necessity would be safe harborage for strangers far from home who are flung into it by night."[11]

But here, too, the Britishers were ready to help. The Motor Transport Volunteers were founded in 1916 by Lady Kaye's husband, Sir John Lister Kaye. The M.T.V. gave free motor transportation to all troops on leave who arrived in London after midnight, when nothing else moved. Most of the volunteers were retired British army officers and all were in uniform. Their motto was *While London Sleeps.*

"As [a] troop train draws into the station they range themselves along the platform, each one calling out 'King's Cross' or 'Paddington' or 'Union Jack Club,' or whatever is the particular station or sleeping place to which it is his special duty to conduct a busload of soldiers," Lady Kaye assured American moms and pops. "The men gather around the M. T. V. officers like sheep around a shepherd. They have many questions to ask: 'What time is the next train for Leeds?' or 'Train doesn't leave till 8:30. Where can I catch a bit of sleep?' And the M. T. V. man answers all questions, and does it, too, in a friendly and cheery way and with an extra welcome for the American boys so far from home."[12]

Yes, the Britishers were doing whatever they could for the Yanks. And darkness and Gotha raids weren't the only hardships in the city that spring, burdens that fell mostly on the hosts. The Air Service boys in their camps and aerodromes had plenty to eat, while Londoners had it harder. Since February, they'd needed ration cards even to buy butter, margarine and meat— if they could find them at all. An adult got twenty ounces of meat a week, kids under ten only half that, and the butter or margarine ration was four ounces per person a week. A healthy sailor or Air Service mechanic could've eaten a Britisher's weekly allotment for lunch.

"The effect of the new scheme will be to abolish public dinners in clubs and hotels, unless they are confined principally to fish and vegetables," the *New York Times* said when rationing started. "There already is talk in certain clubs of combining to stock lakes or private waters with fish for their own use."[13]

Even with ration coupons, Londoners had to stand in line for everything. *Queues*, they called these lines, and they could stretch for a quarter-mile. When people finally got their margarine or mutton, they would go stand in another queue for tea or something else they needed. *Queue* might have meant *quite impossibly long.*

"It was great to get white bread here," London Americans pitcher Leon Vannais said back home in Hartford. "Over in England wheat flour is diluted with barley flour and other products and the war bread is fierce. Breakfast is minus bacon. You know what that means to a Londoner. There are marmalade and tea but not too much. Marmalade is reasonably held for men in uniform. Tea is thin."[14]

People were growing vegetables in tiny patches of soil everywhere, in London and little villages alike, just for the extra food.

"We were in Kensington Palace Gardens, leaning on the fence that goes around the palace—the palace where a little girl named Victoria was born and brought up, and where a lot of high hats went one morning to give her the unexpected news that she was the queen of the British," George Bye wrote for his doughboy readers. "A choice part of Kensington Palace Gardens has been given over to the raising of cabbages, spuds and other munitions of war. Each interested family was loaned, free of any cost, a plot equal to about 300 square feet. ... These allotments are all over Great Britain. Every section of London has them, and all villages and towns and cities. Vegetable patches extend along the railway right-of-ways. They have taken all the vacancy out of empty lots. Hotels have their own garden plots. Consequently, England has an abundant supply of vegetables each year and that's one of two reasons why she faces the submarine menace so complacently. The other reason is her unshakable faith in her navy."[15]

Darkness and *food* popped up over and over in dispatches from London. The nighttime metropolis was "so dark that it is quite impossible to recognize your best friend," a Canadian editor said that summer. "All the shops are, of course, closed at night. It is absolutely impossible to buy milk anywhere in England, except for very young children and persons who are ill, and the same is true in Paris. But England is more closely rationed than France. There is no white bread to be had there at all."[16]

The Air Service boys and all the Yank soldiers and sailors in England were learning fast just what the Britishers had been living with all this time, while Americans were still safe at home. And if they read any newspapers, the boys maybe learned, too, why the Britishers were so good about letting them play ball. British sports were in ruins. Week after week, the local sports pages carried photos of athletes lost in action. On April 12 alone, the casualty lists included a captain who'd rowed at Henley, a shooter from Malvern College, a long-distance runner from Oxford, a golfer and a rugby player—all killed, wounded or missing

The American boys couldn't imagine their own heroes paying that kind of price. What if Jim Thorpe, Barney Oldfield, and Eddie Collins had all been killed? Or Jess Willard, Walter Hagen and Chic Harley wounded or reported missing? And what about the Yankee athletes who were already in uniform—Hank Gowdy, Eddie Rickenbacker, Hobey Baker, Eddie Grant, "Death Valley" Jim Scott and so many others? Which of them wouldn't make it home again, once the Yanks really got into the fighting? It was sobering to think about.

No wonder, then, the Britishers cheered the baseball games, which were as much a mystery to them as cricket was to a fellow from Silver City or Apalachicola. Baseball helped give life and energy to a country where there wasn't much left to cheer about. Say, a guy practically felt like cheering them right back, just to appreciate the fact that they were cheering *him*.

"The arrival in England of so many stars in every branch of sport from America and Canada has awakened new life on every athletic field and set the ball in motion for the enjoyment of quite the best season on record since the outbreak of the great war," said a newspaper in upstate New York. "After four years of fighting, the ranks of British sportsmen have been thinned to alarming proportions, and enthusiasm for sports was on the wane until the Americans and boys from Canada arrived and put fresh life into every indoor and outdoor game."[17]

The paper didn't add that the Canadian boys had suffered severe losses of their own, or point out that two of the four Canadian teams in the AABL represented convalescent hospitals. Sometimes, just a little truth was all that anybody at home wanted to know.

7

Over There

The Yanks weren't playing ball only in the Anglo-American Baseball League. Lots more American boys were serving in France than in England, and they were equally crazy about the national pastime. The circuit they put together in Paris made the eight-team AABL look like a sandlot league.

"A real baseball league, that is what is in store for Parisians this summer," the *Stars and Stripes* said in April. "Yes, it is going to be an honest-to-goodness baseball organization, with from 12 to 16 A.E.F. teams comprising the circuit. ... Arrangements have been completed to obtain the use of the big athletic field at Colombes, a suburb of Paris, where all the league games will be staged. The field is over 50 acres in extent, and at least ten games can be played at the same time. A monster grand stand with a seating capacity of over 25,000 persons, surrounds part of the field."[1]

The Paris league got even bigger and grew to thirty teams, all but two of them from the A.E.F. The league got so big, in fact, that it had five divisions of six teams each. There was an official schedule, with the season set to begin on May 12, the Sunday before the AABL opener. The winners of each division were to play a series for the pennant at the end of the season.

The Y.M.C.A. and the Knights of Columbus (the "K. of C.") had lots of athletic programs for the doughboys in France. The Y thought baseball was so important that it even tried to enlist one of the game's biggest names as something of a baseball czar. The doughboys had even voted for him as the man they most wanted to come over and take charge of diamond activities. That man was Christy Mathewson, Big Six himself, the great New York Giants twirler who now managed the Cincinnati club.

"To meet the imperative demand overseas, the War Personnel Board of the Y.M.C.A. is asked to send this month 1,000 men prominent in business and professional life, including a large number of athletic directors," a Y executive telegraphed to Matty in April. "Special cables from those in authority urge you to come over with important relation to the promotion of baseball for the entire American army. Such an opportunity has never been presented to any man."[2]

Matty replied that he'd think about it and he did. He'd already visited Camp Sheridan, Alabama, over the winter, and played checkers and visited with the boys in the Y.M.C.A. hut down there. He'd also taken his Reds team over for spring training games. Now the Y wanted him to leave his club altogether and come to France, which was no small thing to ask. After thinking about it for a week, Matty said he'd go if the Y could convince him that he'd really make a difference and help boost the morale of American boys. The problem was that nobody could ever spell out exactly what he was supposed to do once he got there.

Still, the *Stars and Stripes* was all for it.

Christy Mathewson, manager of the Cincinnati Reds (Library of Congress).

"COME ON, MATTY," the headline said.

"Baseball philosophers are considerably wrought up by the rumor and hundreds of thousands of words are being written daily as to whether Christy will go abroad or remain at Cincinnati and uphold the national pastime," the army paper added. "'Big Six' is evidently up against it on the checker end, too; but it would be fine if he could land in the Kaiser's king row."[3]

In the end, politics got in the way.

"Must defer action regarding baseball," a Y man wired Matty. He added in a personal letter that they'd had a cable from France, saying that the timing of the thing just wasn't right. "Then, too, the French people, whose viewpoint in athletics is not in accordance with our own, may possibly misunderstand our whole idea, in which event there is possibility for unfavorable reaction."[4]

What exactly did that mean? Basically, that the war-weary French—whose blue-helmeted poilus had been fighting on their own soil since 1914—thought that the Yanks should send over someone slightly more useful than an aging ballplayer, even the great Matty. The *Brooklyn Eagle's* man in Paris "very frankly pointed out in a number of stories that the increase on French soil of American civilians who had nothing more serious to do than to exploit amusements was causing unfavorable comment. Later a story from France stated that because of that growing feeling the offer to Mathewson had been withdrawn, as had the offers to several other non-combatants."[5]

So, that was that.

Matty never said a bad word about the whole mess, but no doughboy would've blamed him if he had. The Reds' skipper would stick with his club until the season was over, then sign up as a captain in the army's Gas and Flame division. He'd do it even though he was old enough that he didn't have to serve at all. Ty Cobb, Branch Rickey and Boston Braves president Percy Houghton all became Gas and Flame officers, too. Nobody could call any of them slackers and get away with it.

Once overseas, Matty would be hospitalized with a bad case of influenza. When he finally got back on duty, he'd breathe in deadly mustard gas during a training accident, which most people wouldn't know anything about until the Georgia Peach wrote about it many years later. The gas could have something to do with Matty's early death from tuberculosis in 1925.

If only the Y hadn't bungled their call in 1918. ...

There would have been lots for Matty to supervise in France. Yanks were playing ball all over the country, and every kind of outfit was looking for games—army, navy and marines; supply companies and infantrymen; ships' crews and repair battalions; stevedores and engineers; navy dirigible stations and military police. In a segregated army, this included even the Negro units, who fielded one of the best teams in France. The 312th Labor Battalion club at St. Sulpice was so good that the *Stars and Stripes* went out of its way to cover it. Unfortunately, the paper used language that would get anybody's block knocked off for using it today.

Doughboys in France played anywhere they could pull out bats and balls and lay down the bags. They'd get up a game in rear areas, where the only thing that could hurt anyone was an up-and-in fastball. And they'd play so close behind the lines that a German in an observation balloon with a good pair of binoculars could've called balls and strikes. Just about every Yank outfit in France had a fast nine, which often included someone you might have heard of back home.

They called the big circuit in Paris the American Soldiers Baseball League. Although much bigger, it really wasn't in the same class as the AABL. Oh, sure, you might see a guy from the old Wisconsin State League, or somebody who'd been a decent hurler for a land-grant school or even an Ivy League college back home. But you wouldn't see many big leaguers like Ed Lafitte or Herb Pennock or Mike McNally. Journeyman Gabby Street, "Old Sarge," would pop up in a *Stars and Stripes* story about the league ... but only because he was too sick to play for his army engineers team.

The Paris league played in a safe rear area. But the army needed its athletes at the front, and big-time ballplayers often wound up in infantry outfits. Hank Gowdy of the Braves was already there with the Rainbow Division. Former Giant Billy O'Hara was an officer in a Canadian outfit, but back home now recovering from wounds and illness. Leon Cadore of the Dodgers would soon lead Negro troops in combat. Grover Alexander and a handful of other big leaguers in the 342nd Field Artillery were on their way over, and would be in action until the very last minute before the Armistice. Alex and the gunners had one hell of a good ball club, but they didn't play in the Paris league and they didn't play at all up on the line.

There were lots of other boys from the American and National leagues up there, too. Even tiny Brownie Burke, an old Cincinnati Reds mascot, had talked his way into uniform and gone to France as a clerk, probably the smallest soldier in the National Army. Eddie Grant, the Giants' old third baseman, would die fighting in the Argonne in October. His teammate Harry "Moose" McCormick would ship home suffering from shell shock even before Eddie's death. There was a war on.

Three hundred thousand Yanks were in France by March 1918. Tens of thousands more stepped off troopships every week. After a very slow start, the American buildup was now an avalanche. Naturally, the boys wanted to play ball when spring arrived. The Y.M.C.A. ordered a thousand gross of bats—144,000 Louisville Sluggers—to equip them. Each bat was branded with the Y's distinctive triangle. Add to that the baseball gear sent over by the Knights of Columbus, the Clark Griffith Ball and Bat Fund, the National League and other groups and you still didn't have enough equipment for all the boys. It didn't help that baseball gear "acted as a sort of loadstone toward German submarines" or that the torpedoed liner *Oronsa* went down with thirty thousand dollars worth of the stuff.[6] The Y had to get creative.

"Score another run for France," a *Stars and Stripes* story told doughboys in early June. "A French manufacturer has made a baseball glove—a fielder's glove, to be exact—working from specifications and blueprints furnished him by the Y.M.C.A. For you might as well know the truth first as last. The shortage of athletic equipment is serious."[7]

The army paper thought the French glove was good stuff, except that the thumb and forefinger were held together by cord instead of leather straps. The bigger problem was the continuing shortage of bats. If a dough-boy wanted to get unpopular real quick, all he had to do was crack the only bat for miles around. There just weren't enough bats arriving from the States and there never would be. "Bats are easy to make, if you have the wood and the machinery—an ordinary turning lathe. So if any enter-prising French wood turner will write to THE STARS AND STRIPES, a con-tract will be placed in his hands that will keep him busy as long as there's an American army in France. No hand carving, no filigree, just plain, hon-est wagon tongue—those are the specifications."[8]

The French bats weren't terrific—the country's ash was a little too heavy, and the first models "resembled the club affected by Jack the Giant Killer"—but they would do in a pinch.[9] The Y ordered a thousand right away and the Knights of Columbus pitched in for 3,000 more. That just left the question of baseballs ... and here the French fell woefully short. What did anybody know in Paris or Lyon about winding and stitching a good horsehide ball?

"One K. of C. man, who wants the best on the market, recently tried out a baseball of French manufacture," the army paper reported. "He hit in regular Polo Ground form, and whish! Where the baseball had been was a white puff resembling a burst of shrapnel. That particular brand of baseball is no longer eligible for championship A.E.F. honors."[10]

The doughboys soldiered bravely ahead, using whatever diamond equipment they could beg, borrow or steal. The game had to go on.

You couldn't say that the French themselves were ever big fans of the American game. They had even less reason than the Britishers to catch the fever, in fact. They knew nothing in Paris about rounders and they didn't play cricket or any other bat-and-ball games.

A few Americans had tried to get the game going there in 1914 before the war, with modest results. "The Frenchmen have taken very kindly to our American sport," the president of the Spalding Athletic Club of Vesinet had said. "They have no professional ball teams, but many amateur organ-izations, mainly run under the supervision of the Racing Club of France, are flourishing. The game is played exactly as it is here [in New York], but the players usually wear a costume similar to those of track athletes here."[11] That didn't sound much like real baseball.

The French showed a little more interest once Yanks started coming to help fight the war. People gathered around doughboys playing catch in the street or tossing a ball around the Tuileries. They'd *ooh* and *ahh* at how the boys handled the horsehide, but stayed safely out of the way in case a ball got away. Sportswriter Heywood Broun once watched a poilu wearing the *medaille militaire* and the *croix de guerre* with two palms set down his gear to join a game at the *Esplanade des Invalides*. He circled under the first fly that came his way, then let it bop him right on the nose. The poilu got up bloody but grinning. *"C'est dangereux,"* he said as he left for the safety of the front.[12]

His countrymen tended to agree, which would spark a nice crack in a Washington sports page a few months after the war: "In England baseball is compared to the 'tame game of rounders' and in France the American pastime is shunned as 'too dangerous.' And people still wonder why differences crop up regarding the league of nations."[13]

"Baseball was almost unknown here," a correspondent would write from Paris the day before the Armistice. "Not many Frenchmen had even seen a game. None understood it with the exception of a travelled editor or so. When the famous Bois de Boulogne was taken over for baseball somebody had to tell them what it was all about, whereupon the American Soldiers and Sailors' Club, after having planned the games, wrote a vocabulary in French so that the poilus and Parisiennes could follow the plays. They called it 'Code Simplifie du Baseball.'"[14]

The Yanks handed out copies of the *Code* during the ball games. It didn't do a lot of good. A quartermaster sergeant even got poetic in the *Stars and Stripes* about the problem of taking a French girlfriend to the ballpark.

> *When you and I were watching while*
> *The Doughboys battled the Marines,*
> *Did classy hitting make you smile?*
> *Did you rejoice in home run scenes?*
> *Ah, no: when Meyer slammed the pill—*
> *They couldn't find it for a week—*
> *You turned to me and said, "Oh, Bill,*
> *I zink his uniform ees* chique!"[15]

The average French soldier didn't have much talent when it came to baseball. He'd never played it, and unlike the poilu with the *medaille militaire*, wasn't very eager to try. Y.M.C.A. volunteers saw the difference right away as they drove toward the front, tossing oranges to allied troops as they passed.

> The French soldiers had a high catching average if he caught one out of 10 oranges as we pitched them, but the Americans caught nine out of 10. The American lad could catch them with his eyes shut or on horseback as

many an American officer did do that day. He could catch a third orange if his two hands were already full. He could jump into the air and nab an orange while he munched another one. He could catch them as they whizzed his way, and at the same time wink at a pretty girl, or hand an orange to a French child. ... The Frenchman reaches up both hands, with a desperate effort to protect his face. But the American forgets his face and nabs the orange out of the air. He is sure of himself when it comes to catching.[16]

The Yanks could not only catch, they could also throw like the devil. This talent came in handy with bombs and hand grenades and such. Seattle Bill James, who'd won twenty-six games hurling for the Miracle Braves in 1914, was even a camp grenade instructor in the States. French officers were impressed by how well and accurately Yanks actually *threw* their grenades, instead of lobbing them with a stiff arm like the poilus. A Yank in the Foreign Legion would set a record at Fontainebleu in August by tossing a grenade two hundred fifteen feet, breaking the record set by another Yank by over twelve feet. Both boys had played ball back home.

"Few games develop the co-ordination of mind and muscle and judgment of distance like baseball," a sober-sided *New York Times* reporter explained. "The truth of this statement is borne out by the fact that the army leaders have found that in grenade throwing, where accuracy in distance is essential, men who have played the national sport are more expert."[17]

In other words ... *hum baby! Chuck that pineapple!*

The French army eventually connected with baseball, but it took

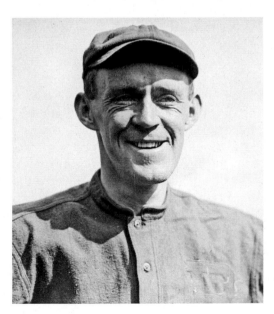

Johnny Evers of *Tinker to Evers to Chance* fame to make the breakthrough. Retiring as a player after sixteen seasons in the bigs, Evers signed on with the K. of C. in June 1918. The newspapers called him "the generalissimo of baseball in France."[18] In other words, the Trojan had the sort of job that the Y had imagined for Christy Mathewson, except the Knights actually made it happen.

Johnny Evers, who went to France with the Knights of Columbus (Library of Congress).

It would be August before Johnny got overseas, but once he's there the French would warm to him—as unlikely as that seemed to anybody who actually knew him. "French Army Adopts Baseball With Johnny Evers as Bawler Out," a headline would say.[19] The French newspapers would call him *Monsieur Jeannot Evers, ancien champion de baseball de Chicago.* "All right, if they say so," he'd grumble, "but what did they want to tack on that 'ancien' business for?"[20] (He probably didn't realize that *ancien* just meant *former.*)

A French general would like what he saw in Johnny, and invite him to teach his poilus the basics of baseball as part of their physical training. "[A]s these fellows couldn't understand English and never had seen a ball game, and I couldn't speak French, you can imagine the job I had. However, they jumped into it with all the enthusiasm in the world and we got along famously—with the aid of an interpreter." Still, Johnny wouldn't see a lot of potential for baseball until the French kids grew up. They were the ones who really liked the game.

"Another thing that will hinder the advance of baseball over there is the scarcity of paraphernalia," Johnny would say once back in the States. "Dealers handled baseball stuff because the Doughboys bought it. But home consumption was nothing to brag about, and it's doubtful whether or not sporting goods houses will carry much of a stock of baseball tools after the Doughboys leave unless baseball propaganda is worked to the limit."[21]

Unlike Johnny, who seemed strangely diplomatic to fans who called him The Crab, Christy Mathewson would shake his head at the notion of French ballplayers. "They are more afraid of a hard hit grounder or liner than they are of a German shell," Matty would say. "Their infield work is bad. They can run bases all right, but have little opportunity because they cannot bat. The thing which the French players cannot do is to stand up close behind the batsman and catch. Nothing can persuade them to stand up and get them right under the bat like our catchers do. They want to retreat about ten yards and catch the ball."[22]

After his work with the poilus, Evers would move along and visit three Yank divisions. He'd talk it up with the boys and give them a few pointers. The Trojan would come under shellfire, too, along with Lieutenant Joe Jenkins of the White Sox and a poor kid who "ducked like a scared rabbit into a dugout. I followed just like that rabbit's brother."[23] Johnny would also meet an army chaplain who'd tell him about an old baseball he'd found on a battlefield in the pocket of a kid killed in action. Touched, the Trojan would ask if he could have it.

"Not for a million dollars," the chaplain would say. "I'm too big a fan, and this is too precious to me. It will be more precious to others. If I can find them when we get back that boy's baseball belongs to them. If not, then I'll keep it as one of the biggest prizes of my life."[24]

Baseball would spread everywhere that the Yanks went during the war and just afterward. Maybe the sport wouldn't ever be popular in lots of these places, but it'd be there nonetheless. Doughboys and bluejackets would play ball in Rome and Antwerp and Rotterdam. A few Yanks serving with the Britishers would even put on a few games in Jerusalem. A Texas paper would look back at it all after the Armistice and wonder where baseball might yet go.

> *Now that the Yanks have taught the French*
> *To root in decent style,*
> *And even Englishmen have looked*
> *On baseball with a smile,*
> *And Italy and Belgium both*
> *Are tickled with home-runs,*
> *How's Yankee baseball going to take*
> *When they play it 'mongst the Huns?*[25]

8

The Stunt

On the other side of the English Channel, the idea behind the King's Game had come early. It hadn't come from the king, although George V apparently saw its merits and possibilities as soon as anybody and acted on them as only he could. Who, then, could claim credit for dreaming up the great Chelsea baseball match? As with everything else surrounding that fabulous, whirring, clicking, rolling, Rube Goldbergesque event, it depended on who (*whom, old boy*) you asked.

There isn't much doubt that British officers at the Ministry of Information helped get the thing rolling. One of the main functions of its American Section in London was to send upbeat war news (what there was of it—the *dope*, they called it) to New York. Officers in the section also kept track of American VIPs in London and helped them to meet all the right Britishers. Every once in a while, too, their duties might involve helping some gorgeous but dim film star who thought that surely the Ministry of Information must know what had become of her missing steamer trunk. Even the people who worked in it thought the proper name for the place should have been the Ministry of Propaganda.

"We used to think up stunts together," recalled Major Ian Hay Beith, a writer and decorated British soldier who had charge of the American Section. "The biggest stunt we pulled off—important because it led to something bigger—was the official celebration in London for the first time in history, by the English people, of American Independence Day!"[1]

Blessedly, calling it Inter-Dependence Day never really caught on. It was a big scheme that involved public meetings, concerts, church services, parties and sports. Arranging it all wasn't simple. Looking around for a spot to hold the speeches, Beith thought the Guildhall was just the ticket. The Lord Mayor of London loved the idea, but had a few questions for the major.

"When did you think of having the celebration?"

"We thought of having it on the Fourth of July, sir."

"I see. Is it absolutely necessary to have it on the Fourth? Won't the Third or Fifth do equally well? You see, the Guildhall is already booked for another meeting on that date."[2]

Fortunately, the Central Hall was available—disaster averted.

The idea for playing an army-navy AABL game on the Fourth came from the U.S. Army team. According to Floyd C. Mims, the army skipper, so did the inspired notion of inviting the royals. Mims wasn't a former pro ballplayer like so many of the others, but a colorful Regular Army soldier from Georgia serving in the Quartermaster Corps. As an enlisted man in the Philippines, he'd once been an orderly for General John J. "Black Jack" Pershing, who now commanded the American Expeditionary Forces. Soon after arriving in France in August 1917, Mims had been ordered across to England to help set up the army's London headquarters.

"I was appointed first-lieutenant and detailed as detachment commanding officer of all our enlisted personnel, soon to arrive," Mims would write many decades later. "I had to locate living quarters and messing facilities as well as fabricate some kind of recreation program. My first thoughts of recreation turned toward baseball. We got a few balls and a bat from the American Red Cross, and held our first practice in the garden behind the Goring Hotel. At that point, we were furnished with all the baseball equipment we required and informed of where we could play golf, tennis, and rugby. Whenever time allowed, we would go to Chelsea Soccer Field, choose up sides, and have a scrub game."[3]

Mims helped form the U.S. Army team for the AABL—"not exactly an amateur sandlot league," in his words. "One rainy day, we sat in a hotel lobby and discussed the necessity of a special game on the Fourth of July. Whom should we invite as celebrity guest? We decided to go whole hog and ask Their Majesties, King George V and Queen Mary, or the Prince of Wales, later to become King Edward VIII, or the Lord Mayor of London. Why not invite them all?"[4]

An old soldier with pull and experience, Mims wasn't shy in making suggestions to the brass. He promised his boys that he'd talk things over with General Biddle, "a kindly and gentle officer of the old school, not given to rash or speedy decisions." Biddle didn't think Mims was serious, but the baseball skipper pressed his case. "I have discussed this with several British people I know," Mims insisted. "They all think it is a great idea."[5]

Biddle said he'd think it over.

Afraid that the general would take too long deciding, Mims suggested that he (Mims) go to see Admiral Sims—the navy ball club would be involved, too, after all. Biddle let him go, and Sims pounced like a destroyer after a U-boat. The admiral telephoned Biddle with the quartermaster still standing in his office. "John," he said, 'I have Captain [*sic*] Mims in my office, and we are talking about an Army-Navy game on the Fourth of July. I think it's a splendid idea.' With that concurrence, General Biddle's inertia evaporated, and he quickly consented. Our project began to roll."[6]

The idea wasn't completely screwy. There was even a nice historical precedent, although nobody knew it at the time. Frederick, the Prince of Wales, and his pal Charles Sackville, the Earl of Middlesex, both middle-aged men, had played an early sort of baseball in 1749. "On Tuesday last, his Royal Highness the Prince of Wales, and Lord Middlesex, played at Bass-Ball [*sic*], at Walton in Surry; notwithstanding the Weather was extreme bad, they continued playing several Hours."[7] Frederick's son grew up to be George III. Now here were the Yankees, their former colonials, wanting to invite George V to a ball game.

American officials dithered, as officials would, over the protocol for inviting the king to the army's home field at Stamford Bridge. "No one knew who ought to meet the royal couple and escort them to their box."[8] They finally managed to extend an invitation, which the king quickly accepted. Pick Cross probably was the person who actually invited the royal family. He couldn't just ring up the palace, of course. (*"George? Listen, the boys are playing baseball on our big national holiday next month. I'm leaving six tickets in your name at Chelsea."*) No, Cross exchanged elegant notes with the king's private secretary, Lieutenant-Colonel Arthur Bigge, the first Baron Stamfordham.

> 8th June, 1918.
>
> Dear Mr. Wilson Cross,
>
>   In reply to your letter of the 7th instant, I am glad to be able to tell you that the Queen and Princess Mary will accompany the King on the occasion of the Baseball Match between the American army and navy on the 4th of July.
>
>   I note that the Match will be on the Chelsea Football Ground and will commence at 3.30 p.m.
>
> Yours very truly,
> Stamfordham[9]

That same day, a short article appeared in the *Times* under the headline "THE KING AND BASEBALL." "The King has announced his intention of being present at a baseball match at Chelsea on the Fourth of July between the United States Army and Navy 'nines.' The day will mark the 142nd anniversary of the independence of the United States, and the King's decision has given great pleasure to Americans in London."[10] This only told Britishers what Americans had read in their own papers two days earlier.

So, who gets credit for creating the King's Game?

Certainly, a team of army ballplayers, their commanding general, an American naval Anglophile, a few British propagandists and a well-connected AABL pooh-bah from Pittsburgh all "did their bit." But it was George V himself—the actual king—who set the whole thing in motion. All he had to do to start the mechanisms whirling was say "Yes," or "right-io," or "delighted, old chap," or whatever a British monarch said when accepting an odd invitation from a rowdy new ally. Nobody had any idea what a big, important thing it would become, but the gents at the AABL were very happy.

"We feel tremendously honoured that the King is gracious enough to place the seal of his approval upon baseball and particularly upon such an occasion," Wilson Cross said for the league. "Baseball is particularly associated with the Fourth of July spirit in the States. But both the game and the day will take on fresh significance for us now that a King of England has 'played the game,' so to speak, on Independence Day."[11]

The "baseball match" quickly picked up momentum. Behind the scenes, George V, grandson of Queen Victoria and cousin of Kaiser Wilhelm II of Germany, helped keep it moving. His greatest strength during this time— his extraordinary gift, in fact—was just how *ordinary* he seemed to Americans. George III hadn't fared well in his dealings with Yanks, but George V had a sort of genius for it.

Aside from being the king, the king didn't seem to have a lot going for him. He wasn't a romantic figure like his grandfather, Prince Albert of Saxe-Coburg and Gotha, whose early death had sent poor Queen Victoria into lifelong mourning. He wasn't an impeccably dressed charmer like his father, Edward VII, "the uncle of Europe," whose style defined an era of fashion. And the king's wife, Queen Mary, was rather matronly, nothing at all like his fabulously beautiful mother, Alexandra. No, George V seemed just a small, shy fellow with a tidy beard. Admirals, generals and ramrod-straight soldiers waiting to be decorated usually towered over him. George looked as if he had to be talked into wearing his tailored military uniforms out of a sense of duty. He seemed to wear them during the war only to declare, *Well, you see, I am the king.*

But this modesty was a sort of strength. For one thing, it made him much easier for Americans to appreciate and like—certainly more than they did Wilhelm II. (And, say, wasn't *he* the perfect target! Cartoonists couldn't have invented a better villain than Kaiser Bill, with his pointed helmets and funny moustache.) American newspapers picked up a story that the king had bought a civilian suit that cost "exactly 57 shillings, or $14.25. ... Maybe some tailor is palming off on George a fancy twenty-pound suit for a 57 shilling one. But the point is, the king is honestly trying to set a good royal example in apparel. He is economizing."[12]

A little later in the summer, George would inspect a Yankee battleship anchored with his Grand Fleet off Scotland. The monarch would pick up a shovel and heave a bit of coal into a boiler to help keep up steam. "It is not the first time I have done this," he'd say, laughing, remembering his time in his grandmother's navy. This little tale would rocket through both fleets. "Perhaps the King has heard of Theodore Roosevelt's custom of clasping the hand of the engineer of every train he rides on," an American paper would say. "Certainly he knows how to gain the good will and admiration of men of inferior station, a point that in old times was of small concern to crowned heads."[13]

The wartime king tried hard to set a good example for fellow Britishers. This meant he took a huge interest in his Yank allies and everything American. Take the day in late June when the king decided it would be a jolly good idea to stop by the Y.M.C.A. Eagle Hut in Aldwych with Queen Mary. He wanted to see how the American lads were getting on there. It was all very informal, or as informal as anything gets for a king. The Palace just rang them up: "The King and Queen desire to call at the Eagle Hut, and will be there in a few minutes."[14]

The Eagle Hut wasn't actually a hut, but an attractive collection of red-roofed wooden buildings. Aldwych wasn't a neighborhood, either, but a wide road that curved out away from the Strand and back again. The Eagle Hut was between the two streets, at the foot of Kingsway, in a pretty spot with grass and trees. Waterloo Bridge and the big bend of the river were only a couple of blocks away. The boys liked to get up a ball game occasionally in the lots around the Hut, and the Yank women who worked there were known to grab a mitt, too. "Never a day passes without a regular 'corner lot' game, while the Londoners stand and stare, and Master Bobby never says 'Move on,' so much is he amused himself."[15]

Five Yank sailors were tossing a ball around with three British Tommies, in fact, when the royals drove up. The sight no doubt cheered George V. The king and queen then went inside, where Allied troops were taking it easy, eating, writing letters and playing pool. The monarchs stopped to chat with a Mrs. Brown from Chicago, who ran the information bureau. She usually spent her shifts answering questions from the boys, everything from how to find the Old Curiosity Shop (a stone's throw away) or a copy of the *Saturday Evening Post* to how a fella could rightly get married there in England. Everybody called her *Mother*.

"How many questions are you asked in the course of a week?" the queen wanted to know.

"About eleven hundred, Your Majesty."

"Do you ever get any questions you can't answer?" the king asked.

"I live in hourly dread of being asked to spell a word I can't spell," Mrs. Brown said, making the king laugh.[16]

A Y.M.C.A. secretary then gave George and Mary a little tour. A secretary in the Y didn't type or take dictation, but was a pretty important guy. "What is the most distinctively American dish you have here?" the king asked. "I want to sample it."

"Buckwheat cakes is the best thing we have," the fellow said.

That sounded swell. "The King and Queen sat down at an oilcloth covered table beside a group of khaki-clad American aviators and two bluejackets from an American battleship. They each ate a plate of buckwheat cakes hot from the griddle, with a generous covering of genuine maple syrup. Having finished their portions, they politely refused a second helping, but declared themselves unanimously in favor of the adoption of buckwheat cakes into the British national menu."[17]

A newspaper up in Minnesota would later crack that the king must've agreed with a legendary Englishman "who urged his companion at an American breakfast table, when buckwheat cakes were served: 'Try one; they're not hahlf so nawsty as they look.'"[18]

George and Mary looked into the kitchen and then the dormitories and chatted with a few of the boys. The king said that he liked a higher pillow than the ones they handed out at the Hut. He laughed when he heard it was a good idea to sleep with your clothes tucked under your pillow and one leg of the bed in each of your boots. "I couldn't do that with mine," he said, pointing to his gleaming leather beauties.[19] A Tennessee boy stepped into the room. "They tell me the king is here," he said, "and I want to shake hands with the head of this beautiful country."[20] George obliged and asked where home was, being unfamiliar with the soft drawl of the Volunteer State. All in all, the king and the queen had a high old time, and the boys cheered them when they left.

"It was the most natural thing for George, every inch a democrat, to do," the *New York Times* said about the visit. "On the Fourth of July (will George III turn in his grave?) the king is to 'pitch out' the first baseball in a game between American teams. Arlie Latham, one of our most unabashed Diamond heroes, has been coaching George in the right delivery, and

Cartoon from an American newspaper (*San Antonio Light*).

probably the king is a bit nervous about his performance. He is certainly more concerned than Arlie Latham, a king of baseball comedians and always a complete stranger to embarrassment."[21]

Oh, yes, Walter Arlington Latham was smack in the middle of the mounting excitement over the King's Game. Stamfordham had asked Wilson Cross if he would bring a ball to the palace one morning, to show the king how to throw it. But having Arlie teach him instead was a brilliant stroke. Just imagine—the Freshest Man on Earth, giving pitching lessons to His Majesty George V, by the Grace of God, of the United Kingdom of Great Britain and Ireland and of the British Dominions beyond the Seas, King, Defender of the Faith, Emperor of India. It boggled the mind! American newspaper editors ate it up with a spoon.

> At the request of the King, Arlie Latham, a former big league player, who will umpire the Fourth of July game, sent the King a regulation baseball a few days ago. The next day Latham called at the Palace and gave the King a brief lesson as to how the baseball should be handled. The proper form in pitching was rather hard for the King to get as he is used to a different type of throw, as in cricket, but the Royal student finally began to get something approaching the right swing. Since then the King has been practicing in his spare moments on a blank wall in the garden.[22]

Arlie's pitching advice to the king: "Speed! and More speed!"[23]

Oh, Americans could just picture the king tossing the old horsehide around his back garden at Buck House. "Isn't it enough to make the crickets whistle?" asked a newspaper in Pennsylvania. Even British subjects were tickled. "The gardens of Buckingham Palace have seen many astonishing changes during the war," quipped a newspaper in New Zealand, "but probably the most remarkable of all is the sight of King George practicing the true Yankee method of 'pitching' a ball."[24]

The wartime odd couple was catnip to American sports editors.

"Arlie Latham is teaching King George how to throw a ball," the *New York Tribune* noted. "We trust King George won't teach Arlie Latham how to wear a crown."[25] And Arlie might not have been the monarch's only instructor. Floyd Mims, never a completely reliable source, wrote decades later that he had visited King George at the palace on the morning of the Fourth, to "coach him a bit about the game, and show how to throw out the first ball."[26]

A paper in San Antonio, Texas, captured Americans' delight in the George and Arlie Show. It ran six cartoons in a large panel across the sports page, under the headline "KING GEORGE ENJOYS 'STACK OF WHEATS' AND TRIES BASEBALL." A sketch in the lower-right corner showed the king fretting to a butler about accidentally breaking a palace window with an errant throw.

> "Grimes—perhaps it would be just as well if you didn't say anything to the Queen about this!"
> "Yes Sir! I'll intimate it wus [sic] an air raid Sir."[27]

Blame it on the Gothas.

9

Old Hands

An *old hand* was worth ten ordinary men in wartime. The term, long used by soldiers, sailors and cowboys, meant an experienced person or expert. You could say *old bird* or *old dog* and mean the same thing.[1] Old hands knew how things worked and how to keep them working. Every first sergeant or chief petty officer wanted them, no matter if they were regulars, volunteers or draftees. No outfit could have too many old hands. The navy nine in the AABL had several, including Mike McNally, Herb Pennock and a fellow named Stuart Hayes.

These boys were old pros, although each was still in his twenties. They had almost nothing else in common. In the way of armies and navies down through the ages, they would all serve together on the London headquarters baseball team, bound like an old ball in a new glove wrapped by string.

After receiving orders to ship out from the Charlestown Navy Yard, Mike and Herb had packed their sea bags, said their goodbyes to Jack Barry, Chick Shorten, Rabbit Maranville and the rest of the Wild Waves and left Boston. They'd first traveled to the League Island Navy Yard in Philadelphia, probably together. Later, they went north again to New York, where they shouldered their sea bags and reported on board the elderly USS *Glacier* for transportation to Ireland.

Glacier wasn't much to look at, no sleek greyhound of the sea like the navy destroyers that had preceded her to Ireland. *Glacier* was built in 1891 as a merchant ship called *Delmonico*. The navy had taken her over in 1898 during the unpleasantness with Spain and had kept her on duty ever since, transporting ice and meat and stores to various parts of the world, mostly in the Pacific. Now *Glacier* was a Naval Overseas Transport Ship ferrying troops to Europe.

She started her first trip across the Atlantic on June 2 with Mike and Herb on board. She would have made the hazardous crossing in a convoy, a large number of vessels steaming together in formation, escorted by destroyers to protect them from German U-boats. Any convoy's speed was determined by the slowest ship in it, which wasn't a very comforting thought when you were facing submarines. A guy naturally wanted to cross the ocean in one of the fast converted ocean liners, maybe even one that the U.S. had seized from Germany, but definitely not on some floating meat locker with about as much speed as a peddler's cart. *Glacier* probably wasn't the pokiest ship in the convoy, but she didn't

Mike McNally, with the New York Yankees after the war (**Library of Congress**).

exactly push the destroyers and she certainly was never admired for slicing cleanly through the sea. It took a while to reach Ireland. *Glacier* didn't return Stateside until July 26, so Mike and Herb likely left her in Queenstown sometime in late June.

Mike probably had orders to report to USS *Melville* in Queenstown. He, Barry and Shorten had all been photographed in navy blues back in Boston wearing *Melville* ribbons on their caps—which was odd, because *Melville* wasn't anywhere near Boston and sailors' cap ribbons generally said only *U.S. Navy* in wartime. *Melville* was a destroyer tender, launched in 1915 and not much better to look at than *Glacier*. She was Admiral Sims' flagship in Europe, although he didn't come on board much. *Melville* wouldn't see much of Mike anytime soon, either.

When the two former Wild Waves arrived in Queenstown, Herb expected to catch another ship and keep on going to Gibraltar, the great British naval base at the entrance to the Mediterranean. Instead, "we found a searching party looking for us," he recalled years later. "It developed that some naval officers in London were arranging a Fourth of July celebration to be featured by a ball game with the army. Learning we were aboard, they arranged for our transfer to London, where Mike and I fought the rest of the war with baseballs."[2]

This was the sort of thing that happened to Michael Joseph McNally.

Mike McNally was born on September 13, 1893, in Minooka, Pennsylvania, which today is part of Scranton. His parents were both Irish immigrants. His pop was a coal miner, normal in a town where many men worked either in the mines or on the railroad. Lots of families were like the McNallys, including the O'Neill clan, their friends and neighbors for years. The only boy among three sisters, Mike worked as a depot agent before he turned seventeen. But what he really cared about was baseball.

Minooka was crazy for baseball. Quite a few boys there would make the majors, including four from one family—brothers Jack, Mike, Steve, and Jimmy O'Neill. The pride of the town was the fabled Minooka Blues, a semipro club that played in a league sponsored by a Catholic temperance group. Paul O'Neill, a fifth brother, coached the club. Lots of his ballplayers were teenagers—"the young Blues," the newspapers called them.[3]

Hughie Jennings, the Detroit Tigers manager, took a paternal interest because he was from the Lackawanna Valley, too. One of baseball's "mighty mites," he helped several of the Blues break into the big leagues, including the O'Neill brothers, outfielder Chick Shorten and third baseman Mike McNally.[4] Mike would always be grateful.

When he broke into the majors, people from elsewhere inevitably would will call him "Minooka Mike" McNally. It was a good nickname, but the original Minooka Mike was Mike O'Neill, who managed in the New York State League after retiring as a player for the Cardinals and Reds. O'Neill signed Mike for his Utica Utes club in the winter of 1911. Standing five-eleven and weighing less than a buck fifty, Mike was so skinny that his nickname was Ghost.

The 1912 season was something of a gift for the kid, whose stats don't even show up in the modern record. Mike helped out around the ballpark, learned the finer points of the game sitting next to Mike O'Neill and once in a while got into a late inning of a game. He made his professional debut during a road game in Scranton—in another good deed by O'Neill—after the Utes' second baseman got himself tossed. Young Mike's hometown pals gave him a suitcase and a traveling bag to celebrate.

Some sportswriters thought O'Neill was letting emotion cloud his judgment in carrying a kid who was "little more than a bat boy."[5] But Minooka Mike No. 1 knew what he was doing. Minooka Mike No. 2 played a graceful shortstop for the Utes the next season, stealing twenty-four bases and hitting .268 against strong pitching. Boston scout Patsy Donovan thought he was "the best ball player for his age that I have ever seen."[6] The Red Sox believed him and bought Mike's contract for thirty-five hundred dollars in August 1913, a month before he turned twenty. The club shipped him to the American Association for seasoning with the St. Paul Saints.

The skinny infielder got noticed the next season. *Sporting Life* said Mike "fields his position well, has a deadly peg, and looks as if he would develop into a fair hitter."[7] The *Pittsburgh Press* called him "the sensation of the American association."[8] He had vision problems late that year—some reports even had him going blind—but Boston called him back that winter and Mike reported to the Red Sox in 1915. "There is no more popular local base ball product than McNally," said *The Sporting News*. "The fans like him because he is the same Mike McNally today that he was when he was on the amateur lots."[9]

The kid from Minooka made the big club, mostly filling in at third base, his old position with the Blues. *Sporting Life* mentioned his "sensational fielding" and "circus stuff" around the bag. Even the *New York Times* noticed the Red Sox's "accomplished new infielder."[10] Mike soon met a raw young pitcher who had arrived in Boston the previous season. That was George Herman Ruth, who would be his teammate for almost a decade and his friend for much longer.

"I learned to laugh and have fun with him," Mike said later of the Babe.[11] Well, sure ... didn't everyone? "The Babe, an innocent minded, simple country boy from Baltimore, was easily influenced by McNally's wiles as a city slicker from Scranton," a New York scribbler wrote later of the friendship, tongue practically poking through his cheek. "They became great cronies. McNally leered an evil Scranton leer as he taught the Babe to eat hot dogs and to guzzle pop right out of the bottle without even using a straw."[12]

Mike didn't stick with Boston that first season, getting sent back to the minors in June. He did okay down there, hitting .253 for the Providence Grays. When the big club made the World Series that fall, the Sox voted to give him a fraction of a player's full share of the proceeds. The 1915 Red Sox team was the first of six pennant-winning clubs that Minooka Mike would play for in the big leagues.

The flashy infielder made the big club again in 1916 and stayed there. He hit a measly .170 in eighty-seven games, but made a name for himself on the bases. The kid was whippet fast and sly as a coyote. "MIKE McNALLY'S DASH BEATS THE SENATORS," the *Boston Globe* headlined in June.[13] "McNALLY'S DASH BEATS YANKS, 1–0," it echoed after the last game in September.[14] But he also proved his head wasn't always as useful as his feet, once batting out of turn in an error-filled loss to the St. Louis Browns.

The second game in the Boston-Brooklyn World Series of 1916 gave Minooka Mike a chance to flash his speed on the big stage. Boy, did he ever make the most of it. The score was 1–1 and the field was getting dark in the bottom of the fourteenth. Red Sox first baseman Dick Hoblitzell was on second after a walk and a bunt. That's when Boston manager Bill Carrigan started pulling levers, sending in Mike to run for Hobbie and Del Gainer to pinch hit. Del sliced a liner between third and short. Mike ran on contact, "off for the promised land," according to the *Globe*. Brooklyn left fielder Zack Wheat caught the ball on a bounce and fired home, too late. "McNally went over the plate like a hound after a fox and the game was over."[15]

Ruth had pitched for Boston that day, earning a complete-game win over Sherry Smith, who also went the distance. The Babe later called it "one of the greatest World Series battles ever put into the book."[16] It's still tied as the longest game in Series history for innings played. The Red Sox went on to take the championship in five games.

Mike got a hero's welcome back home in coal country. A huge crowd was waiting when the train carrying him and Chick Shorten steamed into Scranton station. "Father Minooka, his wife and children were ready early in the evening and they came to the city with Bauer's band and a few tons of fireworks." The folks escorted the boys through the city with "demonstrations at every corner." The Blues team lined up in Minooka to greet them. "It rained rain in Scranton last night, but out in Minooka, it rained enthusiasm."[17]

That marked the end of the last prewar baseball season. America got into the fight beside the Britishers the next spring. Mike enjoyed his best season at the plate in 1917, hitting .300 in forty-two games as the Red Sox finished second behind the White Sox. Then the young speedster joined Jack Barry, Chick Shorten and the others at the Navy Yard in November.

The rest, as they say, was history.

Stuart Slade Hayes was another old hand on the London navy nine. He probably confused a good many folks in England. He was either a ballplayer-turned-consular-officer—and who else had ever made that transition?—or an American diplomat who had once played professional baseball. It was a little less strange if you knew that he hailed from the American capital, where he'd earned a fine reputation as an athlete.

Stuart was a city boy, born in New York and reared in Washington. He got his education at a military prep school in Virginia and at Catholic University. The District sports pages called him Skeets, and when people bothered with his first name they usually misspelled it *Stewart*. His dad was an old New York newspaperman who'd given up bylines for a career in the Government Printing Office and risen to head the Congressional Record. The Printing Office was so important in the District that a local newspaper devoted a whole column to it. Skeets' name often popped up in the paper for his baseball exploits.

In 1909, not yet twenty years old, Skeets starred for the champion Brentwood club in the Suburban League. They gave him a cup at a banquet that year for being the top hitter in the postseason. "Hayes in his answer to calls for a speech, said that he was only sorry that there was not a cup for each member of the team."[18] Yes, that Hayes boy was a natural for foreign government service someday.

Roger Bresnahan, the St. Louis Cardinals' manager, scouted the kid the next year. By then Skeets was working and playing ball for

Stuart "Skeets" Hayes, ballplayer and consular officer (passport photo).

the American Security and Trust Company, which had a very fast club in the District's Bankers League. "Hayes is a clever infielder, fast on the bases, and has always had the reputation of being a heavy hitter. His many friends in Washington believe he will make good in fast company."[19]

Nothing happened with the Cards, but Skeets was still young and hopeful. He played for Catholic University in spring 1911, missing several games for not having enough credit hours. This was a tune-up for playing shortstop that summer for both the bankers' nine plus a second squad in the Capital City League. "Always in the game and a royal good fellow, 'Skeets' is one of the best sports who ever wore spiked shoes."[20]

He stuck with what worked for him and played for American Security again in 1912. It was one heck of a squad and he would know some of the guys for years. They included a future government colleague in London, George Van Dyne, and brothers Reggie and Shag Rawlings, who were both known in the District as classy outfielders and pitchers.

The big leagues kept calling as Skeets played in leagues around the capital. The Indians were interested in 1914. Brooklyn came sniffing around the year after that, and there was some noise that they would draft him and send him to Harrisburg. Neither deal worked out. Skeets finally broke into pro ball in 1915 at shortstop with the Martinsburg Champs in the Class D Blue Ridge League. Their ballpark in West Virginia's eastern panhandle was only seventy-five miles from downtown Washington—as close to the big leagues as he'd ever get.

Skeets worked for a power company in Martinsburg for a while but had bigger plans. By late 1916, he was a clerk in the U.S. consulate in Dundee, Scotland. He was a tall, slender fellow, about to turn twenty-seven, with blue eyes and rapidly thinning brown hair. He looked handsome and studious in his passport photo, perfect for a career with the government. A month before the Americans jumped into the war, Skeets was appointed a vice-consul in London. Soon he was playing with George Van Dyne for J. G. Lee's London Americans. His bosses at the consulate also put Skeets' knowledge to good use and had him whip up a report: *War Demand for Sporting Goods in England.*

"The extent to which the war has diminished the demand for athletic goods in England has been estimated by the head of a prominent firm, manufacturing and importing sporting goods, as being about 60 per cent on all goods except footballs, boxing gloves, and baseball equipment," Skeets wrote. "In these lines this particular firm has experienced an increased trade, due to orders from the Army far in excess of the pre-war Army requirements. ... At present, when the American Army and the American Navy have forces in England, stocks of baseball goods are almost exhausted, and it is impossible to satisfy a constantly increasing demand from camps and stations for balls, bats, gloves, masks, shoes, protectors, etc. It is estimated that there will be a demand for baseball gear during the present season to outfit 2,000 teams, and all of it must be brought over from New York."[21]

The report came out the first week of April 1918, six weeks before the AABL kicked off its season. There might not have been enough baseball gear to go around in England, but Stuart Hayes wasn't about to miss an opportunity to play in the new league. Although a civilian working at the consulate, he somehow managed to play the first two games of the season at shortstop for the U.S. Army club. Somebody then ruled him ineligible, probably following a kick from the navy. That's when things really got interesting. A wire story from London explained the situation in June with the usual journalistic errors. At least they didn't call him *Stewart.*

> S. S. Hayes, known to baseball fans as "Shortstop" Hayes, of the Brooklyn Nationals will have to enlist either in the army or navy to be permitted to play with American teams in the Anglo-American Baseball League. ... It is known that he has been considering enlistment in the army, and the Base

section was hoping to have him in the game against the navy before the King and Queen on the Fourth. Today it is said that Hayes has been negotiating with the navy.[22]

It's easy to see Admiral Sims' hand at work. The old sea dog had already rerouted Mike McNally and Herb Pennock over to London, so what was a little subversion of an army player—especially one who wasn't actually in the army? Before you knew it, Sims' latest diamond star was Ensign Stuart S. Hayes, USNRF. He probably looked great in his navy uniform.

When Skeets switched sides, the sailors suddenly had two commissioned officers on their roster. Ensign Fuller of Harvard, who had been the team captain at the start of the season, was the senior man because he'd earned his single gold stripe months earlier than Stuart. But a pro infielder from rough-and-tumble Martinsburg trumped a catcher from the Ivy League, so for a little while Ensign Hayes became the team captain. Since rank counted for little even in a military baseball league, both ensigns stepped aside when another old hand showed up.

The captain who would lead the boys into the King's Game was Yeoman First Class Michael J. McNally.

10

Two Fronts

The war had raged for nearly four years. Both sides were exhausted and neither side was really winning. Sure, the American army was fresh, with half a million troops overseas by May 1918, including the fifteen thousand Air Service boys in England. But as much as the Britishers needed and appreciated their help, there just weren't enough Yanks at the front yet to tip the fight for the Allies.

Most Yank units were still training and learning how to fight. The French and British brass wanted General Pershing to mix his regiments into their divisions as soon as possible, but Black Jack wouldn't hear of it. He withstood every pressure, waiting until he could put an American army into the field—a *whole* American army. It was a gamble, no doubt about it. The Russians were pretty much out of the war after their October Revolution, and the German armies that had been fighting in the east had started shifting west to France and Belgium. When the Germans launched huge offensives in March 1918 with 300,000 more men than the Allies, things couldn't have been a whole lot worse.

"The baptism of fire has come to several detachments of the American Expeditionary Forces during the last week," the *Stars and Stripes* said on its front page. "On Friday, March 1, the Boche artillery opened a destructive fire on the trenches and dugouts of an American regiment on the sector north of Toule."[1]

The blows kept coming. "*GERMAN ATTACKS FUTILE ATTEMPT TO SPLIT ARMIES*," the army paper trumpeted in April.[2] Then at the end of May: "*THE NEW GERMAN ATTACK*. The third stroke of the German offensive—long expected as an inevitable move—was finally delivered on the morning of Monday, May 27, a little less than one month after the final check of the second stroke in the region of Ypres."[3] And again, a week later: "*AMERICAN HELP TO STEM GERMAN DRIVE ON PARIS. Hold Up Advance at Three Points on Far-Flung Battlefront.*"[4]

Despite the confident headlines, the war on the Western Front could still go either way. Black Jack himself cabled to the army chief of staff and the secretary of war: "Consider military situation very grave. ... Our 2d Division entire is fighting north of Château-Thierry and has done exceedingly well."[5]

He wasn't exaggerating a bit.

Hugh Stanley Miller knew how bad things were in France. He was a washed-up old ballplayer who'd once guarded the first sack for the St. Louis Terriers in the Federal League. The league, like his baseball career, didn't exist anymore. Instead, Hugh now had a box seat at the front.

If his life had followed a slightly different path—if he'd caught a break here or there, or been a little smarter about one thing or another—Hugh might've been the starting first baseman for the navy nine in London. Mike McNally could easily have shifted to another position to make room for

him. But Hugh hadn't been luckier or smarter. Instead, he was now sneaking out of a hospital to return to his buddies at a place called Belleau Wood. Hugh Miller hadn't been much of a ballplayer, but he was one hell of a United States Marine.

Born December 22, 1886, Hugh was the son of Scottish immigrants in the Cote Brilliante neighborhood of St. Louis. He learned to play baseball on the sandlots and in the Trolley League, a hot semipro circuit, and two of his pals made it all the way to the big leagues. Hugh himself grew to over six-feet-one, a hundred seventy-five pounds, with black hair and a hunter's gray eyes. Teammates sometimes called him Cotton,

Hugh Miller, with the St. Louis Terriers (Library of Congress).

a nickname that rarely made it into the newspapers. His regular job back then was bookkeeping in a soap factory, but fans knew him as a rangy first baseman. Hugh turned pro in 1908 and spent three seasons at Keokuk in the Central Association.

He didn't hit much but was terrific running the bases once he got on. Best of all, he was a glove man who got noticed even in the other guy's ballpark. He played "spectacular ball" at Waterloo, Iowa, "pulling down a number of bad throws with one hand and covering his position in elegant style."[6] When the Philadelphia National League club picked him up late in 1910, *Sporting Life* called him a "natural born ball player and one of the greatest fielding first basemen the minors have produced in a long time."[7]

Hugh battled for a spot in the Phillies' lineup the next spring but didn't get it. Sportswriter J. B. Sheridan wrote that the reason was that Hugh "did not get along with Charley Dooin, who was then managing that club, and there was some trouble. ... He never could get away from the Phillies and never could get along with Dooin."[8]

He got into just one game, as a pinch runner in the last frame of a road loss in Chicago. Like Archibald "Moonlight" Graham of the New York Giants before him, Hugh didn't get to bat and never played in the National League again. But he didn't move on to a fine career in medicine like Archie. No, he trudged back to the minors, playing in Buffalo, Sacramento and Montreal. When the Federal League came along in 1914 offering fresh starts to guys like him, Hugh signed with the hometown Terriers.

Sportswriter Hugh S. Fullerton thought Hugh was "a corking man who can hit in slashing solid fashion."[9] He started the year fast before slumping badly with the rest of the Terriers, who finished last in the eight-team league. Fielder Jones replaced Mordecai Brown as manager late in the year. He cleaned house the following spring and swept the whole Terriers infield out the clubhouse door. "Years of squabbles with his managers and absences from the game handicapped Miller, and he failed as a player even in the Federal League," Sheridan wrote later. Hugh was "a very good ballplayer," but had a weakness "for late hours and good times that seriously interfered with his success at his chosen profession."[10]

Hugh went down to the Colonial League, "the dumping-off place for the Feds' excess baggage," doing well enough with Taunton and Springfield to get called back up that fall.[11] He hit .500 in seven late-season appearances with the big club, and even got a game-winning double in a twelve-inning thriller with Brooklyn. The Terriers lost the breathless 1915 pennant race to the Chicago Whales by one percentage point—the closest race ever in big-league baseball. Then the Federal League folded and Hughie became the property of the St. Louis Browns. The Browns tried to send him to Spokane, then to Memphis. Hugh wouldn't have anything to do with either burg and quit baseball.

He'd always been "a very quiet player," Sheridan wrote. "Indeed, it was held against him that he always kept his head down, never said a word and while he played good ball, he also played 'dead' ball. His friends are wont to hold that Miller would have been a very successful player had he shown any 'life.'"[12]

Hugh had been out of the game for a year when America jumped into the World War. He signed up with the marines two months later. He was thirty years old, elderly for a private, but they took him anyway. Like a lot of other guys, Hugh knew he needed discipline and found purpose in the corps. "Had I kept in the condition when I played ball that I am in now," he wrote, "I could have been a better man than [Hal] Chase."[13]

He shipped out to France with the Sixth Marines. The regiment was assigned to the Fourth Brigade, attached to the army's Second Division. The brigade went into the trenches in March 1918. Two months later, the Second Division rushed to block the German drive toward Paris. "What made us fight harder than anything else at Chateau Thierry probably was the sight of the refugees we passed going in," Hugh said. "There was a continuous stream of them for miles, old men and women and children, and the most woebegone objects of humanity you ever saw."[14]

The Yanks helped stop the Germans, sure enough, then counterattacked on the sixth of June. Hugh had been in the hospital with a high fever, but a doctor's orders didn't mean much to him and he slipped out to rejoin his company. The battle at Belleau Wood is famous now. When Hugh's platoon came under heavy machinegun fire, the marines could've fallen back to regroup and nobody would've blamed them.

"Cut that stuff about retiring," Hugh barked. "I am too weak and too tired to do all this work over again. Come on. Let's go."[15]

"He dashed for the machine gun positions," Sheridan wrote. "His company went after him. The men who were with him say that he performed prodigies of valor, tore right into a machine gun crew, bayoneted two Huns and took two more prisoner, made them carry their gear and march back to the rear."[16]

Hugh won the Distinguished Service Cross that day. "Private Miller captured two of the enemy single-handed. Although ordered to the rear twice because of illness, he returned to his command voluntarily and continued to fight with it vigorously throughout the advance."[17] That's from the official citation. Black Jack Pershing shook Hugh's hand after giving him the medal on July 12.

"It was the greatest moment of my life," Hugh wrote. "I shall never forget it."[18] Editors and sports scribblers finally gave him all the applause he'd never earned as a ballplayer. "HAIL HUGH MILLER, HERO WITH MARINES," the *Sporting News* said in a swell headline.[19]

The private wasn't in the States to read it. He just went back into the hospital to finally kick that fever. Later, back up at the front, he'd be wounded twice. The second time would be bad. "A Boche airplane which was flying high, almost out of sight to the naked eye, dropped a bomb down on us and it exploded near to where I was. Part of the steel struck me in the leg below the hip and tore the flesh away and broke the bone."[20]

Hugh Miller, "about the greatest living hero in the war that baseball has produced," would miraculously keep his shattered leg.[21] But it would always bother him and he'd never play organized ball again.

While Marines and doughboys fought and died in France, major league baseball tried just to get through the 1918 season. The magnates were smart enough to watch what they said and choose their battles carefully. Baseball's front lines were in Washington, in the front offices and the headquarters of the two leagues and in the hearts and minds of players and fans. Lots of people were pulled in two directions—wishing to see the war fairly won, while still wanting the game to go on as it always had. Then, too, maybe you had a boy "over there" or on the way across. Or, god forbid, maybe you'd already lost him to a training accident or a U-boat's torpedo or a German shell. If that was the case, then baseball didn't matter a damn to you anymore.

Something called an anti-loafing law in Maryland caused more push-and-pull emotions about baseball. Marylanders thought that any male between nineteen and fifty really ought to have some kind of useful employment in wartime. President Wilson thought the same thing and asked Maryland's governor about the bill. The governor sent a copy to the White House. That led to a meeting with Enoch H. Crowder, provost marshal of the army and head of the Selective Service, whose boards sent the draft notices. On May 23, Crowder announced a change in regulations. "This regulation provides that after July 1, any registrant who is found by a local board to be a habitual idler or not engaged in some useful occupation shall be summoned before the board, given a chance to explain, and, in the absence of a satisfactory explanation, to be inducted into the military service of the United States."[22]

In other words, the Selective Service was playing hardball. "Go to work or fight!" screamed the *Washington Times.* "The idler, rich or poor, will find himself confronted with the alternative of finding suitable employment or entering the army."[23] Pretty soon, people across the country started calling the new regulation the *work or fight* order.

The list of idlers was long. At the top were gamblers, fortunetellers,

Editorial cartoon, headlined, "Make 'Em Work or Fight" (*El Paso Herald*).

clairvoyants, palmists, and guys who worked at racetracks. *Okay so far.* Waiters and men who served food or drink. *Sure, they were probably pretty idle, too.* Elevator operators, doormen and several kinds of attendants. *Well, some of them actually worked pretty hard, you had to admit.* Ushers, domestic workers and store clerks. *Hmmm.* And the category that really worried fans—men connected with games, sports and amusements.

Ballplayers? Did they actually mean *ballplayers*? Everyone wanted to know, especially the owners and the guys on the field. But nobody really knew—not even the provost marshal. If it did mean ballplayers, then things looked pretty bad.

"If it is the intention of the Government to close big league parks for the duration of the war the order of Gen. Crowder will bring it about, as it is the one sport which absolutely would be rendered helpless by the strict enforcement of the order," Fred Lieb warned. "Two hundred and thirty-seven big league players, approximately 85 per cent of the men now manning the big leagues, will be affected by the drastic order."[24]

Except for about forty ballplayers over the draft age of thirty-one and a handful of youngsters who were still too young, all big-league ballplayers were already in the draft. The work or fight order just meant that they might have to go sooner than they'd expected. Lots of big leaguers had already gone, in fact, either drafted or enlisted on their own. The holes in the lineups were getting wide and deep. The sixteen big-league teams could each carry twenty-five men on their rosters—four hundred men if every club carried the limit, which a lot of them didn't, eighteen being a closer number. Why, thirty-six men had gone into the armed forces just since the start of the season, which kicked the total already in the services up to a hundred and ten.

The other big drain on the clubs was the group of players who'd jumped to shipyards. If he was swinging a sledge or running a crane in a yard, a fella usually didn't have to go into the army or navy. Uncle Sam needed soldiers to whip the Kaiser, true enough. But he also needed the transports to get them across, destroyers to make sure the U-boats didn't sink them, and all the other kinds of support ships that a big navy required. Ballplayers weren't the only guys who thought that building ships sounded better than carrying a Springfield rifle. It was no big surprise then when some of the shipyard ball clubs turned out to be pretty good.

Why, just look at slugger Joe Jackson. Shoeless Joe left the White Sox in the middle of May during a series in Philadelphia and started a new job the next morning as a painter in the big Harlan & Hollingsworth yard down in Wilmington, Delaware.

Jackson was playing now for a Harlan nine in the mighty Bethlehem Steel League. At the end of the season, he'd help another Harlan nine win the championship of the Delaware River Shipbuilding League. That kind of thing didn't make people like Miller Huggins happy. "A half dozen players on my club have been approached by men who presumably are conducting the welfare work for the Bethlehem Steel Company," the Yankees skipper sputtered, "and I have authoritative knowledge that players on virtually all the big league clubs who thus far have played on the Atlantic seaboard, have received offers similar to those made to my men."[25]

Shoeless Joe and the other big leaguers who'd skipped to the "paint and putty" leagues drew big crowds on the weekends. They heard plenty of nasty catcalls from the stands, too. "Nothing was too mean to call them," wrote a St. Louis ballplayer now in the navy, "and if they got a dollar for every time some one called them 'slackers' or 'trench-dodgers' they must have gotten round-shouldered carrying their money home."[26]

Maybe they deserved it, maybe they didn't. One of Jackson's old teammates, Alfred "Fritz" von Kolnitz, was now an army major. He believed that Joe had every right to hold a shipyard job. "During the draft period, I will venture, there were thousands of men walking the streets in civilian clothes with exemption papers in their pockets with far less claims than Joe," he'd write to a sportswriter.[27] One thing was pretty clear—the country needed those ships. The law was the law, and the shipbuilders were obeying the letter if not the spirit of it ... just like lots of other guys whose names nobody was shouting in the ballparks.

So things were already pretty tough in the big leagues before the Crowder ruling went off like an aerial bomb. With so many ballplayers gone and maybe lots more soon to follow, people wondered what would become of the 1918 season. General Crowder didn't have an answer. He simply told the newspapers that each player's case would be decided on merit. The question of whether all those ballplayers, golfers, tennis pros and the like really were nonessential to the country would only be decided when somebody appealed a draft board's ruling. Not even the secretary of war knew what would happen, not that it stopped the newshounds from asking. "When Secretary [Newton] Baker was informed that some of the baseball Presidents were credited with the statement that the drafting of baseball men might disrupt organized baseball, he said he was thoroughly familiar with the scope and intent of the new regulations and did not anticipate the result feared by the baseball leaders."[28]

The issue still wasn't settled when high summer rolled around.

"This morning found Gen Crowder's 'work or fight' order in full force, but the leagues have games scheduled just the same," the newspapers said on the first of July. "In spite of the provost marshal's edict that all sports come under the head of unessential activities, and that professionals in sport must take up other work, the leagues are determined to keep going. There has been no decision as yet in the case of any major leaguer, though several minor league players have been ordered by their draft boards to go into useful occupations."[29]

The Anglo-American Baseball League in London, it seemed, was in much better shape than any of the big-league clubs from New York to St. Louis.

And who'd ever have figured *that*?

11

Hurlers

Seaman Herb Pennock, USNRF, had thought he was bound for Gibraltar when he hit Queenstown with Mike McNally. But by the time they walked off USS *Glacier*, he had set aside his expectations of destroyer duty in the Mediterranean. He sure wasn't working for Admiral Wood anymore. William Sowden Sims was a different breed of cat, and he had big plans for Herb across the Irish Sea in England. In a way, the southpaw was just going home.

Herbert Jefferis Pennock, of Kennett Square, Pennsylvania, had a pedigree as long as a fungo bat. His family descended from Christopher Pennock, who'd come to America from Ireland around 1685 to settle in the rolling countryside outside Philadelphia. Family lore said that Christopher had been an officer in the army of Protestant King William III. Some even said that he'd fought under King Billy against Catholic King James at the Battle of the Boyne ... although he probably hadn't.

The Pennocks were the kind of people who had a family crest. Theirs had a wren's head on it, and there was a story about that, too. Supposedly one of the wee birds had pecked at food crumbs near Christopher's hand as he slept in camp on campaign. Or some said the wren had pecked out a little tattoo on a drumhead that woke the poor man up, which was even better. Either way, Christopher opened his eyes, saw the enemy approaching, jumped up and rallied the troops to victory—or so the story went. It was the kind of story people were telling again in 1918, to rally the Britishers in the Great War with Germany.

"There are those who say that the other side was victorious," a female descendant would say at a reunion in the 1920s (imagine Kate Hepburn in *The Philadelphia Story* and you've probably got the picture), "and also those who question whether Christopher Pennock was in military service at the time of the Irish campaign, but the wren's [*sic*] heads are on the coat of arms and the story is an interesting one, so we may as well believe it."[1]

Yes, we may as well.

Whatever the real story behind the wren, Christopher Pennock later left the army. He changed his ways when he got to America and threw in with the Society of Friends, better known today as the Quakers. In 1918, young Herbert Pennock was under arms (if not exactly firing them) with a military force allied to another British king. What would Christopher have thought of that?

Kennett Square is a beautiful little place thirty miles west of Philadelphia. Lots of rich families lived out there or in the countryside. Sportswriters in the 1920s would dub Herb Pennock "the Squire of Kennett Square" and they wouldn't be far wrong. The hurler had the tweeds and the horses and the fine family name, true enough, but as a young fellow he more resembled Abe Lincoln of Illinois. He was six feet tall, had a narrow face and weighed just a hundred and fifty-five pounds. Herb wouldn't always be so thin, though. During his later playing days, he'd balloon all the way up to one sixty-eight. Other ballplayers, no big fans of rich guys, called him Peanuts.

Born on February 10, 1894, Herb grew up playing baseball. It was in his genes; his dad and his Uncle Charlie had both played for the Mohican Baseball Club of Kennett Square. Herb was covering first base for the Cedarcroft Boarding School one day in the spring of 1910 when a coach told him, "Pennock, you pitch this next inning."[2] It wasn't his natural position, but he went in during the ninth and struck out the side with a big roundhouse curve. Pretty soon he was the strikeout king of the Kennett Square town team, too. Scouts started to pay attention.

The next year, still in school, Herb hurled in Atlantic City for a semipro club called the Collegians. He got board and a hundred bucks a month. Right off the bat, he tossed a no-hitter against an independent African American team, the St. Louis Stars. His catcher was Earle Mack, whose dad, Connie, managed and partly owned the Philadelphia Athletics. Earle told Herb he'd start getting telegrams from all over the place after the no-no, and that he shouldn't sign with anybody until he talked with the old man.

"I was just a kid, seventeen years old," Herb remembered years later. "I didn't know what I wanted. But I knew Earl [*sic*]. We played on the streets together. And Connie Mack was my idol. The A's were to me the greatest team in the world. I had never even dreamed of playing for them."[3]

A Washington paper said Mack signed Herb for the Philadelphia club a few hours ahead of Clark Griffith of the Senators. The deal was that Herb would finish his last year of school at Wenonah Military Academy in New Jersey. Mack waited until 1912 to call Herb up to Philly, before he'd spent one day in the minors. Mack told him just to watch for the first two or three weeks to get a feel for things. Then on Peanuts' second day, with Jack Coombs on the hill against the White Sox, the old man called down the bench. "Hey, Boy. Go down in the corner and warm up. You're going to pitch the next inning." The rookie couldn't believe that Mack actually meant *him*. "Yes, you. Go down and warm up."[4]

Walking out to the mound felt like wading through a swamp. The rookie thought he'd never make it. Half the Athletics' famous $100,000 infield was waiting for him out there. "When I got to the diamond, Eddie Collins, Jack Barry and the catcher all met me and talked to me, telling me to pitch just as I did on my academy team and not to worry about a thing. They sort of calmed me down."[5]

Herb pitched four innings and gave up just one hit and a run in his big-league debut. This was the start of his adult life, which like every life would sometimes be hard, especially at the beginning. Jack Barry would be an important part of it for years. Eddie Collins would be a friend for life, and one day his son would marry Herb's daughter. Tough times would come first, though.

The young southpaw pitched fifty innings that first year but missed most of the following season, appearing in just fourteen games in 1913. The official explanation was that he was sick, but family trouble played a part, too. Herb's Uncle

Herb Pennock, with the Philadelphia Athletics (Library of Congress).

Charlie had disappeared one night that May after a meeting in Philadelphia. Charles J. Pennock was a banker and businessman, the former state ornithologist for nearby Delaware, and one of the most famous birders in the country. He also knew his baseball. He had pitched in college, played on the town team, and probably helped Herb with a hurling tip or two. To the rest of the world, Charlie Pennock was a charmer, an "ornithological good fellow ... one of almost everybody's favorite birding companions."[6]

Nobody had a clue what had happened to him. *Poof,* he'd just disappeared from the Broad Street station instead of hopping his train home. Private detectives searched the country and came up empty. People figured Charlie was dead—maybe murdered, maybe snuffed out in some strange unseen accident. Six years later, it would turn out that Charlie had simply changed his name and started a new life in the Florida swamps. He couldn't resist birds, though. He started writing about them again, which gave him away.

The family's story was that Charlie had wandered off while suffering from an attack of aphasia, which he'd had once before. Mostly, it seemed he'd just wanted to get away. "There is not much that I can say," he told friends on the way back home. "I was sick and wanted to go away. My affairs were in good order, I know, and I went to the South and spent my time studying birds and writing."[7]

When the prodigal uncle got back to Kennett Square in the first week of 1920, none of the Pennocks had a word to say to the panting newshounds. But folks had another fine new story to add to the family's history in Chester County.

Herb had returned to Connie Mack's Athletics in the fall of 1913 while the birdman was still missing. He made the club again in 1914 and played well all season, his good luck (if not his uncle) having also returned.

"What were you doing when you were twenty years old?" a sportswriter asked in print on July 4. "Were you a hero all over the land? Were you collecting a handsome salary for six months' work? Were you traveling in parlor cars, living in swell hotels, and seeing the sights? Were you hooked up with a world's champion outfit? No? Well, that's the tale of Herb Pennock, a schoolboy two years ago, now an accredited member of the world's champion Philadelphia Athletics."[8]

Well, sure, it was a nice piece—and just imagine what the guy would've written if he'd foreseen the Fourth of July in 1918! But Herb wouldn't lead the sort of charmed, easy life the scribbler described or that he probably imagined for himself. Yes, the Squire would become one of the greats of the game, but not for a long time. He certainly wouldn't be anywhere near great when he landed on Admiral Sims' squad in London. People could see the potential in him, though. Take Opening Day in Philadelphia in 1915, for example.

Herb started the opener and was almost perfect against the Red Sox. He had a no-hitter going with two out in the ninth, with Harry Hooper up, when the no-no skittered away.

> Hooper, a left-hand hitter, was at the bat and the crowd was preparing an ovation for the youngster, who was to enter his name in the hall of fame, when Hooper tapped a slow bounder through the box. Pennock stood rooted in the spot and made no attempt to field the ball, evidently thinking it would be easy for Lajoie.
>
> The ball took a nasty hop and Lajoie made one desperate attempt to field the ball with his bare hand to make a hurried play, because Hooper is too fast a man to catch without a perfect play on such a hit. The ball struck Larry's hand and bounded off to one side, while Hooper reached first easily.[9]

Everybody in Shibe Park screamed for an error. Nap Lajoie, then in his twentieth big-league season, said straight out that he should get the E. But the scorer disagreed and the pride of Kennett Square ended with a one-hit victory over Boston's Ernie Shore. How many times must the two of them have talked about that game later up at the Navy Yard, when they both suited up for Jack Barry's Wild Waves?

Opening Day was the highlight of Herb's 1915 season, which soon slid out of control like a wild pitch. By the end of May he was three and six, with an ERA a little north of 6.00. The old man decided to cut his losses. "The sale of Herb Pennock, Connie Mack's youthful southpaw, to the Boston Red Sox, at the waiver price of $1,500 was announced last night by Connie Mack. No reason was given for the sale, except that Mack said he did not believe Pennock would ever be a winning pitcher for the Athletics."[10] All of the kid's friends and family could've read that in a local paper in Kennett Square.

"When Herb came to me in 1912, he was very young, too young," Mack would say a long time afterward. "He had speed and he had a good curve. But while I had him he never seemed to fulfill the hopes I had for him." Looking back, the old man knew he'd been wrong. "I have always felt that letting Herb go was my greatest mistake. My experience with Pennock was a great lesson to me. That lesson was, never to let go of a young pitcher who had speed and a curve."[11]

But lots of folks agreed with Mack's move at the time. It wasn't much of a surprise when Boston turned around and sent Herb to the Providence Grays. About the only thing that did go right for the left-hander that year came after the season, when he married Esther Freck of Downingtown, Pennsylvania. He was twenty-one and Esther just twenty.

Herb went back up to Boston in 1916, got into just nine games, then spent most of the year throwing for the Buffalo Bisons. He said later that he'd learned how to pitch in Boston, though—not from the Red Sox but from Hank Gowdy, the blond, freckled World Series hero of the 1914 Braves. The National League catcher was a nice guy and he'd taken a shine to the hurler. He ran Herb through morning workouts, tossing balls at a car tire for a strike zone. "Gawdy [*sic*] made me keep throwing the ball through that tire for two hours at a time. And for weeks, he'd only let me throw a straight ball. After I could put that through the tire, he let me perfect control of my curve. Then I spent years on the bench watching every move players made on the field. That's how I learned to pitch."[12]

Herb developed a smooth, deliberate style, more like a modern pitcher than a hurry-up-and-throw hurler of his own deadball era. Players, managers and even his wife might've kidded him about his slow work, but he was a wonder to see. The southpaw's form would thrill Britishers when he got to England. A cricket writer would even compare him to the Discobolus of Myron—the famous Greek statue of a discus thrower. "His every action was grace itself, and his subtle variations would have made the best of our bowler envious," the fellow would write. "In cricket there have been many left-handed bowlers whose style has been impeccable, but we cannot remember any one who has had as graceful a style as Pennock."[13]

Still, the private lessons from Gowdy and all the watching and learning from the bench—all of that *maturing*, as a pitcher and a ballplayer and a man—took time. Herb didn't have much of a season in 1917, after America had joined the war against Germany and Hank Gowdy became the first active big leaguer to sign up. Herb played through the season and went five and five in twenty-four games. That brought his big-league totals after six seasons up to twenty-three and twenty, nothing to take anyone's breath away.

The war gave him a break from the game that was so hard and disappointing. Herb and Sox pitcher Lore "King" Bader signed up at the Navy Yard in the middle of December, a month after Barry and the first wave of yeomen had gone in. They brought the number of Red Sox on duty there to seven and the total in the U.S. armed forces to an even dozen. Bader reported for duty right away but Herb went home to Kennett Square to put his affairs in order. The yeomen billets were filled by January and Herb went into the navy as a seaman, a humble rank that never seemed to bother him any.

The newspapers, of course, noticed the constellation of players at the Navy Yard. Herb's name popped up in nearly every article about them. "The sailors have a regular big league staff of boxmen, with Ernie Shore, Herb Pennock and King Bader of the Red Sox, and Chippie Gaw, who played with the International League team at Buffalo last season."[14] And it was true, as far as it went. The hurlers were all on the great Wild Waves roster and they all won games in their too-short season. Everyone, that is, except the Squire.

Herb didn't appear in a single game for Jack Barry's club. He didn't toss one strike or ball. He was never quoted in the newspapers, and no writer ever wondered about him in print. He was the man who wasn't there. Maybe Jack was saving him for later in the longer season they all expected—the team sure didn't lack for pitchers. Maybe there was some lingering bad feeling after he was used so little during the 1917 regular season. Or maybe Herb had just lost his love of the game, or had set it aside for the duration. Whatever the reason, he left for Europe with Mike McNally on USS *Glacier*, expecting destroyer duty in the Mediterranean.

Except, of course, life tossed a few curves of its own at Seaman Pennock. The two Red Sox teammates were shanghaied to England practically the minute they reached Queenstown. Admiral Sims was out to defeat General Biddle's boys and impress the king of England.

"I was on my way to Gibraltar when they cooked up that big service baseball game in England, the army against the navy," was how Herb put it years later. "So they threw the switch for me and I went to naval headquarters, London, so that I could do the pitching for the navy in the big game."[15]

Then there was that other line of his, too—*"Mike and I fought the rest of the war with baseballs."* It was wise-ass and funny, especially all those years later when he said it, after he was finally a big star. But that was only the first part of the quote. The rest of it was, "And to think I had enlisted in the navy to get out of the game!"[16]

Shades of Uncle Charlie.

Unlike Herb Pennock, Ed Lafitte wasn't a bit tired of baseball. He hadn't joined the army to get away from it, but rather to do some good with his other abilities.

Ed was a captain—not a team captain like Mike McNally, but an honest-to-god army captain with two silver bars on his shoulders. He was also a dentist, which is how he got the nickname Doc. On top of that, Captain Lafitte was an old hand, one of thirty-five doctors and dentists serving in the U.S. Army's first Oral and Plastic Surgery Unit.

A husband and father, Doc looked older than his thirty-two years. Many of his U.S. Army teammates were ten years younger and a few still dreamed of making the big leagues. Doc had already been there, hung on a while, and come back down to make a life among the mortals. Oh, Doc knew the score, all right. He was the unsmiling hurler in an old Detroit Tigers cap, the natural-born leader the boys gathered around, the guy you'd always watch on the diamond or off it. Doc Lafitte was the real McCoy.

When he'd reported to London in June, he probably hadn't given any thought to whether he'd be named the ball team's captain. Floyd Mims was a first lieutenant, one step below an army captain, and Doc could've pulled rank if he'd wanted. But he had bigger things on his mind than skippering an army nine that played once a week. Did it matter who delivered a pep talk or shook some duke's hand? No, Doc was fine with letting somebody else run that show.

Because, you see, even here in leafy England, across the Channel from the front, Doc was fighting the war. He wasn't training for it or supporting it from a distance, he was *fighting* it in the best way a dentist from Philadelphia could. Aside from dashing Ensign Fuller, the Harvard aviator who caught for the navy nine, Doc knew more about the Great War than any Yank in the AABL. How he got that way was a long story.

First of all, there was his name. No, Edward Francis Lafitte wasn't a direct descendent of the pirate Jean Lafitte ... but wasn't it a shame that he'd never pitched for Pittsburgh!

Ed was born in New Orleans on April 7, 1886. His family soon moved to Atlanta, a city that always treated him like a native son. The Lafitte boys were natural athletes. Ed's big brother Jim, named after his father, grew up to be an Atlanta firefighter-turned-catcher—or maybe, more accurately, a catcher-turned-firefighter. The brothers sometimes were the starting battery for local semipro teams. Jim later played and managed for years in the Southern minor leagues.

Young Ed began his hurling career by happenstance. He tried out for the baseball team in 1904 at Atlanta's Marist College, which in those days was both a secondary school and a college. It was a fine place for learning but lacked an adequate supply of pitchers. The Marist coach was a fellow named Joe Bean who'd been in the big leagues.

"What are you, son?" he asked when Ed came out for the team.

Well, he was a catcher, like his brother Jim.

"No, you must be wrong," Bean said. "You look like a pitcher. In fact, you've *got* to be a pitcher."[17]

The rangy right-hander learned fast. Ed starred at Marist for two years and was the best pitcher in the Georgia Prep League in 1905. Then he went off to Georgia Tech, where he played for John Heisman. Coach Heisman also ran the gridiron and hoops teams, but didn't yet have any important football trophies named after him. He got pretty excited the first time he saw Ed toss a fastball.

"Heavens, man, the football season is over and this is gentle baseball," Heisman told the kid. "Slow 'em down a little."[18]

Ed checked in at six-feet-two and one hundred eighty-five pounds.

He was the rock of Tech's pitching staff in 1906 and they elected him captain the next season. He struck out twenty in a nifty 1–0, eleven-inning win over Mercer and eighteen more against Tennessee. He didn't only hurl, but played every infield position and hit almost .300. He also pitched four no-hitters in the Atlanta City League in 1907. Oh, he played forward on the Tech basketball team, too. The *Atlanta Constitution* later called Eddie Lafitte the "greatest college pitcher the south had ever seen."[19]

He turned pro after his father's death, signing with Jersey City in the Eastern League in 1908. His manager was again Joe Bean. Ed went twelve and nineteen in thirty-three games on a weak ballclub. He racked up almost a quarter of the Skeeters' wins all by himself and once tossed nineteen scoreless innings against Newark. That game ended in a tie, called for darkness after three hours and forty minutes, and it ran his scoreless streak to twenty-seven consecutive innings. "I have hit against Mathewson and some of the old Baltimore Oriole pitchers," Bean said a long time later, "but Ed had as much stuff that day as any pitcher I ever saw."[20]

A Detroit Tigers scout heard about it and the big club bought Ed from Jersey City for five thousand dollars, a very big sum at the time. But he was a levelheaded kid and didn't pour all of his hopes into baseball. Nobody could pitch forever. Ed enrolled that fall in the Southern Dental College in Atlanta, "not because he wants to quit the baseball game, but rather to have something for his arm to do when it becomes feeble from the strenuous twirling."[21]

He studied hard during the off-season, then went to 1909 spring training and caught on with the Detroit club. He made his debut in relief that April, at home against Chicago. He hardly had time to unpack with the big club and got into just three games, one a blowout loss to Cy Young on a raw spring day better suited to football. "I guess I didn't have anything that they couldn't see," the rookie said.[22]

Detroit shipped him out to the Providence Grays in the Eastern League. He was a star there, but luck didn't follow him to Rhode Island. Ed lost one shutout after getting tossed from the game in the ninth inning for questioning the umpire. He threw a no-hitter against his old Jersey City club but still lost, 2–0, "robbed of a well-deserved victory through the misplays" of his infielders.[23] Ed was thirteen and eleven when the season ended. Still, another team's manager said the big Georgian had dropped the spitball he didn't need and was "twice as good as he was last spring."[24]

The Rochester Bronchos of the Eastern League bought Ed's contract that fall. (Yes, they spelled it that way, with an *h*.) They sold his contract to the New York Highlanders in July 1910, but Ed stayed with Rochester the whole season anyway and finished twenty-three and fourteen. The

Tigers acquired him in September, before he ever saw New York. Ed made the big club again in spring 1911 and this time he stuck.

Detroit was wickedly good and got off to a seventeen and two start. Ed got off to a great start, too, despite a pal's crack that an "armless man could win for Detroit."[25] Having Ty Cobb playing behind him didn't hurt any. Cobb would be the MVP that season and hit .420. Ed and the Georgia Peach were both members of what a Detroit paper called the Baseball Brothers' Society—they each had a brother playing in the minors. Ed and Jim had even played with Ty's brother Paul on a team outside Atlanta. Ed was so good for Detroit that the sportswriters started calling him "Chateau Lafitte."[26]

The big man dashed back to

Edward "Doc" Lafitte, with the Brooklyn Tip-Tops (*Brooklyn Eagle*).

Atlanta in May to graduate from dental school. By July he was ten and one and leading the American League in wins. He couldn't have known it then, but this was the peak of his career— one half of a great season. His year started going south in June when Doc got a bad case of tonsillitis. He never got his form back and ended the year at eleven and eight. One bright spot came in late August during a miserable loss to Washington when Doc hit his first big-league home run—his only homer, as it turned out—off Walter "Big Train" Johnson.

Doc's 1912 season was lousy. He needed to leave the team for a few days in May to take a test for his dentist's certificate in Georgia. Hughie Jennings, the scrappy Detroit manager who would later help Minooka Mike McNally into the big leagues, now helped Doc Lafitte out of them. He wasn't happy about his right-hander taking time off.

"If you go home, you can continue on to Providence," Jennings said.[27]

Doc went, and finished the season in the minors.

"Ed Lafitte belongs to that class of players who are about two points shy of the major league standard," the *Milwaukee Journal* said, under a headline that read, "NOT OF MAJOR CALIBRE."[28]

The Atlanta Crackers wanted to sign him, but the asking price of three thousand dollars was too steep for a Southern Association club. Doc held out awhile, then wound up back in Providence. He pitched for the Grays the rest of the year, finishing at fifteen and seventeen. He was still there in 1913, going fifteen and fifteen. Then the Federal League came along and Doc jumped.

He signed with the Brooklyn Tip-Tops and had some success hurling with what one paper called his "space devouring stride."[29] On September 19, against the Kansas City Packers at Washington Park, he almost had a moment of glory—or as much glory as anybody got in the Federal League. Doc threw his second no-hitter, the league's first. But just as with the Grays, it wasn't anywhere close to perfect. Doc's "own wildness and errors in the field let the Packers score a brace of runs" in the 6–2 Brooklyn win.[30]

Doc and the 1914 Tip-Tops were a perfect fit. He finished at sixteen and sixteen, the team at seventy-seven and seventy-seven. He hurled more than two hundred ninety innings, second-most on the team, but led the league with a hundred twenty-seven walks. You never knew what vintage you'd get with Chateau Lafitte.

The next year, in 1915, the Brooklyn club was a mess and Ed didn't last. He was six and nine in July when he was released. He shuffled off to last-place Buffalo and wore a Blues uniform for just seven weeks. Doc had "no place to go but home" after that, one paper said.[31] His big-league record stood at thirty-five and thirty-six, his ERA at 3.34. "I was about ready to call it quits as far as baseball was concerned," Doc admitted later.[32]

The rambling wreck from Georgia Tech wasn't quite done yet. They'd always liked him down in Atlanta, and he got a good offer from the Crackers. Doc was the first man into camp in 1916. He whipped himself into shape and won the home opener, 2–1. For a while there, his season looked promising. "I won the first 11 of 12 games [I] pitched for the Crackers," he'd say years later. "I pitched three or four times a week until my arm could stand it no longer."[33]

His wing gave out and Atlanta went into a slide. A headline in July cracked that as a pitcher Ed Lafitte was a fine young dentist. His manager didn't want to lose him, but Doc saw the end coming. He was eleven and twelve when he finally left the Crackers. His minor-league record stood at eighty-nine and eighty-eight. His overall record after nine seasons in organized baseball was even-steven, one hundred twenty-four games on each side of the ledger. He also had five big-league saves. Doc was the poster boy for ballplayers good enough to break into the show, but not great enough to stay there and become stars.

The dentist still wasn't done pitching, though. He went north to Pennsylvania and hurled for Ridgway of the semipro Interstate League. Every once in a while the old magic came back. In an exhibition game with Connie Mack's Athletics, Doc "pitched excellent ball ... striking out nine in the five innings he pitched."[34]

Doc was practicing and teaching dentistry in Philadelphia in 1917. The Tigers bought his contract, but he'd had enough of Detroit. He drilled teeth during the week, then twirled for Chester in the Delaware County (Pennsylvania) League on Saturdays and for the Doherty Silk Sox in the Paterson (New Jersey) Industrial League on Sundays. If that wasn't enough, he tossed a few innings for a wandering all-star team run by an old big leaguer. Doc flat out loved the national pastime, on every level, and played as long as anybody would give him a uniform.

But with America now at war, Doc's thoughts turned away from baseball. His dad had once hoped that Ed might go to West Point. The hurler did have a little military training, in fact, as a cadet at Marist and in a militia company called the Marist Rifles. With the country calling for men from every field and profession, Doc Lafitte stepped forward. He signed up with the army in July, one of the first former or active big-league ballplayers to enlist.

He got a commission in the Dental Reserve Corps and went off to Camp Jackson, South Carolina, then to the School of Plastic and Oral Surgery in St. Louis. He made captain and shipped out in the spring of 1918. Up in Brooklyn, where fans remembered him, the *Eagle* said he was specializing in "the remaking of faces maimed in the war, one of the highest and most important developments of recent military surgery."[35]

Doc's outfit was historic, if not in any dramatic, over-the-top kind of way, and was later mentioned in a history book or two. "On April 4, 1918, the first oral and plastic surgery unit, under command of Lieutenant Colonel Vilray P. Blair, of St. Louis, set sail on the transport America. There were thirty-five surgeons and dental surgeons in this unit. They arrived two weeks later at the port of Brest in France, were immediately sent to Blois, and there received orders distributing them to their different hospitals and stations. The majority of the unit went to Sidcup and Queen's hospitals, London, England."[36]

Doc went to Queen's. The hospital was a long way from the front, but a long way from peacetime Philly, too. Doc saw the face of war there—literally, the *ruined* face of war. The official name of the place was Queen's Hospital for Facial Injuries. It had a thousand beds and treated over five thousand soldiers between 1917 and 1921. Some boys were so badly disfigured that they wore metal masks to hide their faces. Doc was in charge of reconstruction dental work.

He and other dentists "had to possess mechanical skill to construct the proper appliances for holding shattered parts together, then they must assist the surgeon at the actual operation, working with him at all times until the case was finally dismissed, which might be ... after twenty-five operations or more had been performed on one man's face."[37]

We don't know what Doc felt about playing ball on Saturdays. Maybe he loved the chance to take the field once a week and toss a ball for the army headquarters nine. Or maybe he thought it was a waste of time and only played under orders. There's no record to say whether he walked on or the team came and got him. Things worked out for everyone, either way. Sure, he isn't smiling in any of the old photos or newsreels, but Doc wasn't a light-hearted guy. And a funny thing is, the first mention of him in the AABL came in the wire story about Skeets Hayes having to enlist. "To meet the probable loss of Hayes, the Base Section has a new first baseman in 'Doc' Lafitte, who was the great twirler of Hughie Jennings from 1910 to 1913. After leaving Detroit Lafitte went with the Brooklyn Federals."[38]

Fortunately for the army squad, skipper Floyd Mims had the good sense not to use the lantern-jawed old Tiger as his first sacker.

12

Backstops

The army and navy nines both had good catchers behind the dish on the Fourth. Naturally, the two men couldn't have been any more different.

The army's backstop was Sergeant First Class Alfred Edward Bartholemy. He didn't have the talent or the experience of the hurler he caught, Doc Lafitte, but he was a crackerjack ballplayer. Any baseball bug from the Rockies to the Pacific Northwest could've told you so.

Al Bartholemy was a twenty-three-year-old from Portland, Oregon. His dad was a French-born streetcar motorman. His stepmother was French, too, which must've made the war on the other side of the Channel more personal for his folks than for most parents. Al grew up completely American, like lots of immigrants' kids, and made a name for himself playing the national pastime on local diamonds. Half the ballplayers in Portland seemed to be nicknamed Chubby, for reasons nobody remembers today. Even the newspapers called him Chubby Al, which was odd because he wasn't pudgy at all, but a solid, good-looking guy in his baseball and army uniforms. His pals called him Bart.

Bart had broken into pro ball with the hometown Portland club in 1915. "Bartholemy is 20 years old and this is his first trial in fast company," a newspaper said. "He played for four years with the Piedmont club and was accredited the best catcher in the City League for the season just closed. He always has hit well in the bushes, although his batting average in the City League was not much. He bats and throws right-handed, but switched to hitting left-handed during the fag-end of the City League season in an effort to change his luck."[1]

Sergeant Al "Bart" Bartholemy, Army Air Service (courtesy Ed Bartholemy).

The tactic must've worked because Bart enjoyed a nice little tour through the minors, catching on with a different team in each of the three seasons just before the war. First were the Portland Beavers in the Class AA Pacific Coast League. Next, the Tacoma Tigers in the Class B Northwestern League. Finally, the Denver Bears in the Class A Western League.

Bart wasn't exactly a phenom or a natural, but he got some very good press along the way. A Seattle paper in 1916 called him "one of the likeliest looking young backstops that ever donned the wind pad in this neck of the woods."[2] Another paper over in Salt Lake City (where they really knew their baseball) praised him, too. "Bart is a heady player, always on the jump, and is destined to land in higher company in a short time, if not this year." Some of the shine vanished, though, when the writer added, "Bartholemy has made more errors than any other Tacoma catcher in years."[3]

When America got into the war, Bart finished out the season in Denver and enlisted. He entered the Air Service in San Antonio about the time that Jack Barry and his Red Sox players were reporting to the Navy Yard in Boston. He made corporal in no time and by January sported a sergeant's stripes. Bart was assigned to the 155th Aero Squadron, which was a day bombardment squadron. He wrote home from windy Scott Field in Illinois that he expected to ship out to France, Italy or Egypt.

> Al likes the Army work as far as he has gone and his promotion has been rapid. "Bart," as he was known among the semipro baseball and basketball fraternities, is doing the stenographic work for the Aero Squadron to which he is attached and finds little time to write to his former friends in Portland.
>
> Johnny Bassler, Los Angles catcher, who was to receive a trial with

Cleveland this Spring, is a member of Bartholemy's company and the two are having a dandy time. If these two peppery backstops start pegging lead pills or hand grenades at the Huns when they get "overseas" they ought to be able to play havoc with the "Boches."[4]

After a brief stay with his squadron on Long Island, Bart landed in France in mid–March 1918. At least, that was how the word reached home in a cablegram—that he was safely "somewhere in France."[5] Soon the squadron shifted to England for more training at an RAF station on Salisbury Plain. Bart quickly discovered that Yanks were playing ball there and that the natives didn't quite know what to make of it. He sent home a newspaper clipping with a Britisher's account of the mysterious sport.

> Saw some of your chaps playing at that sport one-half day I was in London. My word how they whizzed that ball from one to another—just like lightning—one could hardly see the bloody thing, you know. Then with that pole-like affair, my word, how they could crash it, so high you couldn't see the bally thing. ... Must be a terribly exciting game to learn. Surprising how easily they catch them when they go so high. Can't see how they do it—my word![6]

It wasn't long before the catcher ran into a familiar face, First Lieutenant Roscoe A. Fawcett. He was now an Air Service pilot in England, but back in Portland he'd been the sporting editor of the *Oregonian*. "In one of his letters Fawcett mentioned having seen Al Bartholemy, Portland lad, who formerly caught for the Portland and Denver clubs," the paper reported. "'Bartholemy is doing very well over here,' wrote Fawcett, 'having been promoted to the rank of sergeant first class, which is next to highest rank below commissioned officer. This is quite a testimonial to his adaptability and all around usefulness.'"[7]

Then a United Press story about the Fourth of July baseball match in London hit the papers in the Pacific Northwest. Bart got a swell story with a long headline:

> AL BARTHOLEMY WILL CATCH BALL ON FOURTH IN BIG LONDON BATTLE / Portland Boy Will Receive Slants of Ed La Fitte [*sic*] in Effort to Beat Navy Team at Chelsea Field; Herb Pennock and McNally Are Members of Tars, Among Others.
>
> Playing with the army team in the great Fourth of July baseball game in London, at which the democratic king of England will throw the first ball, a la President Wilson, is Al Bartholemy, the Portland catcher.[8]

Bart had hit a lowly .214 in his three seasons in the bushes, but suddenly he was a big deal in the Rose City. He was the United States Army's starting catcher in just about the biggest game that anybody had ever heard of back home.

Ensign Charles Fairchild Fuller, U.S. Naval Aviator Number 139, caught for the navy nine. If Sergeant Bartholemy happened to meet him anywhere off the diamond, he was obliged to salute and call him *Sir* or *Mr. Fuller.*

Chas Fuller had grown up in an artists' colony in Cornish, New Hampshire. His parents Henry and Lucia were painters. One of their neighbors was the painter Maxfield Parrish. As Chas and his older sister grew up, their mother made them swear that neither of *them* would ever become painters themselves. "Money was thus a difficult and haunting subject in the family," Chas' son Blair wrote a century later.[9]

The family managed to send Chas to Groton at no small expense. He was a terrific athlete there—quarterback of the football team, captain of the baseball squad. Next he went on to Harvard, where he quarterbacked the freshman eleven and caught for the ball club in spring 1916. By then the Great War had been roaring in Europe for a year and a half. Chas and quite a few Crimson jocks, the last of the innocents, could hardly wait to get into it. They even started training for war in something called the Harvard Aero Corps. Frazier Curtis, Class of 1898, started the group that spring after returning from France with a "keen appreciation of the importance which aviation had already assumed in warfare."[10]

About eighty undergrads enlisted in this corps. Curtis started raising funds for a training school at Squantum, Massachusetts, but fell ill and had to stop. Harvard then said it wouldn't support the project because of the risk of accidents. "The objections of the University authorities were finally overcome, the name 'Harvard' was dropped, and the Corps was rechristened the 'Undergraduates' Flying Corps."[11] The Aero Club of America, Harvard grads and a few others kicked in to fund the outfit and the students paid their own living expenses during training. Chas started flying that winter. A couple of the Harvard boys joined the army before America got into the war in April, then the rest signed up with one service or the other pretty quickly afterward.

"About 100 Harvard men have signified their intention to become aviators. Of this number a score are athletes," the *New York Times* said in April, two days after Washington declared war on Kaiser Bill. "Westmore Willcox, the fast college quarter-miler; Joe Knowles, the Varsity outfielder, and Charley Fuller, sub catcher, are already at Newport News enrolled in the Curtiss School of Aviation."[12]

Chas left Harvard for Virginia to learn how to fly for the navy. It was a dangerous business, but the catcher knew how to forget it and have a good time when he wasn't wrestling a boxy seaplane into the sky. *Variety*, of all publications, noticed him that summer in New York.

During the game of the "Follies" and Friars at the Polo Grounds Sunday for the benefit of the "Sun's" smoke fund [for servicemen], a young man named Fuller introduced himself to the Friars on the bench, saying they needed a catcher and he would catch for them. Mr. Fuller was right. ... The "Follies" were stealing bases and getting runs on passed balls. Fuller caught for the Harvard team and is now in the Aviation Corps [*sic*]. The Friars let him catch and there were no passed balls nor any stolen bases after that.[13]

Chas landed in England with the Naval Aviation Service in January 1918. Admiral Sims thought a lot of his flyboys. "The young men of this service are performing their duties in a manner of which the Navy Department should be very proud," he wrote to navy secretary Daniels late that summer. "They are risking their lives every time they make a flight. They are losing their lives at the rate of about one per day. They have received very high recognition from the Allies with whom they are serving."[14]

Chas sent home a picture of himself sitting in an open cockpit with a grin on his face, goggles pushed up on his dark, curly hair. He seemed to be having the time of his life. This was only partly the truth, of course. Two of his good pals would die flying in the war. One of them, Kenneth MacLeish, little brother of poet Archibald MacLeish, would be shot down over Belgium a month before the Armistice. Chas would keep a picture of one of the lost boys on his dresser for all the rest of his life.

"He was assigned to submarine patrols over the English Channel. Flying itself was hazardous; otherwise the duty was relatively safe, and his life was lively," Blair Fuller would write many decades later. "He wrote his sister that he was spending all his money in London on cigarettes and whiskey."[15]

Sent first to the Royal Naval Air Station at Dundee, Scotland, Chas was transferred to navy headquarters in London just before the AABL season began. Sims took an interest in the dashing ensign and put him up for a promotion. Chas eventually got one, too, the only one of eighteen young officers who did. A Harvard bulletin said later that he was a lieutenant junior grade (j.g.) in March, but writers covering the ball club and the King's Game still called him an ensign. The flying catcher from Harvard made good copy and the newshounds weren't likely to mistake his rank during wartime. He did become a j.g. some time before Sims wrote to Daniels in late August.

Chas was thrilled when Herb Pennock showed up in London. The Squire of Kennett Square was the best hurler Chas Fuller would ever catch, and the Fourth of July game was shaping up to be really something.

It isn't unusual for baseball managers or military commanders to use a guy "out of position" if the need arises ... or to keep throwing him out there if he does a good job (and sometimes even when he doesn't). You do whatever is best for the team, or what someone higher up *thinks* is best for the team. So it was no huge shock that the most experienced catcher on either headquarters club and probably in the whole AABL wasn't catching but patrolling left field for the navy.

John Joseph Egan of Bridgeport, Connecticut, had been around. Like Mike McNally, Jack was the son of Irish immigrants. He was twenty-eight years old and a toolmaker by trade, but during baseball season he donned the tools of ignorance and caught for any club that could use him.

Jack was small for a catcher, about five-feet-eight and a hundred and sixty-two pounds. But he was game and talented and knew the minor leagues well. He'd played for Albany in the New York State League (1913), New Britain in the Eastern Association (1914), Lowell in the New England League (1915), then Lowell again and Springfield in the same circuit (1916). He was with the Bridgeport Americans in the Eastern League when America got into the war in 1917.

"I do not want to work in the factories," he'd once told a big-city sportswriter. "I love the outdoor-life, and would rather play ball than eat. I'm down here to make good with the Washington club, if I possibly can."[16] He meant Clark Griffith's American League club in the District in 1913.

Jack had thought he'd break into the show there, but his hopes of reaching the bigs was mostly gone by the time he reached London. Still, Griffith had given him one beautiful moment to remember during all the days scuffling in the bushes. That was in a spring-training game in Charlottesville, Virginia. Like Doc Lafitte, Jack had a fine baseball memory involving Walter Johnson.

> Johnson was on the mound nearly fifteen minutes, and the ball whizzed over the plate with the velocity of a rifle bullet. Little Jack Egan did the receiving and the youngster handled himself nicely. Walter did not attempt to let out or throw any curves but his control was perfect. Out of nearly a hundred pitched ball [sic] it is doubtful if more than half a dozen were out of the strike zone.[17]

The newspaper boys thought Jack might stick with the club in 1913, but a foul tip nearly ripped his thumb off and he was out of the lineup when it most mattered. Griffith shipped him down that April. Charlottesville was as close as Jack ever got to making the majors. He bounced around in the seasons before the war. Catching is hard on the body, so Jack also played a little outfield at Springfield and Bridgeport. "Egan is a natural hitter as well as a fast man on the bases," a Connecticut paper said.[18]

He joined the navy like a lot of guys and somehow landed in London, where a flashy ensign from Harvard was covering the plate. Jack was an old hand and they had to play him somewhere, so there he was out in left field, a guy who'd once caught Big Train Johnson.

Fair enough.

The army team had two ballplayers who could step in if Al Bartholemy ever went down. One was Fred Tober, twenty-four, from Toledo. He had worked before the war as a mailer for the *Toledo News-Bee*. He'd also been pretty good with the Rail-Lights, an amateur team sponsored by the Toledo Railways & Light Company. These days Fred was a private in the 657th Aero Supply Squadron with Shag Rawlings, who'd been drafted into the AABL a couple of weeks ahead of him.

Like Skeets Hayes, Fred had once encountered Roger Bresnahan, a teammate of Christie Mathewson and a future Hall of Famer himself. *The duke of Tralee*, people called him. Bresnahan bought the Toledo Iron Men club in the American Association in 1916—and caught for them, too. The next season he invited Fred down to camp in Dawson Springs, Kentucky, apparently with no thought that the kid would make the team. "Young Tober, the Toledo semipro catcher now working out here, looks like a capable ball player," the *News-Bee* said. "He ought to do the Rail-Lights some good."[19]

His old newspaper bosses were thrilled in 1918 when Fred's name popped up in a wire story about the King's Game. "TOLEDO BOY IN GAME IN WHICH THE KING PITCHES FIRST BALL," the headline declared. "Playing in the great army and navy ball game in London on July 4, in which King George will throw the first ball, will be Fred Tober, a Toledo lad and former News-Bee mailer," Ohioans read. "He was a catcher here, but will play first for the army team."[20]

It wasn't the last swell headline that Fred would get back home.

There was also Gus Moellman (or Moleman or Moelman or Mohlman, depending on which newspaper you read). The Air Service man had started for the army nine in the preseason, but now was a part-time outfielder. The AABL touted him as one of their seasoned pros—"Moellman of the Des Moines Western league team."[21] Nobody by that name appears in surviving Des Moines records going all the way back through 1900, no matter how you spell *Moellman*. (This includes teams called the Boosters, Champs, Underwriters, Prohibitionists, Undertakers, Midgets and Hawkeyes. They had a knack for naming things in Iowa.) But just because his name isn't there doesn't mean it wasn't true or almost true or could-have-been true. There are lots of gaps in the records of the early minor leagues.

One British newspaper, at least, noticed poor Gus. It ran a close, tightly cropped photo of him staring out through the grill of his catcher's mask. There was a brief caption and no story, the point seeming to be what odd creatures these Yank baseballers were. The headline read: "THE CATCHER'S CAGE."[22]

Britishers loved the Yank catchers, even if they didn't understand the first thing about them.

13

Stamford Bridge

The AABL had played on seven consecutive Saturdays before the King's Game rolled around on Thursday, the Fourth of July. Army had a perfect record while navy was a lousy three and four. Hounslow, Northolt and Epsom all stood between them with four wins, the latter two having played only six games apiece.

Navy looked like an underdog going into the holiday, but really all bets were off. The records didn't mean anything now, with each headquarters having a big-league hurler. The game was shaping up to be sweet—husky rightie Doc Lafitte versus string-bean southpaw Herb Pennock, with Mike McNally and all those good minor leaguers and semipros playing behind them. Yank ball fans figured that Londoners wouldn't really appreciate it, but the locals seemed willing to try. A *Times* correspondent took a whack at explaining things on July 3.

> In first-class baseball across the Atlantic every good hitter's weak points are known all over the continent, from Boston to St. Louis, and the pitcher who did not remember them and turn them to account would not be worth his very handsome salary (he generally gets more than the President in a year, but seldom lasts for a Presidential term).

It didn't exactly read like prose from Grantland Rice, but the fellow plowed on as best he could, which meant comparing baseball to cricket.

> An England bowler is not nearly so well acquainted with the peculiarities of the leading batsmen, either in his own country or in the Dominions. But what happens when a new or little-known smiter waits for them to

Mutt explaining baseball to a Britisher (*Boston Globe*).

come over the plate? The catcher's duty is to form a working hypothesis of his psychology and to inform the pitcher of his theory by means of unostentatious signs (e.g., touching his pad with one hand or the other), whereupon the required curve, high up or low down, close to the body or far out, very fast or comparatively slow, is at once administered. And, to take one of many side-issues, catcher and pitcher must also collaborate in schemes for running out a man on first base who is trying to steal second.[1]

It sure sounded like fun, all right.

The AABL did its part to get cricket and soccer fans wise to the ways of baseball. The league turned out a nifty souvenir program for the game titled *Anglo-American League: United States Navy versus United States Army; In the Presence of Their Majesties The King and Queen and Her Majesty Queen Alexandra*. It listed fourteen army players and fifteen for navy, but those were only the numbers on the Fourth of July. Men continually filtered through the two headquarters. By the end of the season at least twenty-six boys would have worn the army's green baseball flannels and more than three dozen the navy's blue.

There was a scorecard inside the program, of course, which made very little sense to most Britishers. It also included a diagram labeled *Plan of Ground* to show the players' positions. (Did a cricket *programme* do the same for Yanks wondering where the wicket keeper stood or where to find *deep square leg* on the oval?) There was also a sort of baseball primer that ran a page and a half. You'd have thought a Cambridge don had written it.

"The players of each club, actively engaged in a game at one time, shall be nine in number, one of whom shall act as captain; and in no case shall more or less than nine men be allowed to play on a side in a game. A game shall constitute nine innings." That was clear enough, although the *shalls* were a little much for Americans. Near the end of the piece you came across this: "A coacher may address words of assistance and direction to the baserunners or to the batsman. He shall not, by words or signs, incite or try to incite the spectators to demonstrations, and shall not use language which will in any manner refer to or reflect upon a player of the opposite club, the umpire or the spectators."[2]

You had to wonder whether the guy who'd penned the program had ever actually seen a ball game. But as any Yank could have told you, once the game started you'd roll the thing up and use it as a megaphone—especially the Britishers, who didn't have a clue how to keep score anyway. Maybe they'd just make notes in those little boxes where Yanks jotted their hieroglyphics. The program was also a nice thing to send home to the folks so they'd know that you'd been there, but otherwise nobody was likely to bother with it. Because, believe you me, brother, the grandstand would get really *loud* at the football grounds in Chelsea when the army and navy boys ran onto the diamond.

"Seats for this match can now be obtained at the offices of the Anglo-American Baseball League, 2, Savile-row, Burlington-gardens, Piccadilly, W.1," read a little notice in an evening paper. "To facilitate the handling of the crowd those intending to be present will greatly favour the management by booking their seats as early as possible."[3]

The league had already sold ten thousand tickets, including all the reserved seats, some for as much as five dollars. Interest in the game ran high on both sides of the Atlantic. Baseball in England even got into the *Mutt and Jeff* comic strip. Cartoonist Bud Fisher was now an American captain in the British army and both his characters were in uniform, too. Mutt (the tall one) was in the A.E.F., while Jeff (the short one) served with the Britishers. In the screwy way that things happened in the comics, the boys still went everywhere together. In a strip that would run a few days after the King's Game, they'd have some fun with baseball slang as Mutt tries to explain the game to a Britisher wearing a top hat, monocle and morning coat.

"It's like this," Mutt says. "The 'ump' yells play ball. The leadoff man steps to the platter with his mind made up to kill the sphere. The twirler's idea is to make him fan. Maybe he'll use a 'spitter.'"

He goes on like that for another three panels, the fancy gent getting more and more confused by phrases like *willow wielder, Texas leaguer, middle sack* and *backstop*. Mutt, of course, doesn't even notice. "It's a very simple game," he assures the toff. "You'll get onto it."[4]

Britishers were never really sure what Yanks were talking about and their slang was a little thing that both sides could laugh about. "If some one would write a baseball dictionary it would be helpful," a good-natured Londoner wrote.[5] Then the day before the Yank holiday, newspapers in the British capital warned about a *real* menace, something that everyone had to watch out for and take seriously. It wasn't a bigger, scarier model of the Gotha or more U-boats menacing the sea lanes or another big push by the German army in France.

No, it was the Spanish Influenza. "No one knows why it is called 'Spanish' any more than why the epidemic of 1890 should have been branded 'Russian,' but whatever the adjective there is no difficulty whatever in detecting the same old signs of the same old genuine 'flu,' that periodically clasps the whole world in all-too-fond embrace."[6]

Deciphering how bad the flu epidemic was depended on which newspapers you read. One in Australia said that half of London was sick. Another in the Big Smoke itself said only hundreds, but added that dozens were collapsing in the street every day. Even the Archbishop of Canterbury was ill. People didn't yet know it, but the war would be over before the flu stops killing people—millions around the globe, including the United States.

"Many London offices were working with half staff," a correspondent wrote later for a paper in far-off Tasmania. "The majority of cases were mild, but others were followed by utter collapse, and a necessary week in bed. Some business men bought supplies of quinine capsules, and asked their staffs to 'take two daily.' Girls in the munition and small arms factories suffered badly from the plague. Many collieries were denuded of workers. At a West End theatre every chorus girl in the general dressing-room was affected."[7]

But it seemed that the flu was easing a little in London and that the worse of it had passed—"let us hope to Hamburg, Berlin, Vienna, Budapest, and Constantinople," the scribbler added.[8]

Papers in London tried to keep people calm and let everybody know that things could've been worse. "There is no need for anxiety, much less for panic, and though some Government departments and many business houses appear to be hit fairly hard, a few days should see the sufferers restored to health," one said the day before the American holiday. Maybe the editors were downplaying the epidemic or following government orders or just didn't know how bad the flu really was. "The greater the percentage of cases, the sooner the epidemic will work itself out. At the same time the actual complaint must be treated with respect. *Get into the open as much as possible, and don't worry about the war—or anything else.*"[9] This was strange stuff for a big daily in London, where they usually kept a stiff upper lip and didn't often use italics, so you knew the editors meant it.

Londoners took this advice by the thousands. They headed cheerfully to Stamford Bridge on the Fourth to enjoy the baseball match, among them dandy folks one doughboy called "them kings and things."[10] The Yanks' and Canadians' favorite royal wouldn't be joining them in Chelsea, however.

Princess Pat was down with the flu.

It finally arrived—the Fourth of July, American Independence Day ... or British-American Interdependence Day, if you listened to politicians and editorial writers who never really understood the glories of baseball.

"As Major Ian Hay Beith, of the British Ministry of Information, wrote Major General Biddle at London A. E. F. Headquarters, it is the intention of the British people to adopt the Fourth as an Anglo-Saxon festival,"[11] a newspaper in Missouri told readers. The Britishers did precisely that, in a huge change from how the Fourth of July had been observed—you couldn't really say *celebrated*—in London for a very long time.

"Up to two years ago," a New York correspondent cabled, "the biggest celebration of the Fourth of July in England was held at the American Embassy, where the Stars and Stripes were displayed and ice cream and lemonade were served to Americans who came to shake the ambassador's hand."[12] A lot more than just lemonade was planned today.

The sun came up and the flags rose with it, Union Jack and Old Glory fluttering together over the British capital. Soldiers and sailors streamed into town on trains and lorries. Londoners flooded the streets, everybody cheerful on this gorgeous English summer day. The fabulous Goldberg machine that people called the King's Game came slowly to life. You could practically hear it start to whir and rattle and whiz and whoosh, a thing so improbable that not long ago people would have thought you were nuts even to imagine it.

The whole idea was about as crazy as polo in Brooklyn. Imagine, the king of England and tens of thousands of his loyal subjects, all turning out to cheer a couple of dozen Yank soldiers and sailors batting a horsehide ball around a diamond wedged onto what the Britishers called a football ground.

"This event will undoubtedly become historic," London's *Times* predicted.[13]

It was a lead-pipe cinch, brother.

The football grounds lay near where Chelsea met Fulham in west London. Seven manned picket balloons—the *sausages*—hovered two thousand feet overhead. You saw them miles before you got there.

Britishers who knew their history might've thought that Stamford Bridge was named for the village in Yorkshire where King Harold had defeated the Norwegians in 1066, a few weeks before he was killed at the Battle of Hastings. Actually, they'd have been wrong. There really had been bridges here once, with names that sounded like *Stamford*, but somewhere along the line things had blurred. The first bridge was built around 1410, which wasn't that long ago in the way that Britishers looked at things. That made the athletic grounds practically brand new, because they'd been built in 1877. They hadn't started playing soccer here for almost thirty years, until the Chelsea Football Club settled in and called it home.

The place wasn't much to look at, to be honest. The long, high grandstand on the east side seated about five thousand people and might have looked better at a racetrack. High oval banks gave everyone a good view of the field, which they called *the pitch* over here. The pitch was surrounded by a track for people, not horses, to run on. The oval banks were made from dirt excavated for the London Underground, which Yanks called a subway and Londoners called the Tube. Out behind the oval, to the left of the big grandstand, you could see a tall industrial building and two tall smoke-stacks. A subway stop was just around the corner—the Tube was actually above ground here—and a railway station was down the opposite way. The West London & Westminster Cemetery was on the other side of the tracks and the old Workhouse of St. George stood a little way up the Fulham Road. The Imperial Gas Works wasn't far, either, over near a creek that flowed into the Thames.

Stamford Bridge wasn't exactly Lord's, with its white flannels and tea. But they probably could cram in a hundred thousand fans for a big match, most of them standing and screaming their heads off from the terraces. The swells in the seats could look across the pitch to a couple of advertising signs that topped the oval. One was for Bovril, a beef extract that Britishers made into a drink and called a war food. The other was for OXO, which was pretty much the same thing. England was never exactly brilliant at preparing food, and the war had made things worse. No, Stamford Bridge wasn't much like any ballpark that the Yanks knew back home.

"The goal posts were somewhat of an inconvenience and the field itself was built on a sort of a bowl-like pattern, which made it more or less inconvenient to play ball on," Arlie Latham wrote later.[14]

The old yarn-spinner probably wasn't exaggerating about the goal posts—they aren't visible in photos or newsreels of the game at Stamford Bridge, but the league had ground rules about them at the Arsenal grounds in Highbury. Arlie certainly was right about playing in a bowl. The pitchers had to toss from flat ground, with no mound to work from. There weren't any base paths, either, just bags and the plate set down at the regulation ninety feet apart. But the diamond was laid out, the football markings were long gone and the grass was beautiful. The Britishers had green thumbs, you had to admit, and the place was big enough to suit the occasion.

"Stamford Bridge ground, with its terraces and spacious arena, makes an ideal place for any national game where the crowds have to be reckoned in tens of thousands," a London paper said. "Everyone who goes there is sure of a sight of the game. It was a wonderful spectacle on this day."[15]

The invasion of Chelsea started early that afternoon. Servicemen and civilians, commoners and shop girls, gentlemen and ladies headed for Stamford Bridge from every direction, mostly from central London. They came on foot, on trains, by the Tube and in coaches, carriages and omnibuses. Some well-off Britishers paid the equivalent of fifteen dollars a seat just to watch the procession from the sidewalk, the money going to the British Y.M.C.A.

"Although American khaki and navy blue have long been common sights on the streets of London, groups of soldiers and sailors on their way to the game were heartily cheered. Outside the entrance to the Chelsea football grounds, where the game was played, the people lined the streets for several blocks and crowded the windows in their homes, as during a world's series in America, to watch the crowds and applaud the arriving notables."[16] By the time Dr. Raiguel (the Y man from Philly) and his party reached this happy madhouse after their taxi ride out from Piccadilly Circus, "the crowds were so dense that we had to leave our taxi a block away and walk to the gates."[17]

"The approaches to the ground were as like as could be to the entrance to the Polo grounds on the occasion of a big college football game," another Yank remembered. "Crowds in the street all surging towards the entrances and, on every hand, men and women selling American flags. 'Buy the thousand stripes!' some of them cried their wares."[18] A correspondent for an Aussie newspaper loved the color all around. "I never saw so many American flags and Union Jacks of all sizes and shapes before. It seemed that every one of that vast multitude carried one, and not only carried it, but waved it frantically. The Americans are a wonderfully enthusiastic people, and they never do things by halves."[19]

An American engineer traveling overseas for Western Electric wandered in through the wrong gate and got mixed up with a bunch of Yank troops. "Right ahead of me was a little soldier about five feet four inches tall, walking arm in arm with a little British farmerette. They looked just as though they were a boy and girl who had been going to games and picnics together all their lives."[20]

The afternoon was warm and perfect for baseball, described by journalist, author and poet Harold Begbie as only a Britisher could: "The sun not merely shone, but blazed; the sky struggled after an Oxford blue and just succeeded in getting a Cambridge shade which had been once or twice to the wash; a gentle zephyr breathed through the streets."[21]

A betting man could get odds of six to four for army over navy in the London clubs, this despite a rumor that the Braves' Walter Maranville had popped up in London a few days ago, another big leaguer snatched up by Admiral Sims. It was bad dope, though—the Rabbit and his battlewagon were still on the other side of the pond, where he would play for the Atlantic fleet on through the summer. Here at Stamford Bridge, the navy nine in their blue uniforms stepped onto the grass to warm up at twenty past two. The army boys in their pale green came out fifteen minutes later. "Bill Smith, of Savannah. Ga., colored, wearing a white suit and red, white, and blue necktie, led the army group upon the field, carrying a huge silk flag. He was the army mascot."[22]

The place was packed, one correspondent recording that "a strangely mixed audience was at hand, wounded Tommies, American soldiers speaking in all the tongues of all the forty-eight states, a number of American civilians from the embassy and the London colony, groups of dignified staff officers from the army and the navy headquarters, and even a decorous group of Britons dressed in the formal garments which are *de rigueur* in England at any high-class sporting event."[23]

The army's seats were to the right of the royal box, the navy's to the left with the Scots Guards' band in front of them. The doughboys had a regimental band of their own. Convalescing Tommies in light blue were especially noticeable, one group sitting on the ground in front of the grandstand. The Yank army and navy boys were already giving it to each other good, everybody cheerful and getting along fine. A newsreel camera captured Doc Lafitte sitting with army officers and VIPs, wearing his Detroit Tigers cap with his army flannels.

It all felt so much like home that Dr. Raiguel thought that about the only thing missing was bags of American peanuts. "This give and take of your men is a revelation to us," said a young British colonel sitting with him in a directors' box not far from the king and queen. "We're glad to learn that you have the same idea of sport that we have. Our understanding was that you are good winners but poor losers." The colonel added dryly, "To be sure, we rarely see you lose."[24]

King George had mostly stopped riding in automobiles during the war, so he and the missus rode in an open carriage. Harold Begbie described the scene:

> His majesty the King, looking as if he had just received the freedom of the United States as Citizen George Windsor, drove down to Chelsea behind a pair of high-stepping Cleveland bays with our sovereign lady at his side in a pink hat, which an American journalist from Pittsburgh, despairing as to its exact shade, told me a million of his lady readers would want to know all about.
>
> Now, the Chelsea ground does not lend itself to pageantry. As a Board-school playground, if you took down the advertisements, or as a grazing ground for a couple of goats, it might serve; but as a great international scene it is dull. But here came thousands of people yesterday, including the Royal Head of the British Commonwealth, and here history was made, or if not actually made, given a most hearty send-off.[25]

A gold-plated reception committee was on hand as the king and queen stepped out of their carriage. Admiral Sims and General Biddle were there in dress uniforms, of course, with Wilson Cross from the AABL and Irwin Laughlin, the Yankee *charge d'affaires*. You could also see Lady Ampthill, Lord Annaly, the Earl of Cromer and Captain B. Godfrey-Faussett of the

George V meets Mike McNally at Stamford Bridge (Library of Congress).

Royal Navy. These folks were all *in attendance upon Their Majesties*, as the Londoners said. It was a nice little get-together.

Admiral Sims escorted the king, queen and Princess Mary to their box behind the plate. The box had gilt-backed chairs upholstered in red and was decorated in the royal colors. The king paused at the rail as an American band played "God Save the King" and "The Star-Spangled Banner." George then kissed his mother, Queen Alexandra, who was more beautiful than anybody's mother ought to be, and "so young-looking that a gentleman from Pittsburgh very nearly called me a liar," according to Begbie.[26] When the king settled into his seat at her side, the navy rooters nearby didn't quite realize he was there. They knew he was *somewhere* in the grandstand, just not right there so close by. The boys did a double-take and started yelling, which turned into a chant.

"'What's the matter with King George? He's all right!'

"The King heard it, knew it was a true democratic welcome, and flushed with pleasure."[27]

A navy cheerleader raised his megaphone and led another chant:

> *Hail, hail, the King is all here.*
> *What the Hell do we care!*
> *What the Hell do we care!*
> *Hail, hail, the King is all here.*
> *What the Hell do we care now!*[28]

And another cheer went up:

> *Hurrah! Hurrah! Hurrah!*
> *King! King! King!*[29]

George popped up and bowed to the boys, being a tremendous sport about it. Then he plopped back down into his swanky chair in the front row and roared with laughter when Admiral Sims told him what it all meant.

"Tempus does fugit," an Arkansas newspaper said later, "—time was when an incident of this kind would have caused international complications."[30] Yep, George was all right with the Yankee bluejackets. The gobs kept him entertained with a roaring exchange with the doughboys above his royal head.

The king meets Lieutenant Floyd Mims. Wilson Cross (in civilian clothes) and General Biddle are to the left, and Admiral Sims and Lieutenant-Commander Blakeslee are to the right (National Archives).

"Oh you Army!"
"Oh you Navy!"[31]

George had lots of fast company in the royal box. Princess Victoria, the Princess Royal and Princess Maud of Fife had come with his mother. Princess Louise, duchess of Argyll, came a little later. The Asquiths and their daughter were there. So were Lord and Lady Chesterfield, Cora Lady Strafford, Lord Farquhar, Lieutenant-Colonel Clive Wigram, Major Reginald Seymour, Lord Herschell, the duchess of Marlborough, Sir Alfred and Lady Mond, General Sir William Robertson, Lieutenant-General Sir Francis Lloyd, Mr. Walter and Lady Doreen Long, Lord Desborough, Mr. G. N. Barnes, M. P., and Lord Hardinge of Penhurst. "Some one circulated the report that the Gulf of Mexico was also there, but that could not be substantiated," McNally joked later, in a letter home to an old ballplayer pal.[32]

Winston Churchill sat with his wife after his great speech, "in a very good looking top-hat and smoking a six-foot cigar."[33] Surrounding them were rows and rows of British politicians, diplomats, industrialists and business tycoons, plus officers of both navies and what Dr. Raiguel called "a huge group of generals, a scattering of princesses and other royalties."[34]

"The stand was full of American sailors, who sang, 'What the Hell Do We Care?' to a tune that was sad and far-away, a melody for grandmother nodding over the fire," Begbie wrote.

> Bands played, but you couldn't hear them. Thousands of people kept up a yell, hundreds kept up a shriek, fifties kept up a shout, scores swung earsplitting rattles and dozens rang dinner-bells, till you might have thought there was no such thing as a ration book.
> In the midst of this din everybody was standing up, changing seats, invading the ground and getting immensely excited. Cinematograph men looked as if they were pursued by bees; camera men as if wasps were after them.[35]

The king left the box after a few minutes and went down toward the pitch. Admiral Sims walked on one side, Wilson Cross of the AABL on the other, with General Biddle and aides bringing up the rear. Cross probably was the "American baseball organizer" who had visited the palace a day or two ago to brief the king on the game. The pair had spent forty minutes together having a good chat. Besides hearing details of the big ball game, George had talked for a while about how English League football (soccer) was played. "What a fine fellow King George is!" the Yank had said afterward![36]

A funny thing happened in Chelsea now as the king walked with his escorts toward the grass. A mongrel dog trotted past in the opposite direction, paying no attention to anyone, especially the monarch. (*'Scuse me, King, gotta see a man about a dog.*) The little pooch disappeared up the tunnel under the stands, and nobody seemed even to notice it except for Sims—who, of course, was an old sea dog himself.

When the king finally stepped onto the pitch, "from every part of the ground and bleachers there rushed across the green American soldiers and sailors, British and Colonial Tommies, and ladies in fashionable costumes to be near the King. No one attempted to check them."[37] They formed a rough semicircle around His Highness, as if this kind of thing happened every day in ballparks back in the States.

Cross first introduced George V to Lieutenant-Commander Edward G. Blakeslee, the navy's communications and athletics officer. (Sadly, Sims' trusted and capable aide would die from the flu that winter.) Next up were the team captains. Mike McNally stepped forward first, smiling and bareheaded in his ball flannels, his plain blue cap folded and tucked into his back pocket. He shook the king's hand and after a few seconds moved to step back, but the king held onto him. They traded a few more words, still pumping hands, photographers snapping away the whole time.

Syndicated photos of the British king mitting the Irish miner's son would run in newspapers across the English-speaking world. "Minooka, the famous little town that has provided at least one man for every branch of service in the army and navy, and has also sent several of its daughters across the water to do Red Cross work, now lays claim to having had one of its native sons shake hands with the king of England," a paper in upstate New York would say.[38]

Another Irishman on the navy nine (probably Jack Egan from Bridgeport), took a little out of the thing for Mike when he hissed, "Did you notice that his nibs never took his gloves off?"[39] It was true—George V kept his gloves on the whole time, with everybody, which they wouldn't have taken kindly from some rich guy back home.

Floyd Mims, the army skipper, was next up to meet the king. He had his cap in his back pocket, too, and an American flag sewn on his left sleeve like everyone on the army team. George again did most of the talking, thanking Mims for the invitation to the ball game. The lieutenant nodded and stepped smartly back.

Next up was the king's pitching coach.

Arlie Latham approached with a grin and a dapper little salute. He was the only umpire on the field today. "His Majesty appears to realize that an American Baseball Umpire is also some autocrat," a newsreel title card would declare later.[40] Arlie looked swell in a blazer and white ducks, and held a straw hat behind him. He would wear this same getup along with his mask during the game—no hot, boring blue for this umpire. He was also the only Yank who talked as much as George did during their quick get-together.

"I am delighted to see Americans and English drawn so close together in national sport," the king said.

"We hope to make it international sport," Arlie replied.

"How long have you played baseball?"

"Forty years."

"What position did you play?"

"I played third base for thirty years."

"I have read a lot about you," the king said. "I take a great interest in baseball. Recently I have been reading the sporting pages of your newspapers, forwarded to me by the Y. M. C. A., and have also been reading 'The Stars and Stripes.'"[41]

He asked Arlie how old he was. The old Brownie answered that he was sixty-three—strange, since he was either fifty-eight or fifty-nine. George replied that Arlie didn't look a day over thirty-five, which wasn't true on any count. This was the silver-haired ump's version of the conversation anyway, but it seems a bit much for a short handshake.

Arlie stepped away only to return a few moments later. This time George handed him a spanking new Spalding baseball with red and black stitches. The king's hope of throwing out the first ball had been scuttled when someone had ordered tennis netting to be strung in front of the grandstand to protect all those titled noggins from foul balls. (*Heads up, Duchess!*)

"By meekly handing the ball to the pitcher at the London game, King George missed being encouraged from the bleachers by the cry of 'Atta-boy!'"[42]

There would be plenty of theories later why he *really* hadn't thrown out the first ball. "As we understand it, King George handed the ball to Umpire Latham because, in practice, he had developed such a muscle it was feared he might damage the pickle sign at the far end of the field," one wiseacre from the New

Spalding baseball with the now-faded signature "George R. I. July 4, 1918" (courtesy President Woodrow Wilson House).

York papers suggested.[43] More probable, somebody in London just knew the joke about a Britisher who didn't pay attention at a ball game and got clocked by a foul. "Good heavens! A fowl? I thought it was a mule."[44]

Whether he threw it or merely handed it over, the plan had always been for the king to autograph the historic horsehide. He had borrowed an American fountain pen to sign it *George R. I.,* underline it with a flourish and add below, *July 4, 1918.* The *R. I.* was Latin for *Rex Imperator,* king-emperor. The original idea was to auction the ball off for a war charity, "but that stunt was called off because it wouldn't be according to Hoyle with royalty," Arlie wrote.[45]

Tea baron Sir Thomas Lipton was standing nearby in the crowd, everybody making a fuss over him. A newsreel camera captured him surrounded by giggling lasses in summer dresses and sashes that said NAVY. ("We recognize one perfectly good sport—Sir Thomas Lipton," the title card would note.)[46] Sir Thomas would have something to say later about the king's baseball.

"I have a baseball at home which will bring more money, if put up for sale, than any ball in existence," he'd declare. "It was presented to me in Ceylon, 1914, and it is autographed by Charles A. Comiskey."[47] This was before the Black Sox scandal of 1919 crushed the value of Commie's John Hancock.

Wilson Cross would tell the palace months later that he had intended to present the king's autographed ball to Woodrow Wilson. The American president was a real fan, a guy who had proposed to his second wife, Edith Gault, then dragged her to Game 2 of the 1915 World Series. Although Wilson would visit London in December, shortly after the Armistice, the ball would take a long time reaching him. Cross wouldn't have a chance to hand it over personally, so would later get it into the hands of a Wilson cousin. This fellow would finally deliver the ball, mounted on a mahogany base, to the White House in November 1919, seven weeks after Wilson suffers a stroke. It's too bad that the *Rex Imperator* ball wouldn't get there any sooner.

"Baseball was his principal love," a modern historian says of Wilson. "He was a 20th century person—loving cars, loving theatre, watching films, listening to baseball games on a crystal radio set. After his stroke, he would listen to the game and recalculate people's averages as an exercise to bring back his mind."[48]

The president loved the autographed sphere from George V. You can still see it today, in a glass case at the Woodrow Wilson House in Washington.

After Arlie stepped away with the ball, the king and everyone with him looked up into the summer sky. A gray British dirigible dipped and wheeled overhead, and "when it had descended very considerably, two enormous flags—the Stars and Stripes and the Union Jack—were produced from its interior, and, somehow or other, the union of the two countries seemed to draw closer than ever."[49]

This was the North Sea non-rigid airship N.S. 6, which could carry ten men, stay in the air quite a long time and scoot along at fifty or sixty knots when it had to. It was a big thing, two hundred sixty-two feet long, with four fins, and a long control car slung underneath it. From the ground you could see the big number 6 painted on its side and hear the Rolls-Royce engines that drove the propellers. Lots of Londoners had seen it overhead already that summer, and it would continue circling all afternoon. The king seemed to enjoy it.

Arlie then went over the Stamford Bridge ground rules with the two captains. They must have been something to hear—rules governing a baseball diamond squeezed onto a British football pitch—and probably took a minute or two. Both men no doubt paid close attention to the old Brownie, especially the sailor. Minooka Mike wasn't about to lose an important ball game in front of the king of England. "McNally, it is rumoured, turned to his men and said: 'I just want to tell you fellows that we are all born free and equal, but if any of you make a bull before the King ...' Here McNally's voice choked, words failed him, and he added thickly, 'Good-night!'"[50]

There hadn't been much of a crowd here at Stamford Bridge five weeks earlier for the Memorial Day game. Today the grandstand was sold out and the surrounds were thick with spectators. Young women workers from the munitions factories in their brown overalls served as ushers. All around them sat men and boys in every sort of Allied uniform.

"Next to a British captain wearing the V.C., D.S.O., M.C. and a host of other decorations sat a young American lieutenant who has not yet been in France. Australians, New Zealanders, Canadians, Scots, Welsh, Irish and English rubbed shoulders with the Yankee soldiers and sailors."[51] Many civilians arrived "armed with clippings and drawings of a diamond showing the position of the players."[52]

George Bye, the *Stars and Stripes'* man in London, was there, too. He wouldn't get a story into the great army paper—the editions came out on Fridays and this was Thursday afternoon, the deadline falling at exactly the wrong time for him—but that didn't keep Bye from thoroughly enjoying himself.

"I was allowed in the grounds and was on the army bench along with Lt. E. J. Kelly, D. R. C., the official score keeper," Bye reported by mail for papers in the States. "When the team was presented to the King we were there upon the King's right—facing two dozen movie cameras including a half dozen of the American Signal Corps. Look for me in the pictures. The King has a beard. I have only a mustache, one like a small scrub broom."[53]

Estimates of the crowd's size were all over the map, from eighteen to seventy thousand. Nobody apparently asked London's bobbies, who had kept their eyes on prewar soccer crowds. One New York daily pegged attendance at forty thousand and added, "Twice that number of tickets might easily have been sold."[54] Mike McNally, who had played in the big leagues and was as good a judge as anyone, wrote to Boston soon afterward, "There were some 50,000 people present. King George, Admiral Sims, and a lot of other 'big guys.'"[55] He'd tack on another ten thousand when asked about it again after the war. "It was the greatest crowd I ever saw gathered at one time. It had the record world's series turnout trimmed to a frazzle."[56] The AABL much later set the official figure at thirty-four thousand—but that might have been only paid attendance, since soldiers and sailors got in free.

"As the greater part of the crowd was not equipped with opera glasses like Queen Mary, and with their eyes really aching to see a ball game, they just naturally swarmed down on the field, and formed on the side lines," Arlie would write. He exchanged the king's autographed ball for the one they'd actually use and fans "were gently persuaded to encroach no further on the field of play; and the game began."[57] As one paper put it: "A timely hint that the 'flammenwerfers' were being prepared pushed the crowd back."[58]

All eyes turned to Doc Lafitte as he walked onto the diamond. Nobody recorded whether Stanford Bridge grew hushed, or if everyone instead was up and cheering. Doc would twirl this afternoon from flat ground, like a hurler from the rough-and-tumble days standing in the pitcher's box. Imagine the big right-hander, then, taking one quick tug on the bill of his Tigers cap with the Olde English D on the front and going into his windup.

He tossed the first pitch at three thirty-seven.

14

Early Innings

First Inning

The first batter up in the King's Game was Joseph Timothy Lee, the navy right fielder. He was a great-looking kid from Endicott in upstate New York who had never played more than high-school ball back home. He'd enlisted at nineteen the month after America got into the war and earned promotions up to yeoman second class—and not for playing ball, either. He'd stick with the navy in London awhile after the war.

All five of the Lee kids were serving Uncle Sam, which was quite a thing. Joe had a brother at the Navy Yard in Boston and another in the AEF. A third brother who'd been in the war with Spain was working now for AT&T on a government project in Oklahoma. Their only sister was a Red Cross nurse in France. The local paper would later run a big story about the siblings along with their pictures. And when the photo of Mike McNally meeting George V at Chelsea hits the sports pages, the headline would be "Joe Lee, He Saw This."[1]

Half the fleet seemed to be watching from the Stamford Bridge grandstand and terraces as Joe stood at the plate, everybody wanting a hit to start off the game. The tall army pitcher held the ball and stared in from beneath the bill of his Tigers cap. Joe surely knew all about him. Meeting Admiral Sims in a passageway at headquarters wasn't half so intimidating as facing Doc Lafitte from sixty feet, six inches away.

We don't know how many pitches Joe saw in his first at-bat, or how many any of the boys would see this afternoon. It might have been one or it might have been ten, with foul after foul whacking into the tennis netting

U.S. Army team. Seated, from left: Bartholemy, Tober, Dorn, Maender, Mims, Rawlings, Dublynn. Standing, from left: Wallace, Weckesser, Blackmore, Moellman, Montgomery, Lafitte (*San Francisco Chronicle*).

U.S. Navy team. Seated, from left: Fierros, Egan, unknown, unknown, McNally, Pennock (white shirt), Hayes, Fuller. Standing, all unknown (*Souvenir of Anglo-American Baseball League*, author identifications).

protecting the king and queen and all those VIPs. We don't know because nobody reported it.

No London newspaper ran a game story that would've satisfied Yank readers. The most complete was by Canadian William H. Ingram in the *Morning Post* (reprinted later by a paper in Utica, a hundred or so miles from Joe Lee's hometown). Ingram had once been the *Brooklyn Eagle's* man in Paris and knew a thing or two about baseball. Although he wasn't a sportswriter and his story had a few gaps and bobbles (he was especially fond of calling lefties *South Paws*), he did a fair enough job to get an *attaboy* later from sportswriter Lawrence Perry in the *New York Post.* "Damon Runyon, Lee Arms, 'Daniel,' Joe Villa, and all the rest of the metropolitan diamond connoisseurs could not have displayed any more *savior faire* in handling the subject."[2]

American editor James Keeley wrote about the King's Game, too, a shorter piece in the *Daily Mail* that helped fill in gaps left by Ingram. Keeley wasn't a sportswriter either, but did his best to use what the paper called "baseball language."[3] The *Daily Mail* also offered a reliable box score, which might have been his work as well. The box score and the two game accounts didn't exactly match but were close enough for government work. Holiday stories from London that ran in American papers added a few tidbits and details later.

There was also Dr. Raiguel, the civilian from the Y. He'd write a long, rollicking account for a big American magazine, mostly describing the giddy and sometimes goofy atmosphere that surrounded the King's Game. His account fills a few gaps, too. We know from the doctor, for instance, that sometime during the first inning *somebody* fouled off a ball. Chas Fuller tossed his mask aside and raced into the crowd of cameramen but couldn't snag it.

"He hit it!" the Britishers yelled.

Dr. Raiguel had been gawking and missed it. "Hit what?"

"The ball!" the British colonel said.

"Oh, that was a foul."

"A what?"

"A foul. It didn't count."

"Do you mean to tell me that it doesn't count when the batsman hit [*sic*] a ball thrown —"

"Pitched," the good doctor said.

"Well, 'pitched,' then, as fast as that?" The colonel went quiet for a second. "Well, anyway, I'm glad I applauded. That catcher deserves all the credit he can get for the splendid attempt to catch the ball and for upsetting those cinema operators."[4]

Joe Lee might've been the batter who smacked the foul, and he might not have been, too. The young navy right fielder did connect with a Lafitte pitch and keep it fair, slapping it back to the box. Doc Lafitte didn't handle it cleanly and Joe found himself standing on first, the bluejackets going nuts. Catcher Chas Fuller stepped up next. Doc promptly fanned him. *Grab some pine, Harvard.* Minooka Mike came up third.

"Captain McNally, after feeling the ball in several foul hits, drove to Dorn on second base, who caught it and retired Lee on first."[5] Was this a regular double play, or did the army second sacker snag a liner and catch young Lee too far off first? Probably the latter, since the box score doesn't show a 4–3 DP. Either way, navy's top of the first was over.

The army and navy nines traded places.

The newspapers and the AABL didn't say much about the top of the army lineup and it's hard to track them down today. They come into only hazy focus. First up was the left fielder, Sergeant First Class Elmer A. Maender of St. Louis. He'd been in the 155th Aero Squadron with catcher Al Bartholemy, then transferred to the 806th Aero Squadron at a place called Flower Down near Winchester. The newspapers found half a dozen ways to mangle Elmer's last name, rarely the same way twice. A ballplayer named Al Maender had bounced around the low minors in Kentucky and Oklahoma a few years earlier. Elmer's middle initial is A, so it might've been him. Who knows?

After Elmer came the second baseman, an army quartermaster identified in the newspapers as "Private Dorn, University of South Carolina." This was probably Alfred M. Dorn, one of a half-dozen guys named Dorn from South Carolina who served in the army during the war. Alfred was the only one in the quartermaster corps and the only one overseas by July 4. He briefly attended Clemson, though, not the university, but that's the kind of mistake the newshounds made. Then again, this Dorn might have hailed from *North* Carolina, for all we know, because that was also the easy sort of mistake the papers tended to make.

The third man up was the shortstop, Private Roy Carl Blackmore from Dowagiac, Michigan. He'd spent time once in the Southern Michigan League. The papers sometime used his initials, R. C., but he usually went by Carl.

We don't know much else about these first three army batters, but we do know exactly how they did against southpaw Herb Pennock. Some accounts said Herb was throwing a spitball, still legal in 1918. The Squire picked up where he'd left off the previous Saturday, when he'd struck out fifteen men from Canadian Records. "Maender ... fanned the ball briskly three times. Dorn, a southpaw, did the same. Blackmoore [*sic*] had no better luck, and the score for the innings was 0–0."[6]

Struck out the side!

Did the Squire think back to Philly and Opening Day in 1915?

The navy boys howled. They and the army rooters had roasted each other pretty good since Opening Day. They flung verbal jabs back and forth now at Stamford Bridge, and once in awhile directed a remark to a Britisher. "Say, King, them fellows never saw a baseball until they got into the army!" a bluejacket shouted toward the royal box.[7]

George V knew this was all in fun. After all, he wasn't a complete baseball rookie. He'd seen the Giants-White Sox exhibition game at Chelsea during the world tour in 1914, when Chicago's Tom Daly had smacked one out to win it in the eleventh. The king had followed that game pretty well, too. "As an instance of his keen perception, King George led the applause at one stage of the contest when with three men on bases and only one man out the Sox were retired on a clever double play."[8] He'd also watched the match between Canadian army teams in 1917, out at Great Windsor Park.

Watching from the front row of the royal box at Stamford Bridge, the king had his head in the game. George did his best to explain the action to his mother, Alexandra, but left it to Irwin Laughlin from the American embassy to make sense of the game for his missus. That scene alone was worth the price of a ticket.

"The Yanks said that Doctor Page, our Ambassador, had 'passed the buck' and gone to Scotland to get another degree conferred upon him," Dr. Raiguel wrote.

> That he was worthy of the degree was proved by his wisdom in going. There in the royal box sat Mr. Laughlin doing the honors. And he *was* unhappy! All dudded up in a cutaway coat and silk hat, he squirmed and screwed about on the plush chair, he grew red in the face, the perspiration broke out on his forehead, he mopped his brow. His job was explaining baseball to Queen Mary!
>
> And worst of all, the Queen tried to understand the game. She asked questions, she knitted her brows, she emphasized the points by tapping her palm with her fingers. How Laughlin worked! And certainly he did his best. We all know: we have all tried it, and we all know that it can't be done! But Mr. Laughlin was not much worse off than some others of us. Every Yank took a London flapper with him to the game, and all suffered.[9]

Second Inning

The fourth man up for navy was Jack Egan, the minor-league catcher turned left fielder. Batting left-handed, he smacked a ball to army's slick shortstop, who threw over to first in time to get him. Ensign Hayes stepped in next, and Ingram's account gets a little hazy. "Hayes, however, had better luck with the same play, and reached the bag, but in endeavoring to steal second, got caught."[10] The box score seems to indicate that Skeets didn't single, so did he reach first on an error and get thrown out trying to stretch it? Or did he make it safely, only to get cut down later by Al Bartholemy when someone else was batting? There's no way of knowing.

Neither pitcher was hitting in the ninth spot today and Herb came up next. "Pennock managed to make it," according to Ingram.[11] This might have meant he walked, since he wouldn't have a hit today, but more likely he reached base on an error. Army would make five miscues today and navy two. Keeley thought the fielding was actually pretty good, "and considering the state of the field the few errors were excusable."[12] The British football pitch probably wasn't as smooth as an American ballfield and lacked any neatly graded base paths.

So it was one on and two out when navy center fielder Phil Maney came up. He was a machinist mate from Dorchester, Massachusetts, on Boston's south side. Phil had played for St. Ambrose, the 1915 champions of the Dorchester Catholic Club Baseball League. By the fall of 1917, the St. Ambrose service flag had a hundred and two stars on it, one for Phil and each of the other parish boys who'd gone into the service.

The AABL was quite a few cuts above a local Catholic league and the navy right fielder went down on strikes, stranding Herb at first. The hurler picked up his glove and headed back out to the center of the diamond.

Fred Tober was up next for army. The Squire soon sent him back to the bench, another strikeout victim. Doc Lafitte took his place at the dish. He smacked a drive ... somewhere, "but it was not strong enough to carry him to first."[13] Al Bartholemy followed his pitcher, and Herb fanned him, too.

The game was already becoming a dandy pitchers' duel. Floyd Mims, the army manager, would always remember Arlie Latham's energetic umpiring—silver hair flying, arms shooting up to signal balls and strikes. The old Brownie usually worked behind the plate, but stood behind the pitcher when a man was on base. "His strident judgment of each pitch was reechoed from thousands of throats at each call, a performance which showed that the British were quick to catch the spirit of baseball," Floyd would write more than sixty years later. From the bench near the royal box, the skipper also watched King George "barely controlling his impulse to leap up and shout with the rest of the crowd."[14]

Attaboy, Your Majesty.

British newspapers often compared baseball to cricket, which was fair enough as far as it went. The two sets of fans were nothing alike, though. Say, even the Canadians had hooted back in 1915 when their ball club stopped for tea at Lord's. A British football crowd, on the other hand, was much different and a lot more like a Yank baseball crowd—rowdy and noisy. And like football, baseball required a lot of energy.

"The dignity of cricket [baseball] disowns; the tremulous tumult of football is as the recreation of well-mannered mice by comparison to it," London's *Times* said. "The players live on springs, possessing the activity of a high-grade machine. They think by lightning, and field, catch, and throw with the certainty of a stop-watch. As if the chaff of the spectators were not sufficient for them, they chivy one another."[15]

The American boys on the field and in the stands at Chelsea would've laughed at *chivy* but still completely agreed. They gave it to opposing players on the field all afternoon. The Britishers just had to shake their heads at the things they heard.

> *What's the good of putting a dead man in to bat?*
> *He's got a hole in his bat.*
> *Show them where you live.*
> *We are the buds on the top of the tree.*
> *It—it—it.*[16]

Even some Yanks didn't understand all of what the boys shouted and hollered at each other on this fabulous day in old London town.

"Much of the slang was new to me, and to interpret it to my English friends, and at the same time explain the game, was a task for a genius," admitted an Iowa minister preaching in London. "Amazement sat upon their faces. They had never imagined that a hard business people could explode in such a hysteria of play. An English crowd is orderly and ladylike in comparison. Of course, the players, aware of an audience at once distinguished and astonished, put on extra airs; and as the game went on, the fun became faster and more furious. My friends would stop their ears to save their sanity, at the same time pretending, with unfailing courtesy, to see, hear, and understand everything."[17]

Any Chelsea FC supporter around must've loved all the cheering and commotion from the football grounds today. Navy fans were outnumbered quite a bit, but their side was a lot louder than army's thanks to sailor cheerleaders with megaphones. Britishers especially got a kick out of a cheer that navy had borrowed from the kind of football they played on Saturdays at colleges and universities back home:

> *Give 'em the axe, the axe, the axe!*
> *Give 'em the axe, the axe, the axe!*

Where? Where? Where?
Right in the neck, the neck, the neck!
Right in the neck, the neck, the neck!
There! There! There!
Who gets the axe?
Army!
Who says so?
Navy![18]

The sailors swung from that ditty into a new one:

Strawberry shortcake, huckleberry pie,
V-I-C-T-O-R-Y!
Are we in it? Well, I guess!
Navy, Navy! Yes, yes, yes![19]

Then sometimes this:

Here we come, all in a rush!
What the hell is the matter with us?
Nothing at all! Nothing at all!
We come here to play baseball.[20]

And when they got tired of giving it to the army, the bluejackets would send up a good-natured cheer for the royals.

'Rah! 'Rah! 'Rah!
'Rah! 'Rah! 'Rah!
'Rah! 'Rah! 'Rah!
King George, Queen Mary,
Great Britain.[21]

Oh, the place was jumping the whole afternoon.

Helpful Yanks tried to explain the rules to flummoxed Britishers. The former colonials were baseball's ambassadors, and Londoners did their best to understand the game. How well would somebody from Kalamazoo or Gila Bend have understood cricket the first time out? Sure, the ins and outs of baseball were clear enough to the Yanks, who'd played it all their lives and followed it in the papers and gone out to the park whenever they had a few spare buffalo nickels to rub together. But spelling it out for a guy who didn't know a bunt from a hit-and-run was tricky. Mike McNally would tell a columnist back home that the Britishers never really understood why a runner couldn't advance on a foul ball, but that they enjoyed a good rundown play.

"The gentleman from Pittsburgh told me that baseball crams into ten minutes all the nervous tension of a three-day cricket match," Harold Begbie wrote. "I am sure it does. He said a good pitcher gets $16,000 a year. I've not the least doubt of it, but if you think I understood his explanation of the game or the brilliant strategy of the players, who wore jockey caps and long stockings and boxing gloves and fencing helmets, and swung Indian clubs, gentle reader, you are in error."[22]

The gent sitting with a young Yank wearing a Y.M.C.A. uniform kept calling a foul ball *one of those licks behind*—like the one that bounced off the grandstand roof and down into either Fuller's or Bartholemy's mitt.

"He's out!" the Britisher cried.

"No! that didn't count—except as a foul strike."

"But he caught it off the roof!"

"That makes no difference."

Just then the batter bounced a foul ball to a fielder.

"But surely, the batter is out now?"

"No—first bound doesn't count: it must be caught in the air."

Tricky stuff. Then Arlie Latham caught the Britisher's eye.

"'Pon my honor! That umpire must have keen eyesight to tell those balls! The bowler is sending them toward the wicket-keeper at a terrible rate."

He didn't much like the two teams' uniforms, though, which weren't anything like proper cricketing whites. "Your men dress like jockeys with their caps and stockings. They wear fencing-masks, I see."

"Only the catcher."

"But they're all equipped with boxing gloves."

At the end of the second inning, the Britisher said, "It's two-ninths played now, isn't it?"[23]

Well, yes. ... Yes, it was.

Third Inning

Prince Albert, George and Mary's second son, came to the ball game late with the duke of Connaught, Princess Pat's father, who'd just returned from touring the front. The royal family called shy, stammering Albert "Bertie." Although he'd graduated from the Royal Naval Academy and served at sea, he'd lately switched services and today wore the uniform of a Royal Air Force captain. One day he'd be King George VI, when big brother Edward would drop the crown into his lap after deciding he couldn't rule England without the help and support of the woman he loved. George VI would see the country through the next World War and his daughter Elizabeth would become the queen after he passed. But that was all so far away and completely unlikely that it would've sounded like a fairy tale to anybody at Stamford Bridge.

Everyone in the royal box stood when Prince Albert arrived. The ballplayers took a breather while everybody cheered. The Britishers were fond of their royals, but the same thing would've happened if President Wilson had strolled in during a Senators game in Washington. As it turned out, Bertie liked the Yanks' ball game almost as much as his pop did. "It was an experience which Prince Albert never forgot."[24]

Navy's third baseman was the first batter up in the bottom of the third. He's a mystery man, a ghost in blue, the only starting player who would elude an inquisitive author nearly a century later. In the official program they spelled his name *Vannatter*, but the *Times* and *Morning Post* both had him as *Vannetter*, while a third paper had once listed him as *Vanatter*. He probably had played pro ball somewhere, but just where was a mystery, too. A wire story in the States had called him "Van Natta, a former Western leaguer,"[25] but the *Times* this morning had said, "First-Class Yeoman Vannetter (3rd base), played in the Southern League in America."[26] So take your pick. You won't find a player with any of these names in the Western or Southern league records today, which might only mean that the records aren't complete.

Vannatter the Ghost doubled off Doc Lafitte.

Next up was the shortstop, Theodore Fierros, the youngest kid on the field. He was nineteen, a graduate of the United States Indian Vocational Training School in Phoenix and "a fullblooded Papago Indian. In school he was an infielder, quarterback on the football team and captain of one of the military companies."[27] It's nice to imagine that he was just plain *Ted* to his pals back in Arizona, but the ballplayers here inevitably called him Chief.

It didn't matter that Ted hadn't played a lick of pro ball. Leo Callahan, the former Dodger and Wild Wave who'd be a member of the London navy nine later that season, would tell a newspaper back home all about the Indian kid who "could throw that ball to first like very few I ever saw. He has one of those Duffy Lewis arms, and the ball would actually knock you off the bag. I know it pushed me off and Mike [McNally], too."[28]

The navy was even more segregated than the army during the World War. It assigned African Americans only to menial jobs and would keep them there for another thirty years, until President Harry Truman (an artillery captain in France on this Fourth of July) desegregated the U.S. armed forces in 1948. But things were somehow different for Native Americans and Ted Fierros was a shipwright and petty officer. He was a good-looking kid in his blues, and he'd marry a British girl named Minnie after the war. They'd have a little girl together called Theodora. Ted would have a little trouble with the navy later, the marriage wouldn't work out and he'd go back to the United States alone. But today everything was still fine, really dandy, and he was playing baseball in front of tens of thousands of soldiers and sailors, not to mention the king of England.

The young shortstop advanced Vannatter to third.

Joe Lee came up again, the top of the order. The bluejackets all around were making a racket, wanting him to knock the runner in. Joe almost obliged. "He struck firmly to first, but was retired, and Vannetter was caught stealing home." Ingram bobbled the sequence but almost got it right. The box score indicates a nifty 4–3–2 double play—Dorn fielding at second, firing to Fred Tober at first for the force out, then another toss home to Al Bartholemy for a tag at the plate.

Side retired!

The Britisher sitting next to the uniformed Yank from the Y peppered him with questions and observations.

"Why doesn't he put a cushion on the other hand, too?" he asked about the catcher.

"That man will get all dirty," he observed when a runner slid into second.

"Wouldn't he be more efficient if he had a flat side on that stick?" he asked about the bat, which he called a bludgeon.

"But surely, he can't hope to hit the ball when it's traveling that fast?" he said of a hitter.

"What is a hit?" he asked. Once answered, he said, "But, my goodness! there are far too many men standing out there in what you call the field. The ball could never get by them."[29]

Explaining the national pastime to a Londoner was exhausting.

At the bottom of the inning, right fielder Shag Rawlings walked to the plate for his first at-bat. It was no mystery how Shag happened to be on the army nine. "'Shaggy' Rawlings, brother of the heavy hitting left fielder of the Martinsburg team, will probably be seen in a Martinsburg uniform this year," a paper covering the Blue Ridge League had reported a couple years earlier. "He was recommended by 'Skeeter' Hayes, and is said to be a heavy hitter."[30]

That was Stuart Hayes, of course, the former London American who'd played for army as a civilian but now held down second base for navy. Neither of them had lasted long in the league beside Shag's flashier brother. These days Shag was on detached duty from his squadron "in the courier service of the aviation section, American army, running between London and Liverpool."[31] At a boxing smoker later that night he'd run into George Van Dyne, another old London American he'd played ball with back home. It was practically old home week.

Right now, Shag laid down a bunt. Herb Pennock sprang off the mound and tossed to Minooka Mike at first for the out.

Next up was the army third sacker, Corporal John E. Dublynn. Like Maender, he'd just been transferred into the 806th Aero Squadron. (Shag and Fred Tober would stay behind with the 806th when their outfit ships out for France, and Al Bartholemy would end up with them, too. It was a strange sort of catch-all squadron.) Jack Dublynn hailed from Brooklyn, where he'd played on clubs in the Inter-City Baseball Association, generally covering first or second base. He hadn't seen any hurlers back in Brooklyn to match the navy's southpaw today, though.

Herb fanned him.

That brought up the last man in the army line-up, center fielder and manager Floyd Mims. The lieutenant had looked fine meeting George V before the game, but the Squire of Kennett Square was a different sort of royalty. Floyd waited for his pitch and didn't see it. Herb notched his seventh strikeout in the first nine batters, still perfect through three innings.

Doc Lafitte wasn't too shabby, either.

"At the end of the third inning, with a score 0–0, it looked as if it were going to be a pitcher's battle."[32]

No kidding.

15

Middle Innings

With so many Londoners and bigwigs watching the AABL for the first time, the Yanks kept plugging away at helping the Britishers understand what was happening. Dr. Raiguel did his best to explain things to Lady Sarah Wilson, the duke of Marlborough's aunt.

"Now tell me all about it," she commanded the Y man from Philly.

The doctor launched into it, because baseball *does* take some explaining.

"Ah, I see, it's like rounders, isn't it?" her ladyship said.

"Yes, with a few essential differences."

The Y man forged ahead, but it was like running on muddy base paths—pretty heavy going.

"Ah, yes, of course," Lady Sarah interrupted. "I see that it is really a very intricate game that one could not learn in an afternoon, isn't it? Suppose, therefore, you tell me the names of all the prominent Americans that are here and I will tell you the names of the prominent British. We might as well have a pleasant day."[1]

Sometimes you had to sacrifice instead of swinging away.

Fourth Inning

Chas Fuller led off the fourth with a walk from Doc Lafitte. Minooka Mike sacrificed him to second, probably with a bunt although Ingram doesn't say. Jack Eagan moved the aviator along with another sacrifice, but "reached first all the same."[2] In the heat of whatever had happened, Chas charged around third and headed for home. The joint was jumping as he slid across the plate—*SAFE!!!*

Alexandra went as politely nuts in the royal box as a crowned head was allowed to go. "I don't know what he did, but I'm for him!" she trilled.[3] Down at the plate, catcher Al Bartholemy didn't see eye to eye with the queen mother. "He's out!" he shouted at Arlie Latham.[4] Arlie wasn't buying it and the navy led, 1–0. The bluejackets roared and the king got a kick out of it.

"Sailor himself, he perhaps was pleased that the navy should make the first run, and he laughed at [*sic*] the batter slid for the home plate and a cheer leader called forth a more than usually energetic shout."[5] Because the swells with him remained standing after the play, His Majesty also heard that time-honored American request, "Down in front!"[6]

"The English, plainly puzzled by the outbreak, sat down. The King laughed heartily but the fans did not care whether he smiled or frowned. In the joy of watching a real game of ball they had forgotten all about having a King in their midst."[7] The doughboys kept hollering, not at the king but at Arlie over the call. Bart had thrown down his mask and was arguing his head off.

"Now what?" several innocent Britishers asked.

"They're protesting the decision of the umpire," Dr. Raiguel explained.

"Protesting—the—decision—of the umpire!" They were dumbfounded. "But his decision is final, isn't it?"

"Yes."

"But if—"

"Now listen, this isn't cricket. It's baseball."

"I see," they said meekly.[8]

In another minute or so, they *really* didn't know what to make of the Yanks' traditional calls to kill the umpire. A chant went up. Some of the more delicate souls in attendance got alarmed that something horrible might happen to Arlie, who was surely doing his best, poor chap.

> *Kill him!*
> *Kill him!*
> *Kill him, kill him, kill him!*
> *Kill him!*
> *Kill him!*
> *Kill him, kill him, kill him!*

A distinguished English lady turned in a tizzy to the Philadelphia doctor.

"They won't—they certainly won't—"

"No, be assured they won't," Raiguel said quickly.

The British colonel chipped in to help to calm the poor dear, too.

"I can see the Huns won't win this war," he said.[9]

Damn straight.

Amid the commotion, brevet sportswriter Ingram forgot to record what Ensign Hayes did as the next batter. Skeets apparently went out moving Jack Egan over to second. Fans in the States must have wept later that Hugh Fullerton or Fred Lieb hadn't gone over to cover the game properly, or that Lieutenant Grantland Rice of the artillery hadn't hopped across from France to represent the *Stars and Stripes*. There's no telling now whether one of those great wordsmiths might have immortalized the King's Game with a classic line or two (*Against a blue-white summer sky...*). Any of them would've come up with a more stirring description than Ingram to wrap up the top of the fourth: "Pennock, a South Paw, then faced LaFitte's right, but failed to reach first on the drive. Egan died at second."[10]

Army tried to rally in the bottom of the inning. Maender popped out to Chas Fuller and Dorn drove to the left side and was thrown out at first for two quick outs. Then Blackmore got plunked, a rare mistake by the Squire, which brought up Fred Tober, the pride of the Toledo Rail-Lights. Fred dug in and "struck viciously, finally reaching second on a fly, fumbled by Maney."[11] E8, with a man on second. Doc Lafitte stepped in now to face the southpaw. The old Tiger "used his head, but it was of no avail against Pennock's bullets"—which probably meant he fanned.[12]

The rally was nipped, navy still up 1–0.

American cartoonist Robert Ripley—an old ballplayer himself—would celebrate the King's Game a few days later in the newspapers back home. His large drawing had John Bull wielding a baseball bat under the headline "ATTA BOY, JOHN!" One of several vignettes showed an excited Britisher (in a top hat and monocle, of course) yelling out, "Well knocked lad! V-very xtrawdinary! [*sic*] Really—Hasten youth. Make haste."[13] Ripley caught the British mood perfectly.

A terrific game was under way amid all the noise and tumult. Arlie Latham later wrote, "With the grandstand filled with royalty, we put on a show that was good enough for the New York Polo Grounds or any other ball park in the United States, and we did not have a regular baseball diamond on which to play, either!"[14]

London's women seemed to enjoy the baseball match as much as their menfolk. There were a lot of them in the crowd. "Why, at the Navy and Army match the other day, I counted quite twenty 'fans' among the women sitting around me," a Yank officer would say later.

"Yes," a sweet old lady would reply, "and I wished I had taken mine, for the heat was terribly trying."[15]

Chorus girls from the London stage sold programs for two shillings apiece, about fifty cents. Dr. Raiguel delighted in unleashing seven of them on the important Britishers sitting around him—although what a Y man was doing with footlight beauties he never explained. If one girl sold a program, it didn't slow down any of the others making the rounds. Tea baron Lipton was a tempting target.

"Ah, Sir Thomas, won't you buy a program?"

"I have several, thank you."

"Yes, but you haven't bought one from me."[16]

Sir Thomas must've looked like one of his own tea bags, with all those programs stuffed in his pockets.

Fifth Inning

The middle inning was a breeze.

Phil Maney flied to right for navy, Vannatter "failed to connect with the sphere," which probably meant another strikeout for the Squire, and Ted Fierros connected but drove it to short.[17] In the army half of the inning, Al Bartholemy made a quick out ... to somebody. Shag Rawlings hit out to the first baseman. Jack Dublynn didn't do any better, making the third out ... again, somewhere. (*Ingram, didn't yer pap teach you how to keep score, fer cryin' out loud?*)

As the game went along, the colonel sitting with Dr. Raiguel asked about the players. What did they call the bowlers? *Pitchers.* And the wicket keepers? *Catchers.* Chas Fuller's tools of ignorance caught his eye.

"Why does he wear a cage?" Dr. Raiguel explained the mask, but the colonel wasn't impressed. "If I feed him bird seed will he sing?"[18]

Another officer was amazed by how fast Doc and Herb threw. It seemed to him that the boys facing them could hit the ball only by accident. And why did they practice so hard, if they were already so good?

"Warming up," the doctor said patiently.

"Warming up! On a hot day like this?"

"He has a glass arm and —," an American officer began.

"A 'glass arm'? Heavens! How can he do that exercise with a glass arm?"

"It's American slang," Dr. Raiguel explained.[19]

Enough said.

Quite a few newshounds from the States sat up in the press box. Most of them, like Ingram, didn't actually cover baseball a lot. Everybody sat at

Unknown army batter, navy catcher Chas Fuller and umpire Arlie Latham (*Gorrell's History*).

a counter covered by a green baize cloth, Yanks on one side and Britishers on the other. A few kept score. When somebody booted a ball down on the field, a voice suddenly piped up from the back.

"Did you call that an error?"

They turned to see a fellow with one pip on his British uniform, probably the pale blue of a convalescent. Obviously, not everybody in London needed help understanding the game.

"Yes, lieutenant," somebody said.

"But—" the officer began, and went into a neat, knowledgeable argument. The American newspapermen were amazed and didn't know what to think.

During the next inning, when either Doc or the Squire fanned a batter at just the right time, they heard a thumping from the back of the box. It was the lieutenant, banging his crutches to applaud the strikeout.

"What are you, Briton or Yank?" the boys wanted to know.

"I'm a full-blooded Yank, from Roslyn, Long Island. But I can find you a few thousand Britishers in the Army that are as keen about baseball as you and I are. Why shouldn't they? They're the same people that we are. I have been with them now for four years and I have yet to find one unlike the average American from home."

"Four years?"

"Yes. I came over in September, 1914, drove a Norton ambulance for a month—to have a look around—and then chose armored cars. I enlisted, but managed to work up to a commission in a short time. Then I was wounded and knocked out for a while. Then they got me pretty badly at the big show at Cambrai. I have been laid up ever since. A few weeks more and I will be fairly fit again."

He wouldn't tell them much more.

"I don't want any melodrama written about me."[20]

The boys were impressed. After the game, one flagged down a taxi with the lieutenant and heard him introduce himself to some Yanks as Oakham.

Sixth Inning

Joe Lee started off the next inning by smacking one straight to the left fielder. That brought up navy's catcher—"Slugger Fuller," Keeley called him—who was already having a nice game.[21] Chas drove "a magnificent two-bagger to centre-field."[22] You can picture the handsome Harvard aviator out there on the bag, grinning as the bluejackets went nuts in the stands and all around on the terraces. Next up was Minooka Mike, the captain, a Red Sox hero in the 1916 World Series. Oh, Mike wanted to win this game in front of the king and queen, show 'em what an Irish kid from the U.S.A. could do in a pinch. Mike dug in and waited for his pitch from Doc Lafitte.

He got it, and drove the ball to the outfield.

Mike rounded first as Chas headed for home. Ingram doesn't tell us which outfielder corralled the ball or where he threw it. But when the play

Navy rooters at Stamford Bridge (*Our Navy*).

was over, Chas was safe at the plate and Mike was standing on second, probably dusting off his flashy blue flannels. The navy boys had whooped and hollered over their first run, but "the greetings were redoubled" now with the second.[23]

The rest of the inning went quickly. Jack Egan hit one back to Doc, followed by an out by Skeets Hayes. The navy nine trotted back onto the field.

"It's two love, isn't it?" the chirpy Britisher asked the uniformed Y man.

"Two to nothing."

"Well, if the Army makes two runs then it's on the level, isn't it?"[24]

Yes, but it didn't look like army would ever push across a run. Just to underline the inning, the Squire came on and fanned the side in the bottom of the frame—Mims, Maender and Dorn, 1–2–3.

Grab yer gloves, boys.

16

Late Innings

Seventh Inning

The noise and cheers went on and on as the afternoon "passed in such a pandemonium as was perhaps never heard before on an English playing-field; not even on a football ground."[1] It was especially true on the navy side, where you'd have thought the bluejackets had just brought a U-boat to the surface and were about to put an end to her career.

The joint was jumping as Herb Pennock stepped up to lead off the seventh. Doc gave the Squire a dose of his own medicine and sent him back to the bench with a lazy strikeout. Phil Maney "tried ineffectually to reach first," and went back to grab some pine himself.[2] Vannatter popped out to the shortstop in foul ground.

Three up, three down.

The Yanks in the stands all hopped up for the seventh-inning stretch.

"On all sides we began to hear enthusiastic praise of baseball," Dr. Raiguel remembered. "Then we had to explain that we were only relaxing and that the most interesting innings were to follow. 'But,' they inquired, 'why stretch after the seventh inning? Why not after the fifth or the sixth?' Of course there was no reason, I explained, except custom."[3] At least no bobbies showed up this time to find out what the disturbance was all about.

Carl Blackmore came to bat for army after the break. He "faded at first, but not without a protest to Umpire Latham"—a beef![4] Fred Tober then walked. Doc Lafitte slapped one to Mike McNally, who threw for the force out at second on a fielder's choice. Al Bartholemy ended the frame with a fly out to Skeets Hayes.

ATTA BOY, JOHN!

Ripley cartoon of John Bull playing baseball (*Boston Globe*).

Eighth Inning

> 1, 2, 3, 4, 5, 6, 7,
>   All the Navy go to heaven.
> When we get there we will yell,
>   All the Army go to—(Groans!!)[5]

The rooting never wound down all afternoon. To deafened Britishers, "all the words seemed to be well-known, but the tone-quality of the voices was rough, and by the end of the game *extremely* rough—what was left of them. They had books of the words, but they waved them about for emphasis."[6]

We don't learn anything from Ingram and very little from Keeley about the eighth inning, though we know from the box score that nothing much happened. "Smart fielding and good pitching," marked the seventh and the eighth, according to Keeley.[7] Doc struck out two of the three sailors (Fierros, Lee and Fuller) he faced in the eighth. Herb then faced just four batters (Rawlings through Maender) in the bottom of the inning, probably walking the extra man with no damage done.

At some point late in the game Floyd Mims pulled himself from center field and sent in R. E. Allen of Harrisburg, Pennsylvania, who'd played a lot for the army squad earlier in the season. One or the other batted in the eighth, though the box score doesn't show an official at-bat for either man.

One thing that everybody at Stamford Bridge *did* know was that the two Yank pitchers were flat-out firing the horsehide. Strangely enough (strangely to the Yanks, at least), their manner of pitching excited the Britishers because it wasn't allowed in cricket. A player flinging a red leather ball in cricket had to *bowl* it, like a catapult lofting a stone at a castle wall, but never *throw* it with a bent arm like Doc or the Squire. And if he *did* throw it, this was called a no-ball and the batter couldn't be put out by it. Baseball was complicated but cricket had it beat by a country mile, and Americans would've thought any rule like that was just nuts. The Britishers, though, loved the clinic the two Yank hurlers put on at Stamford Bridge.

"Cricketers who saw the July 4 baseball match at Chelsea must have been greatly impressed by the beautiful action of the two pitchers, Pennock and Lafitte, who by the laws of their game are expressly permitted to throw," *The Field* would say. "A point which cannot have escaped notice is that their action is as different as chalk from cheese from that of the so-called throwers at cricket. In bygone days it was a common thing to meet bowlers who threw, and were tolerated because they were harmless, but everybody knew perfectly well that they actually were throwers. If Pennock, throwing as at baseball, were to appear to-day in the Army match at Lord's, every man, woman and child in the crowd would instantly recognize that he was not bowling, but throwing. There would be no arguments about it, for the fact would be patent to all the world."[8]

At least the cricket fans could *see* the baseball that the hurlers and fielders were tossing around the diamond in Chelsea today. The White Sox and Giants had pulled a fast one on the crowd at Stamford Bridge four years earlier. "[T]hey played for five minutes without a ball," a London news-paper admitted. "It was a very clever piece of acting; so clever, in fact, that very few of the English spectators present noticed the absence of the white leather covered ball."[9]

Ninth Inning

Doc Lafitte wanted to keep the game close and let his boys break up the Squire's no-hitter during their last time up. Mike McNally wanted exactly the opposite. The navy's captain came to bat first and stroked a clean sin-gle. With Jack Egan standing at the plate, the Red Sox speedster looked toward the next bag and weighed his chances. "While Egan was looking 'em over he stole second—that is he would have stolen it if he hadn't over-slid."[10] Dorn or Blackmore slapped down a tag and Arlie Latham's arm shot up—*OUT!* It was a long hike back to the bench for the pride of Minooka, Pennsylvania.

After Jack flied or lined out to first, Ensign Hayes came up and also singled. (And didn't Mike wish he was still on base!) Skeets eyed second base just as his captain had. With Squire Pennock at the dish, he took off and "got away with a theft of the keystone bag."[11] He died there when his pitcher fanned. The game was now about two hours old—nobody would think to publish the exact length later.

"The pitching and fielding were brilliant," London's *Times* declared, and "it looked as if the Army would be beaten pointless."[12] In fact, army was down to its last three outs and still hitless.

The bottom of the frame was probably when Warrant Officer John Lane, former secretary for the Red Sox and Jack Barry's Navy Yard nine, went in to play right field. His name doesn't show up on any lineup or game story, or in the accounts of any *other* AABL games for that matter, and he didn't get an at-bat. Lane had been surprised to run into Mike and Herb at navy headquarters some days or weeks earlier. As the team's captain, Mike might've done him a favor by slipping him into the historic contest. "Lane said that while he was standing in the outfield a group of 12 soldiers rushed out and surrounded him and he discovered that they were all boys from Andrew-sq section, South Boston."[13]

Lane had entered a truly great game. Even the Britishers recognized that they were watching something special, even if they didn't necessarily understand just what it was. "The players seemed to have touched on light-ning, and it came out of their feet and fingers in wonderful soft streaks," Australian sports fans would read weeks later, when a letter finally made it into a newspaper down under. "The fielding was so accurate that no man seemed able to get round once, and as three men put the whole team out, the number of innings was endless. I enjoyed seeing the Americans enjoy themselves, but gathered no pleasure or information from the game itself. There was any amount of distraction, not the least being the frequent crossings at a low level so as we could plainly see the occupants, of a large and handsome airship with huge United States' and British flags fluttering from the car."[14]

The box score shows skipper Floyd Mims sending in a utility man to bat for Dorn, the second baseman from South Carolina. This fellow shows up as *Weskesser* in the program, *Waeckesser* in the box score and (the most likely spelling) *Weckesser* in several earlier articles about AABL games. Whoever he was, he walked right back to the bench again after Herb fanned him. Next up was R. C. Blackmore, who went out, too—again, it's anybody's guess how.

That brought up the army nine's last hope, Fred Tober. Playing for the Toledo Rail-Lights hadn't prepared this unknown first sacker for a moment like this. Fred came through, connecting for "a splendid hit," even if nobody wrote *where* exactly he hit it. He raced down the line, rounded the bag and kept going.[15] Did he reach second base in a spray of grass, executing a perfect hook slide beneath a tag? Or did he come in standing with a grin on his face? We don't know, but there he was anyway, safe at second, the first soldier to get a hit off navy all day.

Doc Lafitte came to the plate with the game on the line.

The Squire stared in at him from ... well, not any proper mound like back home, but from the shining English grass of a football pitch. The string-bean navy pitcher had been brilliant today. It didn't matter that his record in the big leagues hadn't been much before the war. Standing at the plate, Doc could understand and sympathize. Except for one outstanding half season in Detroit, Doc's own record in the American and Federal leagues hadn't been much to write home about, either. But Herb really was cooking now, and maybe Doc also saw in him the greatness that was coming. Maybe he foresaw that the simmering southpaw from Kennett Square would become one of the best pitchers ever, after the war when he's traded to the team that would make him famous.

Doc's best days on the field were behind him, but he'd shown flashes of greatness himself. He'd hurled two imperfect no-hitters. He'd played for the Tigers with the great Ty Cobb and pitched and batted against Walter Johnson. He'd taken the field beside and opposing the best boys in the sport, including some of the greatest ever to play the game. He'd worn the flannels for money in the show, and he'd put them on for free for scrappy semipro clubs for the pure joy of it. Ed Lafitte was a *ballplayer*.

So here they were, Chateau Lafitte and the Squire of Kennett Square, representing the U.S. Army and U.S. Navy in the middle of a World War, with the king and queen of England watching from gilded chairs and only God knew how many tens of thousands of Yanks and Britishers howling like banshees from the stands and surrounds. All of this on the Fourth of July in England. Who would've believed it back home in Atlanta or Philadelphia?

Doc dug in.

When exactly did Fred Tober steal third base? Was it on Herb's first pitch? The second? Even later? How close was the throw—or *was* there even a throw? Again, we don't know. Nobody tells us. But there Fred stood, with Doc still at the plate just ninety feet away. "A near-riot ensued," Dr. Raiguel wrote. "Greatly encouraged the Army went at it again."[16] The noise was tremendous. Doc strode back to the plate. Maybe he stood there a second or two, remembering the day with the Tigers when he'd homered off the Big Train. The Squire probably took a look over his shoulder toward the Toledo boy dancing off third before squaring up to deliver his pitch.

Crack!

You can picture Herb's head whipping 'round as the ball shoots past. Again, we don't know where it went, but it went a long way, "Mr. Tober riding home mid the yells and whoops of the doughboys."[17] By the time the navy got the ball back to the infield, Doc was standing on second with the second double in a row. Did he give Floyd Mims and the bench a sardonic, lantern-jawed grin? We can only imagine. Army trailed by just a run now, with Doc in scoring position.

When Al Bartholemy came up with his team still alive, editor Keeley could hardly contain his excitement or his prose. "Mr. Bart, the modern Casey, ... had a chance to immortalise himself in the eyes of the King of England and numerous members of the Royal Family and to earn a nitch [*sic*] in the Army's Hall of Fame like his noted progenitor."[18]

Did the Squire fidget out there on the flat grass, or was he still confident about getting the last out? Herb threw to the plate with Doc at his back. Who knows now what the count was when the crucial pitch came? Bart was ready. He didn't whiff ingloriously like the mighty Casey, but put solid wood on the ball—"a hit that sent the ball away high and a considerable distance, but there was one Ferros [*sic*] who calmly waited until it fell in his gloved hand."[19]

And that was it, the last out in a great navy victory.

Imagine the whoop that went up from those thousands of bluejackets. Somehow it seemed only right that a baseball match played on a British football ground should end with a proper British football score: 2–1.

It had been one hell of a game. Doc surrendered just six hits and a walk, a wonderful performance in any league, but Herb had struck out fourteen and held army hitless into the ninth. "Pennock pitched, and that's the whole story—the army could not touch him," Mike McNally would write home later.[20]

Delirious sailors poured onto the pitch. They "formed fours and, arm in arm, started the snake dance," Dr. Raiguel wrote. "Not to be outdone, the doughboys joined them. Together, blue and khaki zigzagged over the field, while the British applauded in admiration of what they thought was another part of the great game."[21]

It was pandemonium, the Fourth of July and New Year's Eve combined. Did Chas Fuller join the snake dance? Or did he just stand there with a smile on his handsome mug taking everything in, maybe suspecting that his life might never get any better?

The Welsh Guards' band joined the throng, the Yank sailors jiggling along behind. The whole place was screaming and hollering, banging and tooting on drums and tin whistles. When the band and the sailors came past the grandstand, somebody gave an order. Impossibly, the first notes of "The Star-Spangled Banner" floated up over the roar. This was the unofficial hymn of the United States, popular since the start of the war but not to become America's national anthem until 1931. Everything stopped in a heartbeat. The king and the allied officers in the royal box rose in the sudden, stunning silence, which was broken only by the musical notes.

"Hats came off. Sailors and soldiers stood to attention, saluting. After all that noise the quietude, accented by the poignant music, came near being painful," the *Times* said almost poetically. "The meaning of this most significant of all ball games was carried along the air. There was more cheering afterwards, but cheering of a radically different kind. The crowd awoke to consciousness that the afternoon had passed into the history of two great nations."[22]

The scene would touch a small-town editor back in Iowa who didn't even see it. "So you see that Britons, even such sober Britons us the Times represents, though they may have some difficulty in understanding a foreign game, have a perfectly darling understanding of significances," he wrote. "Ball games must strike all Britons as extraordinary; but the Times has no difficulty in perceiving that this ball game was even extraordinary among its kind. And perhaps we, too, can perceive it almost as clearly. We certainly should have been able to perceive it had we been there."[23]

When the tune was done, the king turned to Admiral Sims and General Biddle and gave them an American salute rather than the palm-out salute of the British army—"a delicate compliment," Dr. Raiguel thought. "Again the crowd went wild!"[24] A Chelsea veteran in his scarlet coat watched it all from the crowd. "I wonder what the Kaiser would think of it all if he could be here," he said.[25]

Both pitchers got a royal summons to come up for a handshake from King George. The amiable little monarch chatted with Doc for a little while, mentioning the "receiver being padded up like an armchair when the cricketer bowled."[26]

Admiral Sims was so tickled by the navy victory that he'd announce a promotion for his hurler during a banquet at the Savoy tonight. "Pennock, you were a seaman," he'd say, "but you are now a yeoman."[27] Navy secretary Daniels would congratulate the admiral by cable tomorrow for the big win: "It is but one more proof the Navy can do well anything it undertakes."[28]

The Fourth of July in London had been a grand day for everyone, Yank and Britisher alike. King George would jot a note about it in his diary after he got home tonight to Buck House: "We all went to see a baseball match between the American Army & Navy, played at Stamford Bridge. Large crowds, the Navy won by 2 runs to 1. Quite exciting; only got home at 6.0."[29]

Attaboy.

17

Peacetime

The great whooshing, whizzing, whirling machine that was the King's Game had ended. There were no more mechanical toys knocking over rows of dominos or marbles clattering down curlicue ramps. All the king's horses and all the king's men couldn't have put something like this together again with the help of a handful of wizards, a coven of managers and one or two old spitballers. All that remained was the memory, which was terrific.

"One side won, but I do not know which side," a correspondent wrote for Aussies on the far side of the world. "By that time I was quite thoroughly convinced that it did not matter. The sun blazed, the flags blew out. Stamford Bridge volleyed and thundered vast avalanches of noise."[1]

The great machine hadn't produced a shoeshine for a man standing on a box, but an important boost to morale when Britishers needed it most. The *Morning Post* in London called the game "a match of great excellence and excitement."[2] The good gray *Times* got positively misty over what a headline called "REMARKABLE SCENES AT CHELSEA." "It took us completely away to those distant times when we could rejoice under a blue sky without looking for Zeppelins and Gothas."[3] Later, at the end of the AABL season, the starchy old paper would also add this:

> To the Americans goes the credit of arranging for London the most memorable match of any kind played during the summer. When the United States Navy beat the United States Army at Stamford Bridge in the presence of the king, Londoners received the pleasant shock of hearing once again a riot of cheers and of being introduced to other varieties of shouting which will reverberate on grounds once thrilled only by the modest

applause of the cricket or football zealot, and in parks sacred for centuries from any game whatever.[4]

It really was awfully nice, and everybody was pleased as punch that the king had enjoyed the game so much. George V got lots of good ink on the other side of the Atlantic for attending—not that he'd looked for publicity, or not primarily anyway. A syndicated photo of His Majesty with Arlie Latham ran in papers all over the States under a long headline that mentioned the "spirit which war has created among the allied countries."[5] In London, the *Daily Sketch* ran a cheeky poem:

> *King George the Third with cannon balls*
> *did try our brothers to dispatch;*
> *King George the Fifth the country calls*
> *to watch with him their baseball match.*[6]

The *Times'* man in Washington thought the whole thing went much deeper than a rousing holiday. "During the past year especially Americans have learnt to know us as never before," he wrote in August. "The realization of the community of our ideals has forged a new link between us. It has, aided by the knowledge of our common peril, done more to obliterate the old mistrust of British policy than decades of 'Blood is thicker than water' sentimentalism. ... In this process the personality of the King has played a great part. All the United States rang with his interest in the baseball match."[7]

The Fourth of July baseball game in Chelsea was only that, of course—a *game*. Howard Booker said the next day that the action on the field had been "too good for the British public to understand," and he might've had a point. He backtracked a little by adding, "The play was too close for the uninitiated to appreciate it, but they will soon learn to do so. It was as great a game as I have ever seen, even on the Polo Ground in New York."[8]

He certainly was right about the greatness of those nine innings. Thanks to the King's Game and all the others on the AABL schedule, the league was able to donate almost fifteen thousand dollars to British war charities, the net profits of the season. The league's angels agreed with Booker that Britishers would soon take to baseball in a big way. Nobody seemed to doubt that new, professional leagues would spring up in Great Britain, Ireland and France once the war had ended.

Things looked a little different on the other side of the Atlantic. A columnist in the Windy City pointed out that in its first season the AABL had fielded teams of Yanks and Canadians who had grown up playing the game. "That is an entirely different thing from attempting to stage a league season between teams made up entirely of Englishmen who had acquired their knowledge of the sport from their cousins from over here." He added this zinger: "We imagine such a series of exhibitions would rank alongside the games played for the championship of the Chicago South Side Grammar School League."[9]

Lots of Britishers doubted baseball's future, too. Some even thought the sports tide might flow the other way—that baseball would flop in England while British football became the next big thing in America, brought home by returning doughboys. You had lots of wonderful arguments about it.

Meanwhile, there was still a war to be won. The Britishers and Yanks got on with the business of winning it. A few hours after the final out, a big London newspaper ran a headline that cheered Britishers more than any score from Stamford Bridge: "THREE MILLION 'YANKS.' / The American Army's Strength By September 1."[10] The wire story said America now had better than two million men in uniform and expected four million by 1919. A million of these boys were in France or on the way across. Although the numbers weren't yet public, a Yank force equivalent to thirty-four Allied infantry divisions was already at the front.

The Germans, whether they knew it or not, were about finished. Black Jack Pershing wrote later,

> Thus at this time the American combat reënforcements to the Allies more than offset the reënforcements which Germany had been able to bring from the Eastern to the Western Front after the collapse of Russia. Without the addition of the Americans the Allies would have been outnumbered by nearly 400,000 men.
>
> Now that the Allies were no longer in jeopardy, it seemed opportune to push the formation of our own army near Château-Thierry for use against the Marne salient in the counter-offensive which I had frequently urged.[11]

The Yanks and the French launched their big push on July 18, two weeks after the King's Game. The Germans never went on the offensive again. A wholly American army took the field in August and pushed on until the Armistice on November 11, 1918—one week and four months following the game at Chelsea.

Although they had won the King's Game on the Fourth of July, Admiral Sims' boys couldn't edge out General Biddle's nine for the AABL championship. Floyd Mims' squad finished one game ahead of the bluejackets at the end of play on August 24. The final standings couldn't have pleased the Canadians very much:

U.S. Army	12–3 (.800)
U.S. Navy	11–4 (.733)

Epsom	8–5 (.615)
Hounslow	8–5 (.615)
Sunningdale	5–7 (.417)
Northolt	4–8 (.333)
Canadian Pay Office	2–11 (.154)
Canadian Records	1–7 (.125)

The army players received fine wristwatches after the season, the same sort that many British officers wore in the trenches. They were inscribed: *U.S. ARMY CHAMPIONS 1918. ANGLO AMERICAN BASEBALL LEAGUE. PRESENTED BY MAJOR THE HON. WALDORF ASTOR, M. P.* "The 'M. P.' doesn't stand for military police," Ed Lafitte explained later back in the States. "It means member of parliament."[12] The navy side didn't go home empty-handed, either. Admiral Sims wrote warm, personal letters to several of the boys—probably to all of them—thanking them for upholding the prestige of the United States Navy. Mike McNally and Herb Pennock each got one. "It's a great letter," the Squire said years later. "I wouldn't lose it for anything."[13]

The 1918 season was over, but baseball wasn't yet done in England. The AABL clubs kept playing exhibitions for war charities in and near London. Teams also traveled, if not to France as once hoped. The league had made several road trips during the season, including U.S. Army and Sunningdale in Birmingham (twenty-three thousand fans) and U.S. Navy versus Sunningdale in Glasgow (thirty-seven thousand). Now U.S. Navy defeated a USS *Texas* nine in Rosyth, Scotland, and U.S. Army and one of the Canadian clubs—the newspapers didn't say which one—crossed the Irish Sea to play a benefit for the Blue Cross charity for war horses.

"Had a pretty nice time although it rained for three days while we were in Dublin," wrote Al Bartholemy, who took leave to make the Irish trip. "We only played one game there and beat the Canadians, 13 to 6. Last Wednesday we played them again in Belfast, winning 4 to 3. The attendance all around was very poor, even considering the rain. About 500 at Dublin and less than that at Belfast. They go crazy over horse racing around Dublin."[14]

Two Yank and Canadian teams, apparently not from the AABL, also played at Aberdeen and Dundee, drawing bigger crowds. Altogether, the AABL clubs played one hundred fifty games in 1918, forty-nine of them outside the regular schedule. You really couldn't blame people for getting carried away and thinking such success would continue.

The grand pooh-bahs of the Anglo-American Baseball League thought their circuit had a fine future when the first peacetime spring in five years rolled around in 1919. They again trotted out Arlie Latham, still the freshest man on earth, to spread the good word in England and the United States. Arlie wrote to sportswriter Al Spink that he planned to come home and sign more ballplayers, and predicted an international world's championship series within a year or two.

"Latham is very optimistic over the game's progress in the British kingdom," another article said. "He predicts that before many years have elapsed merry old England will be engaged in an international tournament with clubs of America for the championship of the world. And he goes further and says that when those games are played the crowds in England will be bigger than the crowds in America."[15]

Maybe this was just wishful thinking. After all, lots of the Yank and Canadian boys had already gone home or were headed there. But Arlie wasn't alone if he was really convinced that baseball would fly in England. Bill Lange, an old Chicago Colts and Orphans outfielder turned real estate magnate, was in France thinking much the same thing.

Bill had sailed from New York in January 1919 as the general baseball director for the Y.M.C.A. in Europe. That was only one of his three overlapping missions. Bill was also the chief European scout for John McGraw, now a part owner of the New York Giants. And he was Ban Johnson's man in Europe, charged with looking into taking the American League pennant winners on a European tour that fall to entertain uniformed Yanks. Not only that, he had forty thousand dollars worth of baseball equipment from Clark Griffith's Ball and Bat Fund to hand out to army and navy teams.

The Johnson and Lange plan was to pick up a few good baseball organizers, either professionals or college men, and send them to England, Belgium and Italy to work up what everyone was calling an International Baseball League—a *real* international circuit. Ban and Bill thought all three countries might have low-level leagues of their own by summer. In talking it up before he left, the old Chicago "fence breaker" practically made Arlie Latham sound like a pessimist.

"If the international league thing takes hold, England, France, Belgium, and Italy will have their national series, their European series, and then they will enter a real world series with the pennant winners over here," Bill said. "We could have the games played alternately on this side and abroad, probably running them in order with the teams of the different nations."[16]

The National Sporting Club in London, for one, was happy to hear that Bill was bringing over more baseball. "I believe that his mission of including England and France in the international league scheme is a good one and should be put through," said the group's president. "We will do everything we can to help him."[17]

The Anglo-American Baseball League was already established and had big plans of its own. Nothing proved easy for the AABL in 1919, though. Only two of its eight teams were American—the U.S. Army and U.S. Navy headquarters teams remained, but both aviation nines were gone. The other six teams were Canadian, including reorganized squads from 1918. Floyd Mims, newly promoted to captain, again managed the U.S. Army nine, but he didn't have much left to work with. Many of his boys had shipped home or gone to Europe.

"Captain Mims is to have a baseball team again this year," a pal wrote to Al Bartholemy back in the States, "he feels sore because you, Blackmore, Tober and Dublynn have gone but hopes to get a winning team. My staunch friend Mr. Booker is hanging around here all the time now. ... Gus Mohlman leaves tonight for Hamburg Germany also Capt. Williams they are going to work for the Food Administration. He wants to go and he has my best but oh take me home."[18]

The AABL played games on nearly every Saturday and Sunday from May through August. After the fabulous 1918 season, the league had optimistically taken leases on Stamford Bridge and on grounds in Manchester, Birmingham, Liverpool and Sheffield. It didn't need them. While the league did take the field in 1919, everybody played on the same diamond at Stamford Bridge.

The competition was watered down, too. Instead of facing only each other, AABL teams often played British university nines. These clubs fielded mostly ex–Yank servicemen who'd stayed on in England to study at Oxford, Cambridge and the London School of Economics. (You can imagine Jay Gatsby playing second base during his few months at Oxford, wearing a ball cap and a white cricket sweater, drifting back to snag a lazy fly ball, like a boat against the current in short right-center.) Oh, sure, the AABL squads generally walloped the university nines, but they weren't exactly facing Herb Pennock or Doc Lafitte. Back in the States, about the only way you could follow the league in 1919 was by reading a few short pieces in the *Christian Science Monitor*.

"Attendances were exceptionally good and among the spectators were many Englishmen who had been converted to the game, not only in England but also in France," the AABL claimed later.[19] But that was fudging the facts, really, because it included 1918, when the league drew its biggest crowds. Most of the excitement had died down long before British football got going again in fall 1919.

"The two [baseball] leagues proposed in England have dwindled down to a casual schedule between teams chiefly in the London district," Hugh Fullerton wrote that August. "The sporting goods stores of England are overstocked with goods and no clamorous demand is evident. England has turned down the American game cold and it will be, for a long time at least, class sport with small crowds. The English flocked to see expert Americans play their game, but they neither understand or appreciated the sport."[20]

The Anglo-American Baseball League quietly folded its tent after the second year, although supposedly funded for three. Bill Lange's International Baseball League quickly disappeared, too, and never came close to becoming reality.

Sic transit Gloria mundi, as a tweedy professor must've said somewhere.

William J. Barr was one of A. G. Spalding's men who'd tried to win over Britishers to the national pastime since before the turn of the century. By the start of 1920, he had pretty much given up hope for baseball in England. He wasn't all that sure about cricket, either.

"I find with the exception of the London Baseball Association with a membership of some ten amateur clubs who play at irregular intervals," he wrote to a New York newspaper from Birmingham, "nothing remains of the pioneer work which must have cost the Spalding firm at least $25,000. ... I do not think the climate of Great Britain is favorable to first class play of baseball, for it rains almost every day, even during the summer months. While cricket has had a revival this summer, still it cannot now be called England's national pastime, for association football is played from August 30 until the end of May and thousands attend football games where only hundreds go to even the best cricket matches."[21]

If you wanted to see baseball in England, your best bet was hopping a train to Oxford and the athletic fields spread beneath her dreaming spires. "Here baseball, lusty off-spring of cricket, disports itself. American Rhodes Scholars at Oxford have organized a league with teams representing the various classes and a full season of the national game is in progress."[22]

So, the amateurs had prospered after the pros had all gone home. But the AABL investors still had their fine careers and none was hit too badly when the league went belly-up. Wilson Cross retired as chairman of Vacuum Oil Ltd. in 1936. Newton Crane also did well, and in 1921 became the first Yank to "take silk" as a king's counsel. Being a barrister, he would have noted for the record that Judah Benjamin, former Confederate secretary of state, had served as a *Queen's* Counsel during Victoria's reign.

Howard Booker landed on his feet, too, still hustling. Boxer Jack Johnson asked him to arrange a bout for him in Spain in December 1918. Before long, Booker and a partner were also running dance clubs with American jazz bands—one with a French name in London, another with an English name in Paris. "Europe is just waking up to the dancing craze and moving pictures—comparatively speaking," Booker said. "And Americans are getting in on the ground-floor for the boom that is to come."[23]

Arlie Latham had a more complicated and interesting story. "One of the pathetic figures in London to me is Arlie Latham, the old baseball star and coach," columnist O. O. McIntyre wrote in 1922. "He has the hat checking privilege in a London cafe and is doing well, but London does not know the glory that once was his. He longs for old time friends and the hoarse shouts from the bleachers."[24]

Well, maybe so, but it was hard to imagine a pathetic Arlie, even an ocean away from home. The old Brownie actually seemed to like London and stayed for fourteen years. American pals were delighted to see him, and vice versa, even as he checked their coats at a club called Rector's. Damon Runyon described him during this time as "a short man, with a strangely gnarled countenance. His features suggested the weather-warped knot of an old oak tree."[25]

The Giants and White Sox came through London again in 1924 to play at Stamford Bridge. Arlie was there, of course, in a Giants uniform, chatting with King George and Queen Mary like a long-lost pal. There are pictures to prove it. Loyal John McGraw, before he left, wrote a check to help found a new Anglo-American Baseball Association, a club league that lasted for years in London.

Arlie finally sailed for home in 1931. Although in his seventies, he landed jobs as the press-box attendant at both the Polo Grounds and Yankee Stadium, "a delightful sinecure for an old-time ball player."[26] Columnists still wrote about him, because some stories never get old and Arlie was always great copy. A second world war was fought and won before he died in 1952, still a favorite of fans and baseball writers everywhere. Walter Arlington Latham, his biographer wrote much later, had "served the game in every hands-on capacity, sometimes not wisely, often not well, but always ardently."[27]

The AABL ballplayers did pretty well, too, and one became a star.

Herb Pennock ended the war as a yeoman first class, then went home to play baseball again. Harry Frazee began dismantling his Red Sox club and selling his best ballplayers to the Yankees, starting with Babe Ruth in 1920. Herb followed in 1923 and played in New York for a dozen years. After all the not-so-great seasons, he was resurrected and brilliant. By the time he retired in 1934 after twenty-two seasons, he had won two hundred forty-one games. He'd also won five games and lost none during five World Series.

The Squire stayed in the sport after he hung up his spikes. He was general manager of the Philadelphia Phillies when he collapsed from a stroke in 1948 in the lobby of New York's Waldorf-Astoria hotel. Three thousand people filed past his casket at the American Legion building in Kennett Square. "He reached the top of his profession and gained the acclaim of the whole world for his masterful performances on the pitching mound," a local editorial said, "but he always remained the simple, big-hearted neighbor of Kennett Square."[28] The old southpaw was elected to the National Baseball Hall of Fame in Cooperstown later that year.

The Historic Commission in his hometown wanted to erect a statue of Herb in 1998, marking the fifty years since he'd gone into the Hall. But times change, and the southpaw had lived and died in a very different era. People remembered the racist abuse that his Phillies club had hurled at Jackie Robinson when the Brooklyn Dodgers broke the big-league color barrier in 1947. And somebody repeated what Herb had allegedly said in a phone call to Branch Rickey, who'd brought Robinson into the National League. "You just can't bring that nigger here with the rest of the team, Branch. We're just not ready for that sort of thing yet."[29]

The Dodgers' old traveling secretary had included the remark twenty-two years earlier in a published memoir. Many people believed it, but some didn't. "Whether the conversation was fact or fiction remains a subject of controversy," a Phillies historian wrote later.[30] There's at least reasonable doubt that Herb was the one in the Phillies' organization who'd made the call, and Jackie himself believed it was Bob Carpenter, the club's owner and president.

Local old-timers still stoutly defend Herb's reputation, but no statue of the Squire has ever gone up in Kennett Square.

Ed Lafitte left London for American Base Hospital No. 202 in France while the fighting was still going on. He liked the work and was good at it. He went home to the States in 1919, but stayed in the army for a while. He was promoted to major and served in a base hospital in St. Louis. A few sportswriters thought Doc might try for a comeback in the bigs after his great showing in England. He went home to Philadelphia instead, picked up his dental practice and was happy pitching in a county league. He became the baseball coach at Swarthmore College in 1920 and later coached for the Montgomery School for Boys.

Doc worked as a dentist in Philly for better than forty years, finally retiring in 1961. He died at his home in 1971, a little past his eighty-fifth birthday. His epitaph could've been something that the *Brooklyn Eagle* had printed a long time ago: "Many a soldier today with apparently normal features owes the restoration of his face to Maj. Lafitte's skill."[31]

Mike McNally went to the Yankees two years before the Squire. He had a good season with the club and his old pal the Babe. Still as fast as ever, he famously stole home in the first game of the 1921 World Series.

Minooka Mike played four seasons in New York, mostly as a utility man, then a final dozen games with the Senators in 1925. That was the end of the line. Mike said he would go into the car business in Scranton, but instead headed back to the minors as a manager. He skippered at Binghamton, New York, and at Wilkes-Barre and Williamsport in Pennsylvania. Always a fan favorite, he somehow got it into his head to run for Congress in 1938. He lost the primary election to a powerful incumbent and knew why—"I wasn't quite as good as picking up grounders."[32]

The pride of Minooka later moved into the Wilkes-Barre front office. He wasn't a skinny young infielder anymore—he looked like a barrel, according to the Babe—but Mike stayed in touch with former teammates and liked playing in old-timers games. He was there in uniform when they retired Number 3 on Yankee Stadium's twenty-fifth anniversary, a few months before Ruth's death in 1948.

The Cleveland Indians tabbed Mike as the director of their farm system in 1951. He stayed until 1958, then was a roving ambassador and scout. While he was at it he signed slugger Rocky Colavito, almost in the shadow of Yankee Stadium. Mike died at age seventy-one in 1965 after more than a half century in baseball. He'd said for years that meeting George V at Stamford Bridge was "pretty good for a Minooka boy."[33]

Lieutenant (junior grade) Charles Fuller left the navy after the war, returned to Harvard and graduated with his class thanks to a special program for veterans. Later he went to Columbia to become an architect. He married a sculptor and like other members of the "lost generation" went to Paris. There they met all kinds of artists and expats, including Ernest Hemingway.

The Crash and Depression brought alcoholism and personal problems, and Chas' life grew chaotic. He tried to get back in the navy in World War II. They wouldn't take him, so he joined the merchant marine as an ordinary seaman and sailed in the dangerous Atlantic convoys. After the war Chas was an architect and city planner and for a while advised a new government in Indonesia. He once remarked that he'd probably be remembered as someone who "amused some members of my generation."[34]

Chas died in New York City in 1960 while drying out. Years later his son Blair wrote a biographical sketch of the old man that he titled *The Poison of Non-Fulfillment*. Shortly before his own death in 2011, Blair wrote that July 4, 1918, "might have been the happiest day of my father's life."[35]

Al Bartholemy went home to the Northwest and tried to pick up his baseball career. He didn't hook on as a catcher with a minor-league club in 1919, so signed as player-manager for a team in the Southern Idaho League. "Bartholemy, who has caught great ball and hit hard this semester, manages the Paul team. He is wanted by several clubs, including the Seattle coasters, Los Angeles and St. Paul," a Portland paper reported. "The Angels seem to have the inner track on Al, for Johnny Bassler and he were 'buddies' while both were members of the American air service during the war."[36]

Bart did make the Los Angeles squad in 1920, but got into only one game before being cut. He stayed in California a few more years, playing in the outlaw San Joaquin Valley League. Bart finally hung up the spikes and went home to Portland, where he landed a job with a petroleum company. He played on company teams, coached kids' baseball and kept in touch with Mike McNally well into the 1950s, tipping the Indians exec to prospects in the Portland area.

"Chubby Al" Bartholemy died in 1964, a year before Minooka Mike.

Floyd Mims had a weirdly colorful military career. The army skipper married a Britisher after the war, went home to the States and got out of the army. He worked for a while as a painting contractor in Philadelphia, then went back into uniform as a private first class during the Depression. He stood on the dock with two officers to welcome Black Jack Pershing home from an overseas tour in 1936. The old quartermaster also somehow got himself appointed as a military representative to the National Horse Show in New York.

Floyd became an officer again in World War II, as a major running prisoner of war camps in the States. At least one German POW thought the old boy "seemed somewhat mentally disturbed."[37] Pershing's one-time orderly retired after the war as a lieutenant-colonel, but stayed active and often kicked up a fuss about veterans' issues. He was still around during the Vietnam War, demanding better treatment for American POWs. He died in Florida in 1986, a couple of months shy of his hundredth birthday.

The rest of the boys got on with their lives, in the way that discharged soldiers and sailors generally do. Skeets Hayes became a writer and journalist. Fred Tober went home to Toledo, where he played ball for a shipyard team. Jack Dublynn played club ball in Flatbush. Carl Blackmore suited up for a few games in an obscure league in Michigan. It was probably pretty much the same for most of the others.

The Fourth of July King's Game was remembered only briefly. Newspapers in the States mentioned it often in 1918, then not so much after the Armistice. Dr. Raiguel wrote a nice article titled *The Fourth of July That Rang Round the World: The Greatest Baseball Game Ever Played.* It had lots of photos and ran in the July 1919 issue of *Ladies' Home Journal.* The game mostly faded from memory after that. Details and even the correct year got fuzzy.

According to the Associated Press in 1928, Herb Pennock had pitched in "the famous 10 inning game between American army and navy teams on July 4, 1919, at London."[38] By World War II, the game was only a footnote. The AP's ten-inning goof lived for decades and made it into the Squire's obituary in 1948. Mike McNally's obit in a Scranton paper in the 1960s talked about the game, too, but managed to get the facts right. Doc Lafitte's obit in a Philadelphia paper in the 1970s mentioned his rank in the dental corps, but didn't include the game. Neither did a notice in the *Sporting News*.

Britishers never really threw their arms around baseball, during the war or afterward. There were lots of theories why, one as good as another. Most had something to do with cricket or the British character or both. Sportswriter Thomas S. Rice argued that the generations of Britishers who'd grown up with cricket and football weren't keen to give them up. Baseball itself was partly to blame, too, and Rice pointed a finger at the fans. He wrote from England in December 1918,

> Violent rooting, and the same wrangling with the umpire which have disgusted thousands of Americans have marked many of the ball games here, and have done a vast amount of harm to the baseball propaganda. For some reason, the Britishers have gained the impression that rooting is a form of bluff.
>
> They probably derived the impression from the childish and utterly unprofitable kicking against decisions, kicking frequently indulged in when the umpire was obviously right, just as we too frequently see in the United States. That characterization of rooting as a form of bluff sprang up spontaneously in a number of publications about the same time, and it will take years for baseball to live it down in these islands.[39]

He was probably right. The old dear who'd feared for Arlie Latham's life at Chelsea certainly thought so. A crooked promoter who'd taken off with most of the proceeds from a charity game in the north of England hadn't helped anything, either. And don't forget those screwy baseball primers that an archbishop couldn't have understood. No, Rice couldn't see much chance for baseball catching on after the Yanks went home— "and all tales to the contrary should be heavily discounted."[40]

Leo Callahan of the U.S. Navy nine agreed. "It's no use to talk about England adopting base ball. Nothing to it, and all this talk of the English liking the game is chatter," he said back home. Callahan thought Britishers liked baseball "just as much as Americans like cricket. We played a number of lively games for them, got lots of applause, and went away gladdened by their friendship, anyway."[41]

Ed Lafitte couldn't see it, either.

"I have never seen a Britisher who will admit that baseball is as good a game as cricket," Doc said.

Occasionally one sees youngsters over there playing the game and he is led to hope that maybe the game is catching on. But that is as far as it goes.

The weather over there would make it bad for the owners, too, for there would have to be many more postponements than here because of rain. One advantage the British magnates would have, however, would be that there would not be much mileage.[42]

So despite high hopes in 1918, baseball was never going to catch on in England. A small-town editor in Iowa had explained the Britishers' attitude perfectly a few days after the King's Game: "They like the 'Yanks' and want them, and know that they can not have them without the Yanks' game. They know it is a case of 'love me, love my dog.' But they don't really love the dog. They are just being good sports about it."[43]

And they *were* good sports about it—jolly good sports, too. "If Waterloo was won on the playing fields of Eton," the *Illustrated London News* editorialized, "it may be that it will be said hereafter, in the same symbolic sense, that the Great War was won on the baseball ground at Chelsea."[44] The King's Game had given British spirits a boost and helped to lay the foundation for the special relationship between the U.S. and Great Britain during the next World War and beyond.

Three months after Chelsea, a newspaper down in Hobart, Tasmania, commented that the "Anglo Saxon fellowship was sealed on the Fourth of July, 1918." The ball game, it concluded, was "some match!"[45]

Appendix. Box Score

Navy	AB	R	H	PO	A	E
Lee, rf	4	0	0	0	0	1
Fuller, c	3	2	1	13	3	0
McNally, 1b	3	0	2	9	0	0
Egan, lf	4	0	1	0	0	0
Hayes, 2b	4	0	1	2	2	0
Pennock, p	4	0	0	1	2	0
Maney, cf	3	0	0	0	0	0
Vannatter, 3b	3	0	1	0	1	1
Fierros, ss	3	0	0	2	0	0
Totals	31	2	6	27	8	2
Army	**AB**	**R**	**H**	**PO**	**A**	**E**
Maender, lf	4	0	0	1	0	0
Dorn,* 2b	3	0	0	1	8	0
Blackmore, ss	3	0	0	2	2	1
Tober, 1b	3	1	1	14	1	0
Lafitte, p	4	0	1	0	2	1
Bartholemy, c	4	0	0	8	1	1
Rawlings, rf	3	0	0	1	0	0
Dublynn, 3b	2	0	0	0	0	1
Mims, cf	2	0	0	0	0	1
Allen, cf	0	0	0	0	0	0
Totals	28	1	2	27	14	5

*Weskesser struck out for Dorn in ninth.

Base on balls: Off Lafitte 1, off Pennock 3.
Double plays: Dorn to Tober to Bartholemy; Hayes to McNally.
S. O. by Pennock 14, by Lafitte 7.

Source: *Daily Mail* (London), July 5, 1918

Chapter Notes

Prologue

1. *Emporia Gazette*, July 29, 1918.
2. *New York Tribune*, July 5, 1918.
3. Rupert Brooke, "The Soldier," *1914 & Other Poems* (London: Sidgwick & Jackson, 1915), p. 15.
4. *Daily Mail* (London), July 5, 1918.
5. *Daily Chronicle* (London), July 5, 1918.
6. *Sydney Morning Herald*, September 21, 1918.
7. *Times* (London), July 5, 1918.
8. *Emporia Gazette*, July 29, 1918.
9. *Daily Mail* (London), July 5, 1918.
10. *Sydney Morning Herald*, September 21, 1918.
11. *New York Sun*, July 5, 1918.
12. *New York Herald*, July 3, 1918.
13. *Sydney Morning Herald*, September 21, 1918.
14. *New York Sun*, July 5, 1918.
15. *Chester News*, December 11, 1918.
16. *London Evening News*, July 4, 1918.
17. Alice Ziska Snyder and Milton Valentine Snyder, *Paris Days and London Nights* (New York: E.P. Dutton, 1921), p. 224.
18. *Morning Post* (London), July 5, 1918.
19. *Times* (London), July 5, 1918.
20. *Daily Mail*, July 5, 1918.
21. *New York Sun*, July 5, 1918.
22. Ibid.
23. Ibid.
24. *Emporia Gazette*, July 29, 1918.
25. Ibid.
26. George Earle Raiguel, "The Fourth of July That Rang Round the World: The Greatest Baseball Game Ever Played," *Ladies' Home Journal*, July 1919.
27. *New York Times*, July 5, 1918.
28. *New York World*, October 25, 1918.

Chapter 1

1. W. Heath Robinson, "Making the German Officers' Mess a Success," *The New York Times Current History: The European War* (New York: New York Times Company, 1915), vol. 2, p. 1,082.
2. Brander Matthews, "Chronicle and Comment," *The Bookman*, November 1916, p. 227.
3. *Washington Times*, March 18, 1914.
4. Viscount Grey of Fallodon, *Twenty-Five Years 1892–1916* (New York: Stokes, 1925), p. 20.
5. *Lethbridge Herald*, March 12, 1915.
6. *Windsor Record*, June 26, 1915.
7. *Bath Chronicle*, October 21, 1916.
8. *Lethbridge Herald*, May 22, 1915.
9. *Youngstown Vindicator*, August 29, 1915.
10. *London Standard*, May 31, 1915.
11. *Lloyd's Weekly News*, June 6, 1915.
12. *London Standard*, June 14, 1915.

13. *Milwaukee Journal*, August 19, 1917.

14. *Lloyd's Weekly News*, September 12, 1915.

15. *London Standard*, September 13, 1915.

16. Andrew Horrall, "'Keep-a-fighting! Play the game!': Baseball and the Canadian forces in the First World War," *Canadian Military History*, Spring 2001, p. 32.

17. *New York Times*, June 19, 1916.

18. *Freeman*, Indianapolis, September 19, 1914.

19. Ibid.

20. *Hull Daily Mail*, July 8, 1916.

21. *New York Times*, July 11, 1916.

22. *Washington Post*, July 23, 1916.

23. *Lloyd's Weekly News*, September 17, 1916.

24. *Lloyd's Weekly News*, September 24, 1916.

25. *Boston Globe*, September 28, 1916.

26. *Fort Wayne News*, October 21, 1916.

27. Ibid.

28. *Weekly Dispatch* (London), reprinted in the *Fort Wayne News*, October 21, 1916. The writer used the pen name "Ty Cobb."

29. *Des Moines News*, October 27, 1916.

30. *Lloyd's Weekly News*, October 1, 1916.

31. *Lloyd's Weekly News*, October 8, 1916.

32. J. G. Lee, "A Big Game in London: How Baseball Enthusiasm Grows in the Metropolis of the British Empire," *Baseball Magazine*, October 1917, p. 563.

33. *Hartford Courant*, October 8, 1917.

34. *Times* (London), July 3, 1917

35. *Morning Post* (London), reprinted in the *Schenectady Gazette*, July 14, 1917.

36. *London Evening News*, July 27, 1917.

37. *Milwaukee Journal*, August 19, 1917.

38. *Times* (London), July 30, 1917.

39. Lee, "Big Game," p. 562.

40. Ibid., p. 564.

41. *Times* (London), September 10, 1917.

42. *Daily Missourian* (Columbia), September 21, 1917.

43. Ibid.

44. *Canadian Gazette* (London), November 1, 1917, reprinted in the *Regina Leader*, December 1, 1917.

45. Lee, "Big Game," p. 562.

46. *Ogden Standard*, January 14, 1918.

Chapter 2

1. L. M. Sutter, *Arlie Latham: A Baseball Biography of the Freshest Man on Earth* (Jefferson, NC: McFarland, 2012), p. 10.

2. *Pensacola Journal*, July 23, 1909.

3. *New York World*, December 15, 1888.

4. *New York Times*, December 3, 1952.

5. Sutter, *Arlie Latham*, p. 103.

6. *Pittsburgh Press*, August 1, 1915.

7. Sutter, *Arlie Latham*, p. 103

8. *New York Sun*, January 7, 1941.

9. Sutter, *Arlie Latham*, p. 63.

10. *New York World*, February 13, 1909.

11. *Sporting Life*, June 2, 1894.

12. *New York World*, February 13, 1909.

13. *Spokane Press*, March 2, 1909.

14. *Brooklyn Eagle*, February 21, 1909.

15. Ibid.

16. *New York Tribune*, August 19, 1909.

17. *New York Telegram*, April 20, 1915.

18. Passport application, December 30, 1916. Available at Ancestry.com.

19. Application for Registration—Native Citizen, April 4, 1918. Available at Ancestry.com.

20. Sutter, *Arlie Latham*, p. 220.

21. *Times* (London), July 30, 1917.

22. *Pittsburgh Press*, July 16, 1917.

23. *Fort Wayne News*, August 18, 1917.

24. *Albany Journal*, November 4, 1918.

Chapter 3

1. *Sacramento Record-Union*, October 11, 1889.

2. *New York Sun*, August 5, 1917.

3. Sutter, *Arlie Latham*, p. 214.

4. *Racine Journal*, March 26, 1894.

5. Alfred Henry Spink, *The National Game* (St. Louis: The National Game, 1911), p. 400.

6. *Times* (London), February 27, 1914.

7. *Derby Daily Telegraph*, June 16, 1917.

8. *New York Sun*, February 19, 1918.

9. *Atlanta Constitution*, Oct. 13, 1918.

10. *Sporting Life*, reprinted in *Ogdensburg Republican-Journal*, March 28, 1918.

11. *New York Sun*, February 19, 1918.

12. Ibid.

13. Passport applications, August 22, 1916, and June 29, 1917. W. A. Parsons attested to Booker's identity on the latter application. Available on Ancestry.com.

14. *Boston Globe*, October 18, 1918.
15. Passport applications, September 23, 1913, and December 3, 1919. Available at Ancestry.com.
16. *Boston Globe*, October 17, 1918.
17. *New York Sun*, February 19, 1918.
18. *New York Sun*, January 7, 1941.
19. *Hull Daily Mail*, March 20, 1918.
20. *Stars and Stripes*, March 22, 1918.
21. Ibid.
22. David F. Trask, "William Sowden Sims: The Victory Ashore," *Admirals of the New Steel Navy* (Annapolis: U.S. Naval Institute Press, 1990), p. 282.
23. Edmund Vance Cooke, Today's Poem, *Tacoma Times*, April 29, 1918.
24. *Oakland Tribune*, June 16, 1918.
25. *Sporting Life* (London), reprinted in the *Philadelphia Public Ledger*, April 12, 1918.
26. *Nottingham Evening Post*, April 25, 1918.
27. Horrall, "'Keep-a-fighting!,'" p. 36.
28. *Times* (London), August 30, 1918.
29. *Atlanta Constitution*, October 13, 1918.
30. Unknown publication and date (perhaps *Saturday Evening Post*), in "Newspaper Cuttings: Scrapbook [1918–1924]: Baseball in England," MFF 366, National Baseball Hall of Fame Library.
31. *Newport Journal and Weekly News*, July 12, 1918.
32. *Hull Daily Mail*, May 15, 1918.
33. Ibid.

Chapter 4

1. *New York Sun*, July 21, 1918.
2. *Nottingham Evening Post*, July 12, 1918.
3. *Liverpool Echo*, June 15, 1918.
4. *Nottingham Evening Post*, July 16, 1918.
5. *Stars and Stripes*, May 10, 1918.
6. Ibid.
7. *Lloyd's Weekly News*, May 12, 1918.
8. *Massillon Independent*, June 18, 1918.
9. *Lloyd's Weekly News*, May 12, 1918.
10. *Stars and Stripes*, May 17, 1918.
11. *Brooklyn Standard Union*, May 18, 1918.
12. *Oakland Tribune*, November 26, 1911.
13. *San Jose News*, November 11, 1911.

14. Ibid.
15. *Roman Holiday*. Dir. William Wyler. Paramount Pictures, 1953.
16. *Brooklyn Standard Union*, May 18, 1918.
17. *New York Tribune*, May 20, 1918.
18. *Lloyd's Weekly News*, May 19, 1918.
19. *Fort Wayne News and Sentinel*, May 18, 1918.
20. *Stars and Stripes*, May 24, 1918.
21. *Geneva Times*, May 20, 1918.
22. *Waterloo Courier*, June 6, 1918.
23. *Star* (London), May 27, 1918.
24. Ibid.
25. *New York Sun*, May 20, 1918.
26. Ibid.
27. *London Evening News*, May 29, 1918.
28. "Hitting a Sky to the Bleachers," unknown newspaper and date, in "Newspaper Cuttings," National Baseball Hall of Fame Library.
29. Ibid.
30. *Christian Science Monitor*, June 25, 1918.

Chapter 5

1. *Philadelphia Inquirer*, no date. Quoted in Norman Macht, "Jack Barry," SABR Baseball Biography Project, www.sabr.org/bioproject. Accessed July 20, 2013.
2. *Boston Globe*, July 29, 1917.
3. *Washington Times*, July 29, 1917.
4. *Utica Herald-Dispatch*, August 7, 1918.
5. *Sporting News*, December 20, 1917.
6. Ibid.
7. Frazee letter of January 23, 1918, "Correspondence Concerning Red Sox Players at the Boston Navy Yard, 12/1917—02/1918," National Archives.
8. Telephone Message (Synopsis), February 9, 1918, "Correspondence Concerning Red Sox Players," National Archives.
9. Undated letter, Central Files, "Correspondence Concerning Red Sox Players."
10. *Boston Globe*, January 23, 1918.
11. Endorsement, Commandant to Chief of Staff, January 19, 1918. "Correspondence Concerning Red Sox Players."
12. *Boston Globe*, May 6, 1918.
13. *Boston Globe*, April 23, 1918.
14. *Boston Globe*, April 24, 1918.
15. *Portsmouth Herald*, April 30, 1918.

16. *New York World*, May 6, 1918.

17. *New York Sun*, May 6, 1918.

18. *Boston Globe*, May 17, 1918.

19. *Boston Globe*, May 10, 1918.

20. *Navy Salvo* (Boston), July 15, 1918.

21. *Fitchburg Sentinel*, June 12, 1918.

22. *Utica Herald-Dispatch*, August 7, 1918.

23. *Boston Globe*, August 11, 1918.

24. *Our Navy*, September 1918.

Chapter 6

1. *Stillwell Standard-Sentinel*, March 28, 1918.

2. "Big German Battleplane Splendidly Designed," *Popular Mechanics*, October 1917, p. 513.

3. *Wings*. Paramount Studios, 1927.

4. *Poverty Bay Herald* (Gisborne), March 11, 1918.

5. *New York Times*, May 12, 1918.

6. *New York Times*, March 14, 1918.

7. *Poverty Bay Herald*, June 1, 1918.

8. Edgar S. Gorrell, *Gorrell's History of the American Expeditionary Forces Air Service: 1917–1919* (Washington, D.C.: National Archives, 1974), vol. 24, p. 133.

9. *Gorrell's History*, vol. 22, p. 156.

10. *London Evening News*, May 24, 1918.

11. *Waterloo Times-Tribune*, May 5, 1918.

12. Ibid.

13. *New York Times*, February 26, 1918.

14. *Hartford Courant*, March 18, 1918.

15. *Stars and Stripes*, April 26, 1918.

16. *New York Times*, August 29, 1918.

17. *Rochester Democrat and Chronicle*, June 16, 1918.

Chapter 7

1. *Stars and Stripes*, April 12, 1918.

2. *New York Times*, April 25, 1918.

3. *Stars and Stripes*, May 10, 1918.

4. *Sporting News*, July 4, 1918.

5. *Brooklyn Eagle*, August 24, 1918.

6. *Sporting News*, August 29, 1918.

7. *Stars and Stripes*, June 7, 1918.

8. Ibid.

9. *Sporting News*, August 29, 1918.

10. *Stars and Stripes*, June 21, 1918.

11. *New York Herald*, March 16, 1914.

12. Heywood Broun, *The A. E. F.: With General Pershing and the American Forces* (New York: D. Appleton, 1918), p. 55.

13. *Washington Post*, February 20, 1919.

14. *New York Herald*, November 10, 1918.

15. *Stars and Stripes*, March 8, 1918.

16. *Auburn Citizen*, May 1, 1918.

17. *New York Times*, March 11, 1918.

18. *Syracuse Journal*, June 6, 1918.

19. *New York Telegram*, August 21, 1918.

20. *Utica Herald-Dispatch*, September 16, 1918.

21. *Logansport Pharos-Reporter*, February 4, 1919.

22. *New York Times*, February 18, 1919.

23. *Albany Journal*, December 17, 1918.

24. *Sporting News*, December 26, 1918.

25. *San Antonio Light*, December 30, 1918.

Chapter 8

1. Ian Hay Beith, "As Others See Us," *The Landmark: The Monthly Magazine of the English-Speaking Union* 18, 1936, p. 201.

2. Ian Hay (Beith), "A Memorable Fourth of July," *Landmark* 16, 1934, p. 628.

3. Mims, "Take Me Out to the Ball Game," p. 103.

4. Ibid.

5. Ibid.

6. Ibid.

7. *Daily Mail* (London), June 12, 2013, quoting *Whitehall Evening Post*, September 19, 1749.

8. Elting E. Morison, *Admiral Sims and the Modern American Navy* (New York: Russell & Russell, 1968), p. 425.

9. Letter, Newspaper Cuttings: Scrapbook [1918–1924]: Baseball in England, National Baseball Hall of Fame Library, MFF 366.

10. *Times* (London), June 8, 1918.

11. *Daily Mail* (London), no date, 1918, Newspaper Cuttings file, National Baseball Hall of Fame.

12. *Gloversville and Johnstown Herald*, June 14, 1918.

13. *Utica Herald-Dispatch*, July 27, 1918.

14. *New York Times*, June 27, 1918.

15. *Plattsburgh Republican*, May 4, 1918.

16. Fullerton L. Waldo, *America at the Front* (New York: E. P. Dutton, 1918), p. 23.

17. *New York Times*, June 27, 1918.

18. *Duluth Herald,* July 5, 1918.

19. *New York Tribune,* June 27, 1918.

20. *Edgefield Advertiser,* September 11, 1918.

21. *New York Times,* June 28, 1918.

22. *Binghamton Press,* June 26, 1918.

23. *Schenectady Gazette,* July 16, 1918.

24. *Poverty Bay Herald* (Gisborne), September 6, 1918.

25. *New York Tribune,* June 27, 1918.

26. Mims, "Take Me Out to the Ball Game," p. 104.

27. *San Antonio Light,* July 7, 1918.

Chapter 9

1. John S. Farmer and W. W. Henley, *A Dictionary of Slang and Colloquial English* (London: G. Routledge and Sons, 1905), p. 316.

2. *St. Louis Star,* February 13, 1930.

3. "'Tis a little bit of heaven ...," *The Searcher: Newsletter of the Genealogical Research Society of Northeastern Pennsylvania,* Summer 2008, p. 7.

4. Hughie Jennings' National Baseball Hall of Fame plaque.

5. *Syracuse Post-Standard,* December 31, 1914.

6. *Utica Press,* August 8, 1913.

7. *Sporting Life,* May 9, 1914.

8. *Pittsburgh Press,* September 7, 1914.

9. *Sporting News,* April 8, 1915.

10. *Sporting Life,* May 15, 1915; *New York Times,* May 7, 1915.

11. *Scranton Tribune,* May 31, 1965.

12. *San Jose News,* December 18, 1924.

13. *Boston Globe,* June 2, 1916.

14. *Boston Globe,* October 1, 1916.

15. *Boston Globe,* October 10, 1916.

16. Babe Ruth and Bob Considine, *The Babe Ruth Story* (New York: Scholastic Book Service, 1963), p. 38.

17. *Elmira Telegram,* October 22, 1916.

18. *Washington Post,* October 4, 1909.

19. *Washington Herald,* August 8, 1910.

20. *Washington Herald,* August 6, 1911.

21. *Commerce Reports,* vol. 2 (Washington, D.C., 1918), p. 724.

22. *Hutchinson News,* June 21, 1918.

Chapter 10

1. *Stars and Stripes,* March 8, 1918.

2. *Stars and Stripes,* April 12, 1918.

3. *Stars and Stripes,* May 31, 1918.

4. *Stars and Stripes,* June 7, 1918.

5. John J. Pershing, *My Experiences in the World War* (New York: Frederick A. Stokes, 1931), vol. 2, p. 82.

6. *Waterloo Times-Tribune,* August 20, 1909.

7. *Sporting Life,* November 5, 1910.

8. *Ogden Standard,* September 7, 1918.

9. *Des Moines News,* March 20, 1914.

10. *Ogden Standard,* September 7, 1918.

11. *Sporting Life,* June 5, 1915.

12. *Ogden Standard,* November 10, 1918.

13. *Ogden Standard,* August 10, 1918.

14. *Recruiters' Bulletin,* April 1919, p. 15.

15. *Ogden Standard,* September 7, 1918.

16. Ibid.

17. Harry R. Stringer, ed., *Heroes All!* (Washington, D.C.: Fassett, 1919), p. 278.

18. *Sporting News,* August 29, 1918.

19. *Sporting News,* June 27, 1918.

20. Ibid.

21. *Sporting News,* December 12, 1918.

22. *New York Times,* May 24, 1918.

23. *Washington Times,* May 23, 1918.

24. *New York Sun,* May 24, 1918.

25. *New York Tribune,* May 15, 1918.

26. *The Sporting News,* October 3, 1918.

27. *New Castle News,* February 6, 1919.

28. *New York Times,* May 24, 1918.

29. *Pittsburgh Press,* July 1, 1918.

Chapter 11

1. *Kennett News & Advertiser,* August 8, 1921.

2. *West Chester Daily Local News,* June 29, 1924.

3. Ibid.

4. *Kennett News & Advertiser,* March 7, 1947.

5. Ibid.

6. Joseph Kastner, *A World of Watchers* (San Francisco: Sierra Club Books, 1988), p. 91.

7. *Philadelphia Inquirer,* January 2, 1920.

8. *Washington Times,* July 4, 1914.

9. *Philadelphia Public Ledger,* April 15, 1915.

10. *West Chester Daily Local News,* May 31, 1915.

11. *Kennett News & Advertiser,* May 21, 1948.

12. *Kennett News & Advertiser,* May 7, 1948.

13. *The Field* (London), reprinted in the *New York Times*, August 8, 1918.

14. *New York Tribune*, March 3, 1918.

15. *New York Times*, March 16, 1932.

16. *St. Louis Star*, February 13, 1930.

17. *Atlanta Constitution*, March 9, 1934.

18. *Atlanta Constitution*, May 13, 1906.

19. *Atlanta Constitution*, March 21, 1908.

20. *Atlanta Constitution*, March 9, 1934.

21. *Atlanta Constitution*, November 4, 1908.

22. *Atlanta Georgian and News*, April 23, 1909.

23. *Sporting Life*, July 24, 1909.

24. *Atlanta Georgian and News*, October 1, 1909.

25. Ibid.

26. *Sporting Life*, June 3, 1911.

27. *Atlanta Constitution*, March 29, 1936.

28. *Milwaukee Journal*, April 26, 1912.

29. *New York Tribune*, May 1, 1914.

30. *New York Tribune*, September 20, 1914.

31. *Brooklyn Eagle*, August 29, 1915.

32. *Atlanta Constitution*, March 29, 1936.

33. Ibid.

34. *Sporting Life*, September 23, 1916.

35. *Brooklyn Eagle*, April 10, 1918.

36. Philadelphia War History Committee, *Philadelphia in the World War: 1914–1919* (New York: Wynkoop Hallenbeck Crawford, 1922), p. 775.

37. Ibid.

38. *Hutchinson News*, June 21, 1918.

Chapter 12

1. *Oregonian* (Portland), September 26, 1915.

2. *Seattle Star*, May 11, 1916.

3. *Salt Lake Tribune*, June 24, 1916.

4. *Oregonian*, January 20, 1918.

5. *Oregonian*, March 13, 1918.

6. *Oregonian*, April 28, 1918.

7. *Oregonian*, June 2, 1918.

8. Unidentified newspaper, no date. Collection of Edward Bartholemy.

9. Blair Fuller, "The Poison of Non-Fulfillment," *ZYZZYVA* 50.

10. *Harvard Alumni Bulletin*, May 30, 1918, pp. 671–672

11. Ibid.

12. *New York Times*, April 8, 1917.

13. *Variety*, August 17, 1917.

14. *Hearings Before the Subcommittee of the Committee on Naval Affairs, United States Senate, Sixty-sixth Congress, Second Session* (Washington, D.C., 1921), vol. 1, p. 239.

15. Fuller, "Poison."

16. *Washington Herald*, March 24, 1913.

17. *Washington Herald*, March 13, 1913.

18. *Day* (New London), June 16, 1917.

19. *Toledo News-Bee*, March 21, 1917.

20. *Toledo News-Bee*, July 3, 1918.

21. *Waterloo Courier*, May 16, 1918.

22. *Lloyd's Sunday News*, June 2, 1918.

Chapter 13

1. *Times* (London), July 3, 1918.

2. "Anglo-American League: United States Navy versus United States Army" (London, 1918), pp. 1, 6.

3. *London Evening News*, June 12, 1918.

4. *Boston Globe*, July 8, 1918.

5. *New York Tribune*, July 26, 1918.

6. *Sydney Evening News*, September 28, 1918.

7. *Mercury* (Hobart), October 5, 1918.

8. Ibid.

9. *London Evening News*, July 3, 1918.

10. Raiguel, "Fourth of July," p. 118.

11. *Missourian* (Columbia), July 1, 1918.

12. *New York Tribune*, July 4, 1918.

13. *Times* (London), July 4, 1918.

14. "King Sees Ed Lafitte," p. 70.

15. *Morning Post* (London), July 5, 1918.

16. *New York Times*, July 5, 1918.

17. Raiguel, "Fourth of July," p. 118.

18. Snyder and Snyder, *Paris Days and London Nights*, p. 225.

19. *Brisbane Queenslander*, September 21, 1918.

20. "The Western Front," *Western Electric News*, January 1919, p. 8.

21. *Daily Chronicle* (London), July 5, 1918.

22. *Washington Times*, July 5, 1918.

23. Henry B. Beston, *Full Speed Ahead: Tales from the Log of a Correspondent with Our Navy* (New York: Doubleday, Page, 1919), p. 202.

24. Raiguel, "Fourth of July," 118.

25. *Daily Chronicle* (London), July 5, 1918.

26. Ibid.

27. *New York Times*, July 5, 1918.

28. Snyder and Snyder, *Paris Days and London Nights*, p. 227.

29. Raiguel, "Fourth of July," 118.

30. *Fayetteville Democrat*, July 11, 1918.

31. Beston, *Full Speed Ahead*, p. 202.

32. *Washington Times*, August 9, 1918.

33. *Daily Chronicle* (London), July 5, 1918.

34. Raiguel, "Fourth of July," p. 118.

35. *Daily Chronicle* (London), July 5, 1918.

36. *Weekly Dispatch* (London), July 7, 1918.

37. *New York Times*, July 5, 1918.

38. *Auburn Citizen*, August 2, 1918.

39. *Cleveland Press*, unknown date, Mike McNally player file, National Baseball Hall of Fame Library.

40. Burton Holmes' Film-Reels of Travel, *Seeing London: Part Four, Windsor Castle and Royal Close-ups*, Prelinger Archives.

41. "King Sees Ed Lafitte, Gamma Alpha, Lose Game," *The Delta of The Sigma Nu Fraternity*, October 1918, p. 70.

42. *Boston Globe*, July 6, 1918.

43. *New York Telegram*, July 6, 1918.

44. *Argonaut*, quoted in *The Congregationalist and Advance*, December 19, 1918, p. 723.

45. "King Sees Ed Lafitte," p. 70.

46. *Seeing London*.

47. G. W. Axelson, *"Commy": The Life Story of Charles A. Comiskey* (Chicago: Reilly and Lee, 1919), p. 296.

48. *Washington Examiner*, June 16, 2008.

49. *Field* (London), quoted in *New York Times*, August 8, 1918.

50. *Morning Post* (London), July 5, 1918.

51. *New York Tribune*, July 5, 1918.

52. *New York Times*, July 5, 1918.

53. *Emporia Gazette*, July 29, 1918.

54. *New York Telegram*, July 4, 1918.

55. *Auburn Citizen*, August 29, 1918.

56. *Wilkes-Barre Sunday Independent*, December 29, 1918.

57. *Times* (London), July 5, 1918.

58. *New York Post*, July 26, 1918; incorrectly attributed to *Times* (London).

Chapter 14

1. *Johnson City Record*, August 3, 1918.

2. *New York Post*, July 26, 1918.

3. *Daily Mail* (London), July 5, 1918.

4. Raiguel, "Fourth of July," 119.

5. *Morning Post* (London), July 5, 1918.

6. Ibid.

7. Henry Seidel Canby, "The Fourth of July," *Youth's Companion*, June 1922, p. 309.

8. *Rochester Democrat and Chronicle*, February 27, 1914.

9. Raiguel, "Fourth of July," p. 118.

10. *Morning Post* (London), July 5, 1918.

11. Ibid.

12. *Daily Mail* (London), July 5, 1918.

13. *Morning Post* (London), July 5, 1918.

14. Mims, "Take Me Out to the Ball Game," p. 26.

15. *Times* (London), July 5, 1918.

16. *New York Post*, July 26, 1918, incorrectly attributed to *Times* (London).

17. Joseph Fort Newton, *Preaching in London: A Diary of Anglo-American Friendship* (New York: Harper & Brothers, 1922), p. 99.

18. *Times* (London), July 5, 1918.

19. *Mercury* (Hobart), October 5, 1918.

20. *New York Herald*, July 28, 1918.

21. *Times* (London), July 5, 1918.

22. *Daily Chronicle* (London), July 5, 1918.

23. Waldo, *America at the Front*, pp. 116–117.

24. Sir John W. Wheeler-Bennett, *King George VI: His Life and Reign* (London: Macmillan, 1958), p. 114.

25. *Washington Times*, July 3, 1918.

26. *Times* (London), July 4, 1918.

27. *Tombstone Epitaph*, August 18, 1918.

28. *Providence News*, December 27, 1918.

29. Waldo, *America at the Front*, pp. 115–116.

30. *Gettysburg Star and Sentinel*, March 23, 1916.

31. *Washington Times*, June 16, 1919.

32. *Morning Post* (London), July 5, 1918.

Chapter 15

1. Raiguel, "Fourth of July," p. 118.

2. *Morning Post* (London), July 5, 1918.

3. Raiguel, "Fourth of July," p. 119.

4. Ibid.

5. *New York Times*, July 5, 1918.

6. Raiguel, "Fourth of July," 118.

7. Snyder and Snyder, *Paris Days and London Nights*, p. 226.

8. Raiguel, "Fourth of July," p. 119.
9. Ibid.
10. *Morning Post* (London), July 5, 1918.
11. Ibid.
12. Ibid.
13. *Boston Globe*, July 6, 1918.
14. *The Delta of Sigma Nu Fraternity*, October 1918, p. 70.
15. *London Evening News*, July 8, 1918.
16. Raiguel, "Fourth of July," p. 118.
17. *Morning Post* (London), July 5, 1918.
18. Raiguel, "Fourth of July," p. 118.
19. Ibid.
20. *Sporting News*, July 25, 1918.
21. *Daily Mail* (London), July 5, 1918.
22. *Morning Post* (London), July 5, 1918.
23. *Times* (London), July 5, 1918.
24. Waldo, *America at the Front*, p. 116.

Chapter 16

1. *Times* (London), July 5, 1918.
2. *Morning Post* (London), July 5, 1918.
3. Raiguel, "Fourth of July," p. 119.
4. *Morning Post* (London), July 5, 1918.
5. Raiguel, "Fourth of July," p. 119.
6. *Sydney Evening News*, September 28, 1918.
7. *Daily Mail* (London), July 5, 1918.
8. *The Field* (London), July 18, 1918, reprinted in *Sydney Referee*, October 23, 1918.
9. *New York Tribune*, July 26, 1918, quoting *London Morning Post*.
10. *Daily Mail* (London), July 5, 1918.
11. Ibid.
12. *Times* (London), July 5, 1918.
13. *Boston Globe*, July 20, 1918.
14. *Sydney Evening News*, September 28, 1918.
15. *Daily Mail* (London), July 5, 1918.
16. Raiguel, "Fourth of July," p. 119.
17. *Daily Mail* (London), July 5, 1918.
18. Ibid.
19. *Daily Telegraph* (London), reprinted in *New York Herald*, July 28, 1918.
20. *Auburn Citizen*, August 29, 1918.
21. Raiguel, "Fourth of July," p. 119.
22. *Times* (London), July 5, 1918.
23. *Sioux City Journal*, reprinted in *Estherville Enterprise*, August 28, 1918.
24. Raiguel, "Fourth of July," p. 119.
25. *The Times* (London), July 5, 1918.
26. *Atlanta Constitution*, March 29, 1919
27. *Boston Globe*, July 20, 1918.

28. *Kansas City Times*, July 6, 1918.
29. Wheeler-Bennett, *King George VI*, p. 114.

Chapter 17

1. *Sydney Morning Herald*, September 21, 1918.
2. *Morning Post* (London), July 5, 1918
3. *Times* (London), July 5, 1918.
4. *Times* (London), September 4, 1918.
5. *La Crosse Tribune and Leader-Press*, August 3, 1918.
6. *Daily Sketch* (London), reprinted in *New York Post*, August 7, 1918.
7. *Times* (London), August 6, 1918.
8. *London Evening News*, July 5, 1918.
9. *Chicago Tribune*, December 22, 1918.
10. *London Evening News*, July 4, 1918.
11. Pershing, *My Experiences*, vol. 2, pp. 154–155.
12. *Atlanta Constitution*, March 29, 1919.
13. *New York Times*, March 16, 1932.
14. *Oregonian* (Portland), October 20, 1918.
15. *Union News-Dispatch*, May 29, 1919.
16. *New York Sun*, January 19, 1919.
17. *Oakland Tribune*, February 4, 1919.
18. Letter signed "Chubbie," April 9, 1919. Collection of Ed Bartholemy.
19. *Anglo-American Year Book and International Directory* (London, 1920), p. 35.
20. *Atlanta Constitution*, August 18, 1919.
21. *New York Sun*, January 4, 1920.
22. *Washington Herald*, June 27, 1920.
23. *Hudson Valley Times* (Mechanicsville, NY), December 7, 1921.
24. *Logansport Pharos-Tribune*, September 8, 1922.
25. *Washington Times*, April 23, 1921.
26. *New York Times*, December 3, 1952.
27. Sutter, *Arlie Latham*, p. 242.
28. *Kennett News & Advocate*, February 6, 1948.
29. Harold Parrott, *The Lords of Baseball* (New York: Praeger, 1976), p. 192.
30. William C. Kashatus, *September Swoon: Richie Allen, the '64 Phillies, and Racial Integration* (University Park: Penn State University Press, 2004), p. 28.
31. *Brooklyn Eagle*, April 1, 1919.

32. *Scranton Tribune*, May 31, 1965.

33. *Scranton Chronicle*, May 31, 1965.

34. *ZYZZYVA* 4, 12.

35. Blair Fuller, e-mail to author, February 22, 2011.

36. *Oregonian* (Portland), September 22, 1919.

37. Jeffrey E. Geiger, *German Prisoners of War at Camp Cooke, California: Personal Accounts of 14 Soldiers, 1944–1946* (Jefferson, NC: McFarland, 1996), p. 95.

38. *Schenectady Gazette*, June 15, 1928.

39. *Brooklyn Eagle*, December 8, 1918.

40. Ibid.

41. *Pittsburgh Press*, January 6, 1919.

42. *Waterloo Courier and Reporter*, May 27, 1919.

43. *Waterloo Times-Tribune*, July 9, 1918.

44. Josh Chetwynd, *Baseball in Europe: A Country by Country History* (Jefferson, NC: McFarland, 2008), p. 93.

45. *The Mercury* (Hobart), October 5, 1918.

Bibliography

Books and Articles

Anonymous and Institutional Publications

"Anglo-American League: United States Navy versus United States Army; In the Presence of Their Majesties The King and Queen and Her Majesty Queen Alexandra." London, 1918.

Anglo-American Year Book and International Directory. London, 1920.

"Big German Battleplane Splendidly Designed." *Popular Mechanics,* October 1917.

Commerce Reports. Washington, D.C., 1918.

Correspondence Concerning Red Sox Players at the Boston Navy Yard, 12/1917 —02/1918." Record Group 181, National Archives, Waltham, Massachusetts. Available at www.archives.gov.

Dictionary of American Naval Fighting Ship, 8 vols. Washington, 1959–1981.

Hearings Before the Subcommittee of the Committee on Naval Affairs, United States Senate, Sixty-sixth Congress, Second Session. Washington, D.C., 1921.

"King Sees Ed Lafitte, Gamma Alpha, Lose Game." *The Delta of The Sigma Nu Fraternity,* October 1918.

Souvenir of Anglo-American Baseball League (Season 1918), With Photos of Teams. London, 1918.

"'Tis a little bit of heaven ...," *The Searcher: Newsletter of the Genealogical Research Society of Northeastern Pennsylvania,* Summer 2008.

Works by Named Authors

Axelson, G. W. *"Commy": The Life Story of Charles A. Comiskey.* Chicago: Reilly and Lee, 1919.

Beith, Ian Hay. "As Others See Us." *The Landmark: The Monthly Magazine of the English-Speaking Union* 18 (1936).

_____. "A Memorable Fourth of July." *The Landmark: The Monthly Magazine of the English-Speaking Union* 16 (1934).

Berger, Ralph. "Arlie Latham." SABR Baseball Biography Project. www.sabr.org/bioproject.

Beston, Henry B. *Full Speed Ahead: Tales from the Log of a Correspondent with Our Navy.* New York: Doubleday, Page, 1919.

Bradford, James, ed. *Admirals of the New Steel Navy: Makers of the American Naval Tradition, 1880–1930.* Annapolis: U.S. Naval Institute Press, 1990.

Brooke, Rupert. "The Soldier." *1914 & Other Poems.* London: Sidgwick & Jackson, 1915.

Broun, Heywood. *The A. E. F.: With General Pershing and the American Forces.* New York: D. Appleton, 1918.

Canby, Henry Seidel. "The Fourth of July." *Youth's Companion* 96 (June 1922).

Cheseldine, R. M. *Ohio in the Rainbow: Official Story of the 166th Infantry, 42nd Division in the World War*. Columbus: F.J. Heer Printing, 1924.

Chetwynd, Josh. *Baseball in Europe: A Country by Country History*. Jefferson, NC: McFarland, 2008.

Farmer, John S., and W. W. Henley. *A Dictionary of Slang and Colloquial English*, London: G. Routledge & Sons, 1905.

Foster, John B., ed. *Spalding's Official Base Ball Guide*. New York: American Sports Publishing, 1919.

Fuller, Blair. "The Poison of Non-Fulfillment." *ZYZZYVA, The Last Word: West Coast Writers & Artists* 50. Available at www.zyzzyva.org. Accessed December 25, 2009.

Geiger, Jeffrey E. *German Prisoners of War at Camp Cooke, California: Personal Accounts of 14 Soldiers, 1944–1946*. Jefferson, NC: McFarland, 1996.

Gorrell, Edgar S., ed. *Gorrell's History of the American Expeditionary Forces Air Service: 1917–1919*. Washington, D.C.: National Archives, 1974 (microfilm).

Grey, Viscount of Fallodon. *Twenty-Five Years: 1892–1916*. New York: Stokes, 1925.

Hendrick, Burton J. *The Life and Letters of Walter H. Page*. Garden City, NY: Doubleday, Page, 1923.

Horrall, Andrew. "'Keep-a-Fighting! Play the Game!' Baseball and the Canadian Forces in the First World War." *Canadian Military History* 10, no. 2 (Spring 2001): 27–40.

Jones, Jerry W. *U.S. Battleship Operations in World War I*. Annapolis: U.S. Naval Institute Press, 1998.

Kashatus, William C. *September Swoon: Richie Allen, the '64 Phillies, and Racial Integration*. University Park: Penn State University Press, 2004.

Kastner, Joseph. *A World of Watchers*. San Francisco: Sierra Club Books, 1988.

Lee, J. G. "A Big Game in London: How Baseball Enthusiasm Grows in the Metropolis of the British Empire." *Baseball Magazine* 19, no. 6 (October 1917): 562–564.

Leeke, Jim. "The Delaware River Shipbuilding League, 1918." *The National Pastime: From Swampoodle to South Philly; Baseball in Philadelphia & the Delaware Valley* (July 2013): 58–63.

_____. "Royal Match: The Army-Navy Service Game, July 4, 1918." *NINE: A Journal of Baseball History & Culture* 20, no. 2 (Spring 2012): 15–26.

Matthews, Brander. "Chronicle and Comment." *The Bookman* 44 (November 1916): 223.

Mims, Floyd C. "Take Me Out to the Ball Game." *U.S. Naval Institute Proceedings* (February 1982).

Morison, Elting E. *Admiral Sims and the Modern American Navy*. New York: Russell & Russell, 1968.

Newton, Joseph Fort. *Preaching in London: A Diary of Anglo-American Friendship*. New York: Harper & Brothers, 1922.

Parrott, Harold. *The Lords of Baseball*. New York: Preager, 1976.

Philadelphia War History Committee. *Philadelphia in the World War, 1914–1919*. New York: Wynkoop Hallenbeck Crawford, 1922

Pershing, John J. *My Experiences in the World War*. New York: Frederick A. Stokes, 1931.

Raiguel, George Earle. "The Fourth of July That Rang Round the World: The Greatest Baseball Game Ever Played." *The Ladies' Home Journal* 36 (July 1919): 118–119.

Robinson, Jackie, and Alfred Duckett. *I Never Had It Made: An Autobiography of Jackie Robinson*. New York: HarperCollins, 2003. First published 1972 by G.P. Putnam's Sons.

Robinson, W. Heath. "Making the German Officers' Mess a Success." *The New York Times Current History: The European War*, Vol. 2. New York: New York Times Company, 1915.

Ruth, Babe, as told to Bob Considine. *The Babe Ruth Story*. New York: Scholastic Book Service, 1963. First published 1948 by E.P. Dutton.

Snyder, Alice Ziska, and Milton Valentine Snyder. *Paris Days and London Nights*. New York: E.P. Dutton, 1921.

Spink, Alfred H. *The National Game*, 2d ed. St. Louis: The National Game, 1911.

Stringer, Harry R., ed. *Heroes All! A Compendium of the Names and Official Citations of the Soldiers and Citizens of the United States and Her Allies Who*

Were Decorated by the American Government for Exceptional Heroism and Conspicuous Service Above and Beyond the Call of Duty in the War with Germany, 1917–1919. Washington, D.C.: Fassett, 1919.

Sutter, L. M. *Arlie Latham: A Baseball Biography of the Freshest Man on Earth.* Jefferson, NC: McFarland, 2012.

Trask, David F. "William Sowden Sims: The Victory Ashore." In *Admirals of the New Steel Navy*, edited by James C. Bradford. Annapolis: U.S. Naval Institute Press, 1990.

Tucker, Spencer C., ed. *Almanac of American Military History.* Santa Barbara: ABC-Clio, 2013.

Vaccaro, Frank. "Herb Pennock." SABR Baseball Biography Project. www.sabr.org/bioproject.

Waldo, Fullerton L. *America at the Front.* New York: E.P. Dutton, 1918.

Whale, George. *British Airships Past, Present & Future.* London: John Lane and the Bodley Head, 1919.

Wheeler-Bennett, Sir John W. *King George VI: His Life and Reign.* London: Macmillan, 1958.

Manuscripts and Papers

"Correspondence Concerning Red Sox Players at the Boston Navy Yard, 12/1917—02/1918," Record Group 181, National Archives (www.archives.gov).

Hughie Jennings National Baseball Hall of Fame (NBHOF) plaque.

Ed Lafitte player file, NBHOF.

Arlie Latham player file, NBHOF.

Mike McNally player file, NBHOF.

Newspaper Cuttings: Scrapbook [1918–1924]: Baseball in England, MFF 366, NBHOF

Herb Pennock player file, NBHOF.

Magazines

Argonaut
Baseball Magazine
The Congregationalist and Advance
Delta of the Sigma Nu Fraternity
Harvard Alumni Bulletin
Ladies' Home Journal
Our Navy
Recruiters' Bulletin
Sporting Life
Sporting News
Western Electric News

Newspapers

United States
Albany Journal
Atlanta Constitution
Atlanta Georgian and News
Auburn (New York) *Citizen*
Binghamton Press
Boston Globe
Brooklyn Eagle
Brooklyn Standard Union
Chester (Pennsylvania) *News*
Chicago Tribune
Christian Science Monitor
Cleveland Press
Daily Missourian, Columbia, Missouri
Day, New London, Connecticut
Detroit Free Press
Des Moines News
Duluth Herald
Edgefield (South Carolina) *Advertiser*
Elmira Telegram
Emporia (Kansas) *Gazette*
Estherville (Iowa) *Enterprise*
Fayetteville Democrat
Fitchburg (Massachusetts) *Sentinel*
Fort Wayne News
Freeman, Indianapolis
Geneva (New York) *Times*
Gettysburg Star and Sentinel
Gloversville and Johnstown (New York) *Herald*
Hartford Courant
Hudson Valley Times (Mechanicsville, New York)
Hutchinson (Kansas) *News*
Johnson City (New York) *Record*
Kennett News & Advertiser, Kennett Square, Pennsylvania
Keokuk (Iowa) *Daily Gate City*
La Crosse Tribune and Leader-Press
Leon (Iowa) *Reporter*
Logansport (Indiana) *Pharos-Reporter*
Lowell Sun
Massillon (Ohio) *Independent*
Milwaukee Journal
Navy Salvo, Boston
New Castle (Pennsylvania) *News*
New York Herald
New York Sun
New York Telegram
New York Times
New York Tribune

New York World
Newport Journal and Weekly News
Oakland Tribune
Ogden Standard
Ogdensburg (New York) *Republican-Journal*
Oregonian, Portland
Pensacola Journal
Philadelphia Inquirer
Philadelphia Public Ledger
Pittsburgh Press
Plattsburgh (New York) *Republican*
Portsmouth (New Hampshire) *Herald*
Providence News
Racine Journal
Rochester Democrat and Chronicle
Sacramento Record-Union
St. Louis Star
San Antonio Light
San Jose News
Schenectady Gazette
Scranton Chronicle
Scranton Tribune
Seattle Star
Sioux City Journal
Spokane Press
Stars and Stripes, Paris
Stillwell Standard-Sentinel
Syracuse Journal
Syracuse Post-Standard
Tacoma Times
Toledo News-Bee
Tombstone Epitaph
Union (New York) *News-Dispatch*
Utica Herald-Dispatch
Utica Press
Washington Herald
Washington Post
Washington Times
Waterloo Courier and Reporter
Waterloo Times-Tribune
West Chester Daily Local News
Wilkes-Barre Sunday Independent

Youngstown Vindicator
Australia, New Zealand and Tasmania
Brisbane Queenslander
Mercury (Hobart, Tasmania)
Poverty Bay Herald (Gisborne, New Zealand)
Sydney Evening News
Sydney Morning Herald
Sydney Referee
Canada
Lethbridge (Alberta) *Herald*
Regina (Saskatchewan) *Leader*
Victoria (British Columbia) *Daily Colonist*
Windsor (Ontario) *Record*
United Kingdom
Bath Chronicle
Daily Mail (London)
Daily Sketch (London)
Derby (Derbyshire) *Daily Telegraph*
Hull Daily Mail
Liverpool Echo
Lloyd's Weekly News
London Evening News
Morning Post (London)
Newcastle Journal
Nottingham Evening Post
Times (London)
Weekly Dispatch (London)

Films and Websites

Seeing London. Dir. Burton Holmes. Circa 1920s.
World War I: The First Modern War: Massive Air Attacks, The History Channel, 2014.
www.ancestery.com.
www.baseball-reference.com.
www.britishpathe.com.
www.sabr.org/bioproject.
www.ZYZZYVA.org.

Index

Numbers in **_bold italics_** indicate pages with photographs.